Dining Room and Banquet Management

Anthony J. Strianese

Delmar Publishers Inc.®

NOTICE TO THE READER

DEDICATION

DINING ROOM AND BANQUET MANAGEMENT is dedicated to my love, Pam. Her guidance, assistance, patience and understanding were invaluable for the success of this book.

Cover photo courtesy of L'Escoffier Beverly Hilton.

Delmar Staff
Associate Editor: Cynthia Haller
Project Editor: Laura Gulotty
Production Coordinator: Larry Main
Design Coordinator: Susan C. Mathews

For information address Delmar Publishers Inc.
3 Columbia Circle Drive, PO Box 15-015
Albany, NY 12212-5015

Printed in the United States of America
Published simultaneously in Canada by Nelson Canada,
a division of The Thomson Corporation.

10 9 8 7 6 5 4 3

Library of Congress Cataloging in Publication Data

Strianese, Anthony J.
    Dining room & banquet management / Anthony J. Strianese.
       p.   cm.
    Includes bibliographical references.
    ISBN 0-8273-3307-2. — ISBN 0-8273-3308-0 (instructor's guide)
    1. Food service management. I. Title. II. Title: Dining room and banquet management.
TX911.3.M27S76 1990
647.95'068—dc20

89-39212
CIP

CONTENTS

Preface   v

Part One: The Foodservice Industry

Chapter 1
The Importance of Service   3
Chapter 2
The Importance of Sanitation and Appearance   23
Chapter 3
Styles of Service & Place Settings   41
Chapter 4
Proper Guidelines for Service   73

Part Two: Dining Room Management

Chapter 5
The Styles of Service   105
Chapter 6
Training the Service Staff to Serve the Meal   131
Chapter 7
Organizing the Dining Room to Accept Guests   159
Chapter 8
Planning Reservations and Blocking Tables   179
Chapter 9
Managing the Dining Experience   199

Part Three: Banquet Management

Chapter 10
The Banquet Business and the Banquet Manager   225
Chapter 11
How to Book Functions   245
Chapter 12
The Banquet Function Sheet   267
Chapter 13
Managing the Function   297

Appendix A
Eight Napkin Folds   331
Glossary   339
Bibliography   345
Index   350

PREFACE

Dining out has been a passion of mine throughout my life. Each dining experience brings a new challenge. That challenge is to find a restaurant that offers excellent service to the guest. Whether I am dining at a restaurant in my own region, on vacation or taking one of many soccer trips, I am constantly searching to discover the perfect restaurant that has outstanding **SERVICE.** Each wedding, bar mitzvah or banquet attended is also a research trip. The quest to find perfect service at a banquet is my goal.

My research has taken place in restaurants as diverse as large chain restaurants like TGIFridays, mom and pop operations, such as The Bears, and haute cuisine restaurants like the Four Seasons in New York City. Banquets have been attended at VFW posts, church halls, four star resorts and elegant country clubs. The service has ranged from awful to outstanding.

My first job as a banquet manager was at a hotel in the middle of a decaying inner city. I quickly learned the secret of success in the banquet business. The secret—**SERVICE. SERVICE** was of utmost importance to all guests, regardless of their socioeconomic status or any other classification with which society labels individuals. Day after day this fact was confirmed by letters and thank you notes; but most convincing was the fact that the banquet business increased, when by all other indicators it should have been declining or nonexistent.

My next job was as a food and beverage manager at a brand new hotel. Again the importance of service was taught to the staff. The restaurant and banquet rooms were filled to capacity nightly. Unfortunately, the food was not consistently excellent; in fact, at times it was embarrassingly bad. The conclusion: excellent service will make up for mediocre food.

In 1974, I became a Hospitality Educator at Schenectady County Community College, assigned to teach courses in Dining Room and Banquet Management. In researching material for the courses, I soon discovered the reason for the poor service in America. First, the service person's job was (and is) not considered a profession as it is in Europe. In many ways the job of service person was looked down upon by the American public. Therefore, no one ever took the time to train American workers in the proper methods of service. Additionally, because America is such a melting pot of cultures, the methods of serving have evolved and resulted in a hodgepodge of French, Russian and a made-up type of service, called American.

Like so many of my peers in the Hospitality Education field, I soon discovered that there were very few textbooks addressing this subject. I could find no easy-to-read, easily understood book that explained the importance of service and the proper method of service. I did discover books and articles on the subject, but most of them explain how to serve as it applies to their own particular area of the country. These books are too simple in explaining the importance of service. Other books that tried to take a more professional approach contradicted the proper guidelines of service and were too complex. None of them gave substance to the logical reason for service.

I could not find any book that would be a comprehensive guide to fit the needs of students, dining room and banquet managers. In addition, the few books that were found on the subject either specialized in banquet or a la carte dining. There was no one comprehensive book that addressed the importance of service in both the restaurant and banquet field.

The target market for this book is the student in the two- or four-year college courses in restaurant and banquet management. It is written with the student in mind, and developed after years of research. I wrote many true stories about the type of service I have received in my travels. There also are unique review features that are included to increase the student's learning and interest.

Systematic Sequence of Book

One of the major strengths of DINING ROOM AND BANQUET MANAGEMENT is an easy-to-read format and the smooth flow of ideas. In addition, besides presenting these ideas, it explains to the reader the practical application of these ideas to achieve excellent **SERVICE.** This book introduces new theories in the evolution of service.

The book is divided into three parts. Part one consists of information that every person must know about, regardless of what area of the hospitality industry their career will take them. Part two consists of the important information that is needed to provide excellent service in an a la carte restaurant. Part three consists of information needed to provide excellent service in a banquet facility. Therefore, after completing part one, you may proceed to part three if your interest lies in banquets. Parts two and three are independent of each other. The book follows a logical pattern; one that I know you will enjoy.

Learning Objectives and Problem Questions

At the beginning of each chapter, there is a comprehensive set of learning objectives addressing the main concepts covered in the chapter. In all chapters there are problem questions that allow for an open-ended discussion of the situation. These open-ended questions were designed to make you think. Many of these questions have several solutions—just like the situations you will encounter in the dining room or banquet business. A test bank has been supplied to adopting teachers. This bank of questions will test the reader's knowledge of the objectives presented at the beginning of the chapter.

Problem Cases

All chapters include real life situations describing the problems I have experienced as a banquet and restaurant manager or as a guest at a restaurant. These problem cases are often used to illustrate how not to do some task; but many times you will be asked to explain what is wrong with the situation. These situations are interesting, and also may generate much controversy.

Pictures

This book has fifty pictures. However, one of the unique features of this book is that there are a series of twenty pictures that illustrate both correct and incorrect types of service.

ACKNOWLEDGMENTS

There are many people who made this textbook possible. Without them it would never have been written. I would like to offer special thanks to the following individuals:

Cindy Haller, my editor at Delmar Publishers, who answered my many questions and taught this novice the correct way to write a book.

Karen Lavroff-Hawkins, previously at Delmar Publishers, who first proposed to me the idea of writing a textbook and who got the text approved by Delmar.

Matteo A. Casola, Professor and Chairman of the Hotel, Culinary and Tourism Department at Schenectady County Community College, for providing me the opportunity to share my knowledge with the future leaders in the Hospitality Industry.

J. Gary Brenenstuhl, my office mate, who contributed many insightful suggestions and information needed in this text.

Peter Houghton, Senior Technical Specialist, who took many of the photographs.

My friends at Walt Disney World; Duncan Dickson, Manager of College, International and Professional Staffing who assisted me in obtaining the permission to get pictures from Walt Disney World; Toni Piturro who accompanied the photographer to make certain that the pictures were correct; and Tony Jenkins who gave me my first interview and got the ball rolling on how great service is accomplished.

To all of my former and current students who granted me interviews and obtained pictures for me:

Carol Philippi of the Old Journey's End.

Kim Sibson Williams of the Harry M. Stevens Corporation at the Astrodome in Houston, Texas.

Sue Simpson and Kim Spiak of the Desmond Americana.

Mike Stalica, Franca Ricupero and Colleen Sherman who gave personal interviews to me.

A special thanks goes out to these three individuals for posing for pictures: Marlo Santore, Ken McCauley and to my special friend from the Beijing China School of Tourism Yun (Sonny) Goo.

I would also like to thank the following reviewers who gave me many valuable comments and suggestions:

Natalie Williams
Pensacola Junior College
Pensacola, Florida

Richard Hathaway
1714 Park Avenue #109
Baltimore, Maryland

Ernie Green
14842 Raquel Lane
Canyon Country, California

John Olson
SUNY College of Technology at Delhi
Delhi, New York

Duane Sunwald
Spokane Community College
Spokane, Washington

Phyllis McGuire
City College of San Francisco
San Francisco, California

ABOUT THE AUTHOR

Anthony J. "Toby" Strianese, Professor in the Hotel, Culinary Arts and Tourism Department has been a member of Schenectady County Community College's (SCCC) faculty since 1974. He holds a Bachelor's degree in Business Administration from Bryant College, Smithfield, Rhode Island. He obtained his Master's degree in Educational Psychology from the College of St. Rose in Albany, NY. He was Chairperson of the SCCC Faculty Chairperson from 1983–88. Mr. Strianese was instrumental in getting Schenectady accepted into the Walt Disney World College Program and serves as the Walt Disney World Coordinator for SCCC. He has participated in numerous College Educators Forums at Walt Disney World in Orlando, Florida. Professor Strianese is the author of *THE WINE STEWARD,* a computer software program. He has served as a consultant to many excellent restaurants and companies. Before coming to SCCC he was banquet manager at the DeWitt-Clinton Hotel in Albany and food and beverage manager at the Roundtowner Motor Inn in Colonie. In addition, he has been published in *The Journal of Hospitality Education* and regularly presents lectures on wine and dining room service.

Part 1

The Foodservice Industry

Chapter 1
The Importance of Service

Chapter Objectives:

At the completion of this chapter the student will be able to:

1. verbally define service as it relates to the hospitality industry;
2. give examples of excellent service;
3. list Maslow's Hierarchy and explain its importance in the hospitality industry;
4. distinguish the different types of service the dining room manager and banquet manager must provide;
5. write a definition for the word ubiquitous and give an example of it as it relates to the hospitality industry; and
6. list and explain the qualifications that managers must possess to provide excellent service.

Service for the Present and Future

Guests in the twentieth and twenty-first centuries are and will be no different from guests throughout the ages. All guests want to be and appreciate being pampered. When leaving their homes for an evening out, to spend their hard-earned money, they want an enjoyable, entertaining evening. More and more individuals are choosing a restaurant for their evening out. Many business people choose a banquet facility or restaurant in which to conduct important business meetings. It is up to you, the restaurant and banquet manager, to make their experiences enjoyable.

Reasons to Provide Good Service

Guests enjoy talking about their experiences at a restaurant. They *like* to talk to their friends about good service, and they *love* to tell their friends about poor service. Every restaurant manager or potential restaurant manager should know the following facts about service and customers. Writing in *Nation's Restaurant News* (NRN), Robert L. Desatnick, President of Creative Human Resources Consultants, states: "Ninety-six percent of unhappy customers never complained about rude or discourteous treatment. Ninety percent or more of those dissatisfied with the service will not buy again or come back. Each of those displeased customers will tell their stories to at least nine other people. Thirteen percent of those former customers will tell more than 20 other people."[1] With a little simple math, you can see that a negative experience can affect that restaurant's business substantially. This is called **WORD OF MOUTH.** It is the best and worst type of promotion for a business. Word of mouth has more effect on business at a restaurant or banquet house than any other factor. Why? Because people like to ask other people where to find a great place for dining or holding banquets. They trust recommendations from a friend rather than advertising. The following story illustrates the point.

 ## Word of Mouth

A woman entered a restaurant with her fiancé. Being a vegetarian, she asked for a tuna sandwich on a hard roll. The service person said they were out of that item. The guest patiently explained that she was a vegetarian and asked about the availability of nonmeat items. The service person, by means of body language and nonverbal communication, gave the distinct impression of being annoyed. After visiting the kitchen again, the service person reported that the manicotti was meatless. The woman asked if the sauce was also meatless. The service person made a third trip to the kitchen to inquire, returning with the news that the cook could make a meatless tomato sauce. The guest agreed and placed the order. However, she and her fiance discussed the attitude of the service person and wondered if the sauce would really be meatless. They decided to leave the restaurant, but knew they should first try to find their service person to cancel the order. As they approached the kitchen, they asked another service person to tell their service person to cancel the order. Standing near the opened kitchen door, the couple heard and saw their service person say, "Cancel that manicotti. That witch has changed her order three times!" Furious, the guests sought out the manager and complained.

The woman could not wait to volunteer this story to her friends and her classmates. All of the students in the class wanted to know the name of the restaurant. She gladly told them the name of the restaurant and where it was located.

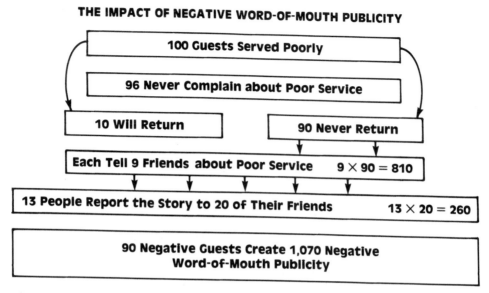

THE IMPACT OF NEGATIVE WORD-OF-MOUTH PUBLICITY

100 Guests Served Poorly

96 Never Complain about Poor Service

10 Will Return

90 Never Return

Each Tell 9 Friends about Poor Service $9 \times 90 = 810$

13 People Report the Story to 20 of Their Friends $13 \times 20 = 260$

90 Negative Guests Create 1,070 Negative Word-of-Mouth Publicity

Figure 1–1. This is what occurs when a restaurant has 90 unhappy guests. By the power of word of mouth, 1,070 people will believe that your restaurant is poor. This is the impact of negative word-of-mouth publicity.

Guests that patronize restaurants and banquet houses love to tell their friends about the service they received from the establishments. Therefore, it is imperative that restaurant and banquet managers strive to provide excellent service and make word of mouth work positively for them in order to make their businesses successful.

What Guests Think of Service

On the cover of the February 2, 1987 issue of *TIME* magazine was the headline, "Why is Service So Bad?" In the story, the author of the article claims that "personal service has become a maddeningly rare commodity in the American marketplace."[2] The restaurant industry was and is built upon excellent food and service. The dictionary definition for service is "the act or manner of serving food and drink."[3] There are many ways to serve food and beverages. Unfortunately many of these ways are poor. Year after year, survey after survey, the number one reason why guests would not return to a restaurant is always **Poor Service!** The National Family Opinion group and the Gallup organization continue to have this fact verified in all of their research. In 1986 NRN reported on a survey of over 12,000 adults who were asked what would cause them not to patronize a restaurant? Eighty-one percent of the respondents cited poor service as the most important factor. In 1988 NRN again reported the results of a Gallup poll; this time the author stated that "greeting regular customers by name does as much to boost their patronage as discounting the price of the meal."[4]

What the Hospitality Industry Thinks about Service

At a 1987 NRN-sponsored meeting of restaurant operators held in Atlanta, Georgia, a panel of industry leaders stated that "customer service has become the No. 1 issue in the food-service industry today, and finding first-rate employees to fill this need is the No. 1 challenge."[5] In today's society, which continues to move toward more computers and impersonal service, the customer wants smiles and human interaction in place of cold, nonthinking, unemotional computers. It becomes essential that the restaurant and banquet managers of the twenty-first century know how to give and train their employees to provide excellent service to their guests.

Who is Responsible for Great Service?

Too many times, the service person is blamed for good or poor service. It appears to the guest that the service person should take the credit or blame. However, the blame or credit falls on the manager. It is up to the manager to set the tone of the business. If the manager cares about his guests, then the message will be loud and clear to the service staff. If the manager gives the impression that he is only there because he has to be and that the guests are an imposition on his time, the service staff will get that message also. Over and over again, the one common thread in all restaurants that are judged to be outstanding is the care and concern of the owner or manager toward the guests and staff.

Three successful restaurant owners are Carol Philippi, Nicholas Morrone, and Beverlee Solff Shere. Philippi, who opened The Old Journey's End in 1979 in West Sand Lake, New York, feels that her success has been the result of an innovative and imaginative menu, attention to details, and making her guests feel as if they are guests in her own home. An accomplished chef, she was asked why she preferred to spend her time in the dining room instead of the kitchen. She replied: "I feel that the front of the house is very important because when people go out for fine dining they expect a great deal of attention. The owner or the manager is the only person who can give the guest that extra recognition." First-time restaurant owner Morrone, citing the reason for the success of Razzle's in New York City, says that "people feel relaxed when they come here." He can usually be found circulating in his dining room, furnishing the key ingredient of warmth to his guests. Beverlee Solff Shere, president of the Coach and Six in Atlanta, Georgia,

Figure 1–2. A restaurant manager (standing) making her guests feel important. Notice the casual fun-filled atmosphere evoked by the guests. (Photo courtesy of The Old Journey's End)

stresses the importance of keeping track of the names of all customers from the time the reservation is made to the end of the meal. Her restaurant celebrated its silver anniversary recently. Since Shere assumed command of the restaurant in 1974, the volume of business has almost tripled. And who makes the best type of manager? The authors of *A Passion for Excellence* state that "the best bosses are neither exclusively tough nor exclusively tender. They are both: tough on the values, tender in support of people who would dare to take a risk and try something new in support of those values."[6] One of the authors' most valuable points is that successful managers "pay an obsessive attention to detail."[7] In the highly demanding restaurant business, the restaurants that succeed and prosper are the ones whose owners take the time to pay attention to details and make their guests feel welcome in their restaurant.

MBWA

The authors of *A Passion for Excellence* state that there are only two ways to create superior performance. The first is to take exceptional care of your customers via **superior service.** One of their techniques is called MBWA, or "management by wandering around." They claim that an effective manager must be where the action is. In a restaurant, the manager should be walking around talking to the guests. In a banquet, the banquet manager should make certain that the guests are happy. By doing this wandering around, the manager can observe all situations and solve problems before they occur.

Service Defined

In the restaurant industry, service is defined by two words—competency and friendliness. Competency can be defined as serving food and drinks in the correct manner to the guest: The service person knows who gets the shrimp scampi and who gets the prime rib without asking the guests; the service person serves all food to women first; the service person removes one course before serving the next. Competent service often is not noticed, but it results in a good feeling about the restaurant by the guests. After the meal is complete, the guests know that they had a pleasant experience, but they do not realize why. The service person paid attention to the details. However, competency alone does not make a good service person.

A service person must also have the other attribute, friendliness. It is much more important than competency. The service person should make the guests feel that they are guests in a private home. Think about it. When someone comes to your house, you ask them if they want a drink. You pay attention to them. You are nice to them. However, the service person must be realistic and not overly friendly to the guest. If possible, a service person should address the guest by name (not first name, of course) and be able to make the guest feel welcome in the restaurant. But—a word of caution—don't be a phony. Too many of the 1980s fern bars had the waiters and waitresses running up to the table with a canned speech: "Hi, I'm Gary (or Sue) and I'll be your waiter (or waitress) tonight. Our specials for the evening are . . ."—and then they went on with what seemed like a five-minute speech outlining specials, pushing drinks and food, and in general boring the customer. A service person should be a professional combining competency with friendliness.

What is Excellent Service?

Excellent service occurs when guests in a restaurant never have to ask for anything. Many times guests do not realize they have received excellent service until they have left the establishment. The service person does everything correctly without the guests knowing it. When guests reach for the coffee cup, the handle is right where their thumbs and fingers naturally go. The water and wine glasses are always filled. It is never necessary to ask for the ketchup or butter or more bread. A second cup of tea or coffee is poured before the guests request it. The correctly added check is even presented to the guests without having to be asked for; and the service person and host thank the guests for patronizing the restaurant. It bears repeating: Excellent service is friendliness combined with competency.

The Best Service in the World

Walt Disney World near Orlando, Florida, has a multifaceted philosophy of food service. One of the points is to have "fast and efficient service." The most important ingredient in successful service is the human element, that is, concern for the guest. Walt Disney World has been praised for its excellent service, and it has been featured in the book and the television show, *In Search of Excellence*. Managing an operation that employs over 32,000 people requires excellent training and attention to detail. How do they accomplish it? That was the question that was put to Tony Jenkins, a College Relations Coordinator for Walt Disney World Company.

Disney Training

According to Tony, all new employees have to attend orientation classes, where they learn about the history, philosophy, and style of Disney.

All service staff employees receive an initial three-day training period with approved trainers. These trainers are employees who have worked at the restaurant for a period of time and who are themselves products of the Disney training classes.

On the first day at the job, the new employees will follow and observe their trainers for half a day. This procedure is called shadowing. During this time, the trainers explain how to present the menu and how to serve the food. All of the methods are standard for all service staff at Disney.

In the second half of the day, the new employees carry out the trays for the trainers. The trainers, since they are regular service persons, have their own stations in the restaurant. All the training in this phase is accomplished on the

Friendliness + Competency = EXCELLENT SERVICE

Figure 1–3. The key to successful service. Friendliness plus competency from all the staff to all the guests.

job, and the new employees have to meet and follow all the standards set down by Disney. For example, every item that comes from the kitchen to the dining room must be carried on a tray. Disney insists on the same standards for all their restaurants, the same service to all their guests at all locations.

On the second day of training, the new employees will have contact with the guests. They will approach the guests, present the menu, and take the order. The trainers are now shadowing the new employees. Throughout the day, the new employees are encouraged, reminded, and taught the correct ways to serve Disney guests.

On the third day, each new employee begins the day by being assigned two or three of the trainer's tables. By the end of the day, the new employee is waiting on and serving all five tables in the station.

"The key to the Disney training is follow-up," says Tony. "Each restaurant has periodic service meetings. Perhaps one or two a month to go over new procedures, price changes and new menu items."

Another key is the use of mystery shoppers at Disney. These shoppers patronize the restaurants for the sole purpose of observing their operation. Included in their observations is a report on the service by the service person. Therefore, the management of the restaurant has an unbiased report on its operation and can take steps to clear up any problems.

All of the above sounds great. But can it really work? The question was posed to Colleen Sherman, who worked as a food and beverage hostess at Disney on the Walt Disney World College Program. She feels, as Tony does, that the follow-up is the key to making the system work. She said, "When I made a mistake the supervisor would take me aside as soon as possible and tell me what my mistake had been. Then I was able to correct it and the Disney service concepts were reinforced."

What is Poor Service?

Poor service is easy to recognize. Every person reading this book can cite many examples of poor service. Ineffective service can be frustrating and embarrassing for a restaurant. For instance, you, as a guest, are served your meal, and a few minutes later your dining companion is served. Or, how many times have you had to wait for a check before you could get to that show on time? And how many times have you been met and upset by rude servers with an "I-don't-care" attitude?

Leonard Roberts, Arby's former president, has said that customer comment cards are almost always focused on how they are treated as people and

Figure 1–4. College students participating in the Walt Disney World College Program in Florida. (© 1987 The Walt Disney Company)

as consumers. Jane Wallace, writing about the explosion in takeout sales in the March 4, 1987 issue of *Restaurants & Institutions,* says: "Eating out has become such a hassle. What the industry seems to have forgotten is that enjoyable eating out is a combination of food and service. Most operators have done a good job tempting the public with food and menu concepts. But when service becomes such a hassle that customers prefer to take food home, things have reached a sorry state indeed."[8]

The Reason for Poor Service

Statistics indicate that ninety-three percent of restaurant failures stem from poor management. People who manage restaurants very often have no concept of how to please their guests. Many managers prefer operational tasks to the actual running of a restaurant. If you are that type of individual, quickly put down this book and change careers!

Employees, during the first thirty days after being hired, will establish their work pattern, often based on their manager's style. If a manager fails to conduct formal training sessions and fails to express the restaurant's philosophy on guest service, the results will be poor service from the employees. After all, the manager doesn't seem to care about the guests!

On the other hand, if you have a manager that cares and trains the staff properly, the business will prosper. Marlowe's restaurant, in Denver, Colorado, had sales shoot up 12%, even though Denver was in an economic slump. It was accomplished by training Marlowe's servers through the use of a videotape training manual, role playing, and written tests. Only about 50% of the trainees pass the seven-day session. After passing training, servers establish sales goals and are evaluated by the use of a point system: certain bottles of wine, appetizers, and desserts are given point values; results are tracked weekly, with color televisions, ski trips, and camping equipment awarded to the ten service people with the highest tallies. Training, attention to detail, and a follow-up system pay dividends for the restaurant.

The Psychology of Service

Every person who considers a career in the restaurant field must realize that most guests do not come to a restaurant or banquet facility merely to eat. In the field of psychology there is a well-known theory formulated by A. H. Maslow called Maslow's Hierarchy. This hierarchy deals with human needs. Maslow cites five basic needs that an average person should possess. These are the physiological need and the needs for safety, love and belonging, esteem, and self-actualization. The first four are referred to as dependent needs because they are obtained from other people. Self-actualization comes from oneself. Restaurant managers should know and understand how these needs affect their guests.

Basically, the theory states that a person must significantly satisfy one need before moving on to the next need. However, it has been demonstrated that it is possible to satisfy portions of two needs simultaneously. Let's relate Maslow's Hierarchy to the restaurant business and understand why this theory is important to a restaurant and banquet manager.

A restaurant and/or banquet manager should realize that two of the needs, the physiological and the need for love, most often will have been met before the guest enters the hospitality establishment. The final need, self-actualization, is an internal need that the manager deals with indirectly. The major needs that the manager and the employees must deal with are those for safety and esteem.

The physiological need means that if we do not have enough money to provide food for ourselves or our family, we will spend the greatest portion of our time trying to earn enough money or to obtain food to satisfy this need. All of our guests have satisfied this need because they are not starving.

Once the physiological need is satisfied, the person moves on to the next need—the safety need. The safety need can play an important part in the success or failure of a restaurant or banquet facility.

Our guests generally have satisfied the safety need, because they probably live in a community that makes them feel comfortable and fearless. However, some restaurants may have a problem in satisfying the safety need. Problems will arise with an establishment located in a dangerous section of town, or one which disruptive customers are allowed to patronize. Guests in these establishments will not be able to enjoy their meals because they will be concerned about their safety after they leave the restaurant. Thus, even though their safety need was satisfied in their own neighborhood, the safety need is not satisfied at the restaurant. Because of this, they will not patronize your restaurant. Therefore, it is imperative to make certain that your guests' safety need will be satisfied. Another part of the safety need can be thought of with regards to sanitation. If your establishment has been shut down by the health department because of unsanitary conditions at any time in the past, guests will most likely not want to patronize your restaurant.

Once the safety need has been satisfied, the guests now move to the love and belonging need. This need refers to being accepted by other people and groups. Most guests have made friends and formed associations with their peers. At times, this need benefits the restaurant and banquet facility greatly, because our guests belong to groups that patronize restaurants and banquet facilities.

For the most part, the guests that we receive into our restaurants and banquet facilities have all significantly satisfied the first three needs: physiological, safety, and love and belonging.

The key need that all restaurant managers, banquet managers, and service staff can satisfy is the fourth need—the esteem need. This need centers on self-respect and is generally thought of as ego needs. It means that someone (namely, you, the manager or service person) gives the people respect and makes them feel important. For example, addressing the guest by his or her name, or inquiring about the guest's family or job are ways to satisfy the ego need. This esteem need is not a new theory. Even back when our country was being founded, Ben Franklin is reported to have said "The taste of the roast is determined by the handshake of the host." Wise men have always realized the importance of being pleasant and building up the ego of their guests. This esteem need should almost always be positive, as it is for the guests shown in figure 1-5 on a Royal Caribbean Cruise, but sometimes it can appear to be negative and still result in ego gratification.

Ego Gratification

There was a local diner in a small community. Since the diner was open twenty-four hours, townspeople congregated there at all hours, and some came in three and four times a day. One guest, who came in more than others, was greeted by the words: "You again Frank. We'll put a bed in the back so you can sleep here." Frank enjoyed this attention so much that he increased his trips to the restaurant. He felt important and his need for esteem was being recognized.

The fifth need is the need of self-actualization, which comes from within the person. This is when the person develops his or her maximum potential. Restaurant managers indirectly contribute to the development of this need because they have helped to satisfy the fourth need—the esteem need.

All restaurant and banquet managers should know how and when to use Maslow's Hierarchy to understand their guests. Of course, many restaurant owners have no idea why they should know or even use this theory. You will enjoy the following story because it illustrates how *not* to treat guests.

Mistaken Identity

Fresh out of college, I invited my two fraternity brothers up for a day of watching thoroughbred racing. After a very successful day of playing the horses, my friends asked me where we should go to dinner. Because my father went to a particular restaurant all the time and was a friend of the owner, I suggested we go there.

As we walked into the restaurant, I could see the line of people waiting for tables. This did not bother any of us. We would go in, ask for a table, and go to the bar and have a few drinks.

Being proud of myself for recommending an obviously fine restaurant, I marched up to the hostess desk and, to my delight, saw the owner.

He looked up, not recognizing me, and said "Yes?"

"Hi, I'd like a table for three," I said. And then I added, "I'm Toby Strianese, Art's son."

In a loud voice he replied, "I don't care who you are, you will have to wait your turn just like anyone else!"

As I walked back to the end of the line, my face was flushed with embarrassment. My friends could not wait to tell me what great influence I had.

A few years later the restaurant closed its doors. However, every time I see my fraternity brothers they still remind me about that restaurant.

Figure 1–5.   Guests being served aboard a Royal Caribbean Cruise Ship. Their esteem need is filled. (Photo courtesy of Royal Caribbean Cruise Lines, Inc)

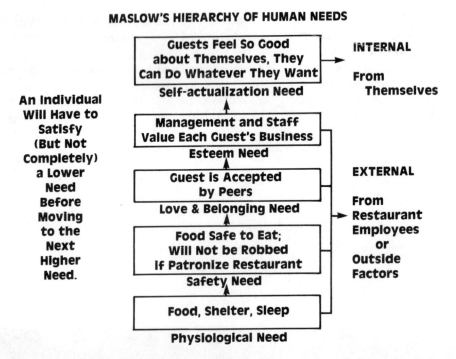

Figure 1–6. Maslow's Hierarchy of Human Needs. Every individual has to satisfy the lower need before moving on to the higher need. The physiological, safety, love and belonging, and esteem needs are dependent needs—they occur with the help of the restaurant employees or outside factors. Self-actualization occurs when the dependent needs have been met. This need comes internally from the individual.

Being Ubiquitous

All individuals who work in a restaurant must be ubiquitous. It is one of the most important qualities for restaurant business employees. Ubiquitous means being everywhere at the same time. The restaurant manager must know what is going on at all times. A ubiquitous manager will appear to have eyes in the back of his or her head. If the manager, host or hostess, is talking to a guest at the guest's table, he or she must also be aware of what is occurring in the entire dining room. If a new party enters the restaurant, the host must excuse himself or herself and greet the new guests.

The same is true of the service staff. An example of an ubiquitous service person occurs when your water glass is filled without your having to ask. The service person knows what you want without you having to request it.

The banquet manager must be ubiquitous also. The main job of the banquet manager is not to serve or cook food, but **to take the responsibility of the party off the host's shoulders and put it on his or her own shoulders.** People hosting parties want to be able to spend time with their guests. Therefore, a banquet manager, such as Kim Sibson Williams at the Astrodome Complex in Houston, Texas, must take care of all the minute details to make the banquet a success. She must be able to handle all problems for the host of the party. One facility she is responsible for is the Astrohall, which can accommodate parties for between ten and one thousand guests.

If the flowers are wrong at a wedding, the banquet manager soothes and calms down the bride and her parents, and corrects the problems. The banquet manager is ubiquitous and ensures that the party runs smoothly. The job of a banquet or catering manager is one of the most exciting and rewarding but stressful positions in the hospitality industry.

Figure 1–7. Exterior of Astrohall in Houston, Texas, where banquets for up to one thousand guests are held. (Photo courtesy of Hall Puckett)

Successful Management

The successful manager, whether it be for banquets or a la carte dining, must have the following qualifications.

1. He or she must know the different types of service, when to use them, and how to serve properly. There are two main types of banquet service: Russian and American. A la carte service is American, French, Russian, or a combination of all three of the styles.
2. The manager must know the proper methods of beverage service, as well as how to organize, plan, and implement beverage service for banquets and a la carte dining. Included are open and cash bars, and proper wine service. The manager must have a knowledge of wines and the proper pairing up of food with wine.
3. The manager must be personable and have a genuine fondness for people. Managers must realize the importance of talking to guests and making them feel important. Knowledge and use of Maslow's Hierarchy must be used to recognize guests. There is nothing as powerful as addressing a guest by his or her name. Both the dining room manager and the banquet manager must be visible in the dining room so they can talk to their guests.
4. Organization is the key for a successful manager. If you are not an organized person, the dining room or banquet room is not the business for you. These two areas run on organization.
5. The manager must possess the ability to stay calm under pressure. This is especially necessary for catering and banquet managers. One factor can be guaranteed at a banquet: No matter how rich or poor, how influential, or how educated the host of the party may be, they are always under a tremendous strain. They want the party to be a success. The banquet manager is the person who must keep them calm.
6. The manager must be in good physical condition to withstand the long, unusual hours and stressful conditions. The job involves much physical labor, since the manager often helps to move tables, transport food to catering events, and lifts up heavy items that are needed either in the restaurant or at the banquet.
7. The manager must be able to resist temptation. Since there is so much food and liquor available, managers find it easy to drink and eat too much.
8. The manager must be able to effectively deal with both employees and guests. Any person considering the restaurant business as a career is

Qualifications for Successful Management

1. Knowledge of Food Service
2. Knowledge of Beverage Service
3. Friendly, outgoing personality
4. Organizational skills
5. Ability to stay calm under pressure
6. Good physical condition
7. Ability to resist temptation
8. Diplomat
9. Knowledge of training employees
10. Ability to handle complaints

Figure 1–8.

advised to take as many psychology courses as possible so they can manage all the idiosyncrasies of their guests and employees.

9. The manager must know how to train employees. In this industry most of the training is done on the job. The successful manager will have a training plan, implement it, and have a follow-through system like that of Walt Disney World Company.

Successful managers have many other qualifications, this is not a complete list. However, there is one more important qualification a manager *must* have. It is the ability to deal with and handle complaints.

How would you have handled the following letter of complaint?

May 28, 1987

Ms. Lori Smith, Manager
The Restaurant
Anywhere, USA

Dear Ms. Smith:

At approximately 6:30 P.M., on Sunday May 20, my family and another family of 4 had dinner at your restaurant. This letter is to inform you about our dining experience.

Our first impression of the restaurant was excellent. The hostess greeted and seated us at the round 8-top on station or table 35, on the second level. Anne (I believe that is the name she wrote on the check) was asked for two separate checks for the two families. She did not appear to be too pleased about the request, but reluctantly complied (check number 614176). Three glasses of Parducci Chardonnay were ordered along with other beverages. Upon receiving and smelling the wine, the three of us knew it was not Chardonnay. I went to the main bar and asked the bartender to smell the wine and tell me its variety. He informed me that he could not and if I had a problem, I should tell my waitress. Doing this, my waitress said she ordered Chardonnay. We stated it was not, so she took the glass back to the service bar to check. She returned and said, "We are out of the Chardonnay, so the bartender gave you Chenin Blanc." I asked if this was the house white wine and she replied "yes." We told her we would drink the wine.

Why would a bartender and a waitress substitute Chenin Blanc for Chardonnay? It would be like a cook substituting a hamburger for the Philly Steak sandwich because they are both beef, which I doubt has ever happened. The waitress would have been informed by the cook that they were out of the menu item and she would inform the customer.

If this was the only problem, I could have overlooked it. Another problem was Anne's attitude. If she said she made a mistake that would have been OK. But she made us feel like the wine mix-up was our fault. The final straw that prompted me to write occurred when we got our bill. The Chardonnay read $2.45 per glass. When we pointed out the mistake on the bill, she said she charged us the right price for the Chenin Blanc, even though the check read Chardonnay. Since we thought we drank the house white wine (as she said before) @ 1.75 per glass we felt overcharged. Then to insult us more, she brought the menu to prove she was right and we were wrong. On the check, I wrote "very poor service, letter will follow." In addition to the above mentioned, she never checked back with us to see if everything was OK nor did she follow any proper guidelines of service. She served the drinks from one spot, just placing them on the table, not asking anyone to pass the drinks, not a friendly word. She avoided the table as much as she could.

On our way out the hostess did an excellent job. She asked if everything was all right. When I told her it was not, she asked what happened. I stated "a lot!" and kept walking. The hostess continued to ask all members of my party what was the problem. Finally, my wife (the last person out) explained the problem. The hostess tried to get my wife to talk to the manager on duty, but since we were on our way home we did not want to take the time. The hostess is to be commended for reacting to the situation the way she did.

In summary, the food and hostess were great, but the waitress and bar people should be trained properly and change their attitude. Remember the customer is not always right, but is never wrong!

Very truly yours,

Wayne M. Bruno

cc: Mr. John Jones
President of the Restaurant Corporation

Chapter Summary

1. Excellent service is defined as competency plus friendliness.
2. Bad service is easy to recognize. One example occurs when the guest has to wait over five minutes to receive the check.
3. Maslow's Hierarchy plays an important part in the restaurant and banquet business. A manager who understands the hierarchy and how to use it will make the guests feel important.
4. The restaurant manager has the choice of giving guests either American, French, or Russian service. The banquet manager can offer the guests American or Russian banquet service.
5. Managers must know, and give the appearance that they know, everything that is occurring in the restaurant or banquet at all times. This is called being ubiquitous.
6. To qualify as a manager of a restaurant or banquet, an individual must possess the ten qualifications listed in Figure 1-8.

Review Questions

1. Define service as it relates to both restaurants and banquets.
2. Give five examples of excellent service you have experienced at a hospitality establishment.
3. List the five stages of Maslow's Hierarchy and explain its importance in the hospitality industry.
4. List and explain the different types of service that the dining room and banquet manager must provide to the guests.
5. Write a definition for the word ubiquitous and give an example of it as it relates to the hospitality industry.
6. List and explain the qualifications that managers must possess to provide excellent service in the hospitality industry.
7. List the three types of a la carte service a restaurant manager can offer to guests and the two types of banquet service that are available to guests.
8. Give five examples of bad service you have experienced in a restaurant and explain why the service was poor.
9. Explain word of mouth publicity. Why is it the most potent form of publicity?
10. What is the key to making the Walt Disney World Company training successful? Explain your answer.

References

1. Robert L. Desatnick, "Seizing The Competitive Advantage," *Nation's Restaurant News,* 28 September 1987, p. F68.
2. Stephen Koepp, "Why is Service So Bad?" *TIME,* 2 February 1987, 48–52.

3. Jess Stein, ed. in chief, *The Random House Dictionary* (New York: Ballantine Books, 1978), 815.
4. Peter J. Romano, "Friendliness Works As Well as Discounts," *Nation's Restaurant News,* 5 December 1988, 3.
5. "Customer Service As Primary Challenge," *Nation's Restaurant News,* May 1987, 25.
6. T. Peters and Nancy Austin, *A Passion for Excellence, The Leadership Difference* (New York: Warner Books, 1985), xviii.
7. Ibid.
8. Jane Wallace, "Eating Out: A Pleasure or a Hassle?" *Restaurants & Institutions,* 4 March 1987, 16.

Chapter 2

The Importance of Sanitation and Appearance

Chapter Objectives:

At the completion of this chapter, the student will be able to:

1. write the definition of sanitation and explain its importance as it relates to management in a dining room facility;
2. know where to find the health regulations for the particular locality (state, county, city) in which the business is located;
3. describe acceptable cleanliness and appearance standards for employees;
4. list reasons for handling utensils, glasses, and plates by their base or rims;
5. identify and write out the "freedoms of soil";
6. verbally explain why tables cannot be set with silverware in advance; and
7. write in essay form about the importance of a clean-looking establishment as it relates to the hospitality industry.

Sanitation

The definition of sanitation is "the development and application of sanitary measures for public health."[1] This simply means that when customers enter a restaurant to eat, the food and the conditions of the restaurant are clean enough so they will not get sick from patronizing the restaurant. The National Institute for the Foodservice Industry (NIFI) defines sanitation this way: "In a foodservice situation, santitation means wholesome food, handled in a hygienic environment by healthy food handlers in such a way that the food is not contaminated with disease-causing or otherwise harmful agents."[2] Sanitation refers to visual as well as physical. Our guests will perceive our restaurant to be dirty, if the restrooms are dirty. Any positive impressions a customer might have about a restaurant can be ruined by a trip to a dirty or a bad smelling restroom. Countertops and other restroom surfaces breed germs which can be transferred to food or utensils by restaurant personnel. It is the responsibility of the manager to keep the restrooms spotlessly clean.

If your guests are waited on by a person with dirty, scuffed shoes, they may think that the cook is not clean. To the guests, the service person is the restaurant. The guests may be right, or they may be dead wrong; but it is their perception which determines if the restaurant is clean. They are the customers and the customers are always right. Oftentimes, if the "front of the house" (the physical area in which the employees serve the guest) appears to be dirty, customers believe the kitchen is dirty even though it is not. They are scared to eat at the restaurant because they may get sick as the result of a dirty kitchen.

History has proven that some of the illnesses that guests pick up at restaurants are no worse than getting the flu, but others can be fatal.

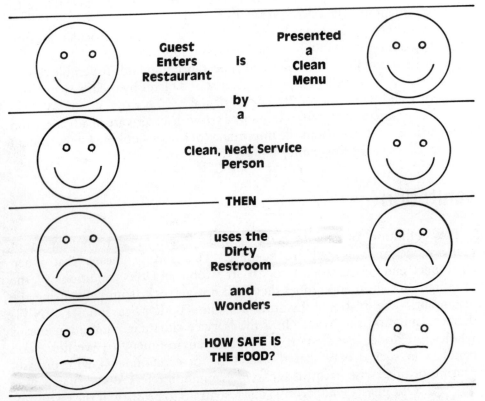

Figure 2–1. Is the food safe to eat? The guest, after being presented a clean menu by a neat service person uses the dirty restroom.

Who Monitors the Cleanliness of the Restaurant?

In each community in the United States there are stringent health rules to protect the public. They have been established because, for many years, businesses lacked concern for both the cleanliness of their establishment and the safety of the food that they served to their guests. Because of this, each state has health laws that restaurant managers must abide by if they are serving the public. In many communities, the restaurant must have a permit to operate, which is issued by the local health department. In addition, the health department of the community in which a restaurant is located will conduct surprise inspections of the establishment. If the health department, when inspecting a restaurant, discovers health code violations, the restaurant could be fined and shut down. The media (tv, radio, newspapers) could report that the restaurant was closed because of unsanitary conditions. They may also use a visual aid like the one in Figure 2-2. The negative publicity will seriously harm the business.

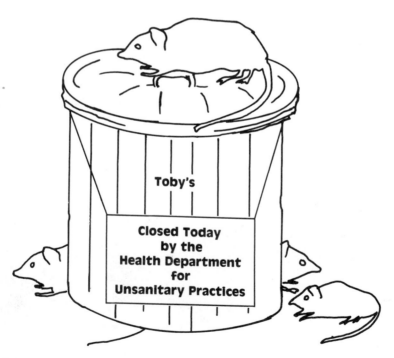

Figure 2–2. An example of graphic publicity that newspapers or television stations may use in order to inform the public about restaurants that have been closed by the health department.

Who is responsible for the sanitation of the establishment? The banquet and restaurant managers are the ones responsible, and they must have a plan to clean the restaurant and enforce the highest standards of sanitation.

First Appearance

The first impression is a lasting one. This has been stressed throughout our lives. Little things mean a lot to our guests. The way the restaurant appears to the guests will influence them in determining if the restaurant is clean. If it is, they will feel safe, have their meals and banquets, and spend their money at your establishment.

Good sanitation begins with the appearance of your building. Guests perceive the whole restaurant based on the appearance of your building, parking lot, and signage. Hotels have to be concerned with the way their lobby and public areas appear.

Figure 2–3. Exterior of an independent restaurant. The building and parking lot appear clean and attractive. The cleanliness creates a positive first impression to the guest. (Photo courtesy of The Old Journey's End)

Figure 2–4.   Interior courtyard of a hotel. The cleanliness of the courtyard gives the guests a positive first impression of the hotel. (Photo courtesy of The Desmond Americana)

A Little Assignment
(to be done on a regular schedule)

Make this an everyday habit. Approach your restaurant as a guest would approach it. Vary your approach daily, so you will view your building from different angles (not all guests enter your establishment from the same direction). Notice the condition of the parking lot; are there any potholes? Look to see if there are any papers on the ground. How does the landscaping and the condition of the building appear? Is the front door dirty? Are there cigarette butts outside the entrance way? Do this assignment during the daylight and evening hours. You are viewing your business from the guests' perspective. This is called **consumer orientation.** Make notes about what is good and bad, and compliment those responsible or devise a plan to correct the problems. And most important, follow through on the implementation of the plan!

The Influence of the Manager

Attention to detail is the key to running a great business. Two of the most influential people in the hospitality industry, Ray Kroc of McDonald's and Walt Disney of the Walt Disney Company, were sticklers on cleanliness. (A little trivia: both of them were in the same ambulance company in World War 1, serving as drivers, both underage). People in the hospitality industry should take their lead from the companies these two men founded when it comes to cleanliness and sanitation. In his book, *McDonald's Behind the Arches,* author John Love states that "the characteristic that was possibly most responsible for creating the family image Kroc was looking for was the cleanliness that McDonald's built into its operating system."[3] He further states that "even competitors concede that McDonald's uncommon dedication to running a clean restaurant set a standard in the industry that others aimed for but seldom hit."[4] Ray Kroc used to say, "If you've got time to

McDonald's Key to Success

Q = Quality
S = Service
C = Cleanliness

The Key to *Cleanliness*
is
Attention to Details

Figure 2–5.

lean, you've got time to clean."[5] He wanted his stores to be spotless! Any person with a free moment was taught to clean. Whenever Kroc would visit one of his units, he would pick up any papers on the ground before entering the store. This demonstrated to the managers and employees that if the owner of the company can pick up papers, then everyone can pick them up. This is how managers set examples. If your employees observe you stooping over to pick up papers, then they will too. This is also done by the managers at Walt Disney World. The effect is lasting. One alumni of the Walt Disney World College Program remarked that she cannot walk by a piece of paper without picking it up.

Kroc's Zeal for Cleanliness

The difference between a good place and a great place is attention to details. One of the reasons that McDonald's is the most successful foodservice company is illustrated by the following story. One Saturday morning at the original Des Plains, Illinois, McDonald's, employee Fred Turner (who eventually became President of the company) saw Ray cleaning out the holes in the mop ringer with a toothbrush. No one else had really paid any attention to the mop ringer. But when Ray Kroc looked at the mop ringer he saw built up crud in the holes. He wanted to clean the holes so the wringer would work better. Ray Kroc built McDonald's on the letters QSC, which stands for Quality, Service, and Cleanliness. Cleanliness was made a key part of the strategy to make and keep McDonald's number one in the restaurant business. Half of the 1958 operator's manual was devoted to describing recommended procedures on cleaning. Today, McDonald's has the reputation of being the cleanest operation in the hospitality business.

Detail is the Key

Ask any parent what factors influence them in choosing a restaurant for their family. Every one of them will rate cleanliness a high priority item—especially the cleanliness of the high chairs. Parents know what a mess little kids can make. Restaurants that have clean high chairs can make quite a positive impression on young parents. Employees should be instructed to thoroughly clean all high chairs after each use. Make certain they are instructed to clean all those little nooks and cracks where the young toddler throws food. After the high chair has been cleaned thoroughly, the tray should be wrapped in a clear plastic wrap. Training employees to do this will increase business, not only when the children are young, but as they grow up.

Appearance of the Employees

Ray Kroc was not the only one who knew that cleanliness would create the atmosphere that families were looking for; Walt Disney did too. Disneyland was founded because there was no amusement park where Walt could take his family to have a good time together. The generally recognized concept of an amusement park was unacceptable to Walt Disney's way of doing things. Almost all had dirty looking employees, too many people pressuring the guests to buy things, and too many barkers (salespeople). When Walt founded Disneyland, he knew that the presentation of the park and its employees had to achieve standards that would earn the respect of the guests. Walt instituted "The Disney Look." It is a major part of the Disney theme parks. The Disney Company stresses to all its employees (called cast

Figure 2–6. Cast members illustrating the "Disney Look" at Walt Disney World. (© Walt Disney Productions, 1984)

members): "The 'Disney Look' is a tremendously important part of the overall show at both Disneyland and Walt Disney World. This employee excellence has brought more than two decades of compliments and recognition from people the world over."[6]

The Service Persons' Appearance

1987 was designated as the year of the waiter. In the October 28 issue of *Restaurants and Institutions* magazine, the perfect waiter is described. Burt Hixson, owner of the Warehouse Restaurant in Marina del Ray, California, states that good grooming is the most important trait of service persons. Owner Benjamin Bernstein of Mike Fink's in Lexington, Kentucky, says: "Their appearance reflects their regard for themselves. Somebody who doesn't have regard for himself can't make the type of appearance that we want."[7]

Each restaurant should set grooming guidelines for their employees. These grooming guidelines should be explained to the employee when hired. Supervisors have the obligation to refuse to allow people to work if they do not adhere to the standards. For example, all Disney employees when hired know they have to adhere to a strict grooming guideline. Male employees cannot have any facial hair, nor can their hair length be touching their costume collar. Females cannot wear long, dangling earrings. The acceptable size of earrings is the size of a dime. Nail polish is limited to a clear color. All new employees have the policy explained to them before they accept the job. It is up to the manager to set the standards, explain, and enforce them.

 Dining Out, a Pleasant Experience?

A couple had invited their neighbors to dinner at a nice, upscale, "Yuppie" restaurant. The couple had been telling their neighbors for weeks about the good food at this restaurant, the reasonable prices, and the enjoyable evening they would have. Once the four people were seated, their waiter approached the table. He had on a white shirt with the sleeves rolled up. He had hair almost to his shoulders that looked as if he hadn't washed it in a week. The neighbor's wife said, "He should have a hairnet." How was the meal? For the four of them it was disappointing, mainly because of the dirty-looking appearance of the waiter. That was the first turn-off. From that point on, all of the guests felt his service was as poor as his appearance. Whether it was or not, in the minds of the four his appearance had ruined their evening out. Do you think the guests will ever return to this restaurant?

Managers should learn from history. Not long ago, it was common practice for a waiter to be clean and well-groomed when he reported for work. In the late 1800s and early 1900s, at places like the fashionable Belmont Hotel in New York, the waiters had to pass an inspection every morning by the headwaiter. If they were not dressed properly, they were not allowed to work. Later on, in the great depression, if they could not pass inspection by the headwaiter they were fired immediately. During the depression, unemployment was so high that people waited outside the back doors of restaurants every morning at lineup time. They knew that if they could get a job in a restaurant they could at least get a good meal. Waiters were clean, well-groomed, and had an immaculate uniform.

Since the 1950s, we in America let people do "their own thing." Restaurant owners allowed employees to dress any way they wanted. Standards were dropped and the appearance of the service person suffered. However, a business that continued to set and enforce standards was The Walt Disney Company. Today, as always, there is a lineup daily. If a male employee has a one-day growth of hair on his face, he is not allowed to work until he shaves—and is issued a warning. One day a cast member appeared at the daily lineup with a new hairstyle. It was too extreme for the rules. The employee was not allowed to work until wearing an acceptable hairstyle. Disney employees are given written notification that violation of the appearance policy may result in dismissal from employment.

Each business and manager has to set guidelines that are correct and appropriate for the particular staff and establishment. The uniform and appearance of the staff have to fit the restaurant. A place like TGIFridays or an independent local mom & pop pizza place have a different concept from Disney. Their uniforms are different from one another. They are less structured than places like McDonald's or Disney, which is fine, as long as they are clean and comply to the standards set by management. Managers must set guidelines for appearance and cleanliness. A checklist (either mental or written) must be developed. Managers must follow this checklist and not let anyone work who deviates from the standards of the checklist.

To reemphasize, the manager must set the standards of grooming, inform the employees, and **enforce the policy.**

In his book, *The Best of Gottlieb's Bottom Line,* Leon Gottlieb writes about the problems with dress codes. "More importantly, do you enforce your dress code? We suggest you do not—not entirely or consistently. Too many houses have allowed their crews to become sloppy, to everyone's disadvantage. You are not a good boss if you allow your personnel to be out of uniform."[8] For example, Gottlieb states: "Grooming: Clean shaven, mustaches trimmed above the lip line, clean fingernails, haircut above the collar or worn in a net, should be the type of professional appearance required in your house."[9]

Cleanliness during the Shift

Being a service person is a demanding job. It requires much physical labor. In addition, the service person can get sweaty and dirty and look disheveled during the shift. As a manager, be aware of this. If an employee looks messy, the supervisor should have that person immediately change into a clean uniform.

In many restaurants, both employees and guests use the same restrooms. After working a few hours on a shift, a kitchen worker may not make a good appearance. The kitchen whites have turned brown, covered with grease and gravy. The manager should insist that when employees leave the kitchen, they are dressed cleanly and neatly. It is recommended that cooks and chefs have an extra uniform jacket available, so they may change into a clean uniform when they have to appear in the "front of the house."

How do My Employees Smell?

Your employees should smell clean. However, some employees have a strong aroma that will turn off your guests for their dining experience. Do not allow service persons to work who are wearing perfume or cologne. Guests become annoyed if all they smell is the smell of perfume or cologne. The chef will not be too pleased with the service person ruining the aroma of the food. At one restaurant, the service person's first customer ordered a glass of wine. When the guest lifted the glass of wine up to smell the aroma, all that she smelled was the perfume of the service person, who had just doused herself with perfume, liberally putting it on with her right hand. When she served the guest the glass of wine, the perfume was transmitted to the glass. Because taste is 85% aroma, the guest tasted only the perfume.

As bad as, or worse, is the problem of body odor. It is a must that all of your service staff use deodorant. One of the worst dining experiences ever experienced occurred because of the waiter's body odor. Each time the waiter approached the table, he reeked of body odor. The entire meal was a revolting experience. The guest has never gone back to the restaurant.

All employees should smell clean. Supply the restrooms with extra soap and deodorant, if needed. Make your guests' dining experience pleasant because they enjoyed the aroma of the food. Don't let other aromas mask the flavor of the food.

The Handling and Storing of Utensils, Glasses, and Plates

Sanitation is extremely important in handling and storing utensils, glasses, and plates. The service staff must be trained to pick up the silverware by the handle, not by the part of the utensil that goes into the guest's mouth, which

Figure 2–7. The incorrect way to hold a glass. Service staff should never handle the glass on the part that will go into the guest's mouth. (Photo courtesy of Peter Houghton)

Figure 2–8.   The correct way to hold silverware. The service staff should be trained to pick up the silverware by the handle, not by the part of the utensil that goes into the guest's mouth.

is illustrated in Figure 2-8. The same is true of plates and glasses. Handle them by their rims. Train your staff not to touch the part of the glass or plate that the guest will drink or eat from. There is an important reason for this. Disease can be transmitted from one person to another by improper handling of serving items. Not only can a disease be transmitted, but guests get upset when they see this type of carelessness on the part of the service staff.

Teach Your Staff How to Handle!

Editor, NRN

Restaurant operators need to start acting responsibly by properly training and supervising their food servers. My husband and I eat out quite often, and it is sickening to observe the way some food servers handle cups, glasses, and eating utensils.

One would not think anybody needs to be trained to handle a glass or a cup that will be used by someone else. Nobody wants to drink out of a container whose rim has been handled by the server.

I have seen this practice in upscale dining establishments as well as in budget restaurants and airplanes. Flight attendants are the worst!

As a food microbiology professional, I am deeply saddened by this apparent lack of regard for the public's health. Sanitation should be our primary concern and especially so during these times of heightened disease awareness.

We need to boost our employee training programs to address these concerns. Health departments are not staffed to police all areas.

Edith A. Wilkin
Denver, Colo.[10]

(The above letter appeared in the October 12, 1987 issue of *Nation's Restaurant News*. Copyright © 1987, Nation's Restaurant News, Reprinted with permission.)

As has already been noted, the lack of sanitation in a food service establishment has more serious aspects beyond the negative impression given the public by unclean conditions. People can die from disease caused by poor sanitation. Unsanitary conditions and careless handling of utensils can result in the spread of disease, food poisoning, and death.

The story of Typhoid Mary should be known by all workers in the foodservice industry. A lot of people know the name but don't know that she became famous because of the havoc she wreaked in New York City, where she was a cook. Wherever she worked, an outbreak of typhoid followed her. Typhoid was an easily transmitted disease. It spread in various ways. One of the surest ways was for the carrier to touch something that could transmit the disease.

Mary probably did not wash her hands with extreme care. Unless extreme care is used in washing the hands, bacteria may remain on the hands and contaminate anything the carrier touches. This is the reason that you see the signs in all restrooms that say "All employees must wash their hands before returning to work."

Hence, the less frequently dishes and silverware are handled, the less chance of contamination. Employees must be trained to keep their fingers out of cups, bowls, and glassware. The eating end of silverware should never be touched after the silver comes out of the machine. Sterile dishes and utensils can be recontaminated by the mere touch of a careless hand.

Setting up Tables in Advance

Health departments have various rules for presetting tables with utensils. Each manager is advised to check his own local health agency to determine how many hours or minutes a table can be set up in advance of your guests arriving. In some localities, silverware must not be preset. It is given to the guests wrapped in a paper or linen napkin when they sit at the table. This is to prevent any germs from contaminating the silverware or cups or saucers. It is possible that germs can be transmitted from people walking through the restaurant if they cough or sneeze.

For a banquet, most health agencies allow the banquet facility to set up from one to two hours before the banquet is to take place. However, all health agencies agree that tables cannot be preset with silverware or dishes overnight. The reason is that a lot of disease-carrying rodents and insects are nocturnal. It is possible that cockroaches and mice could contaminate the silverware at night.

In addition, it is of utmost importance that the manager sees to it that utensils, plates, and glasses are stored properly when not in use. This means a place that is free from insects and areas where they could become contaminated.

Cleanliness of Eating Items (Freedom from Soil)

It is generally accepted that unclean utensils do constitute potential health hazards. Each service person must inspect all utensils before using them to make sure they are clean. Food cannot be considered safe if permitted to come in contact with dishes, glasses, and utensils that have not been properly washed.

Guests are concerned with the appearance of the utensils. If they see any food leftover on the plate or knife from a previous meal, they will become upset. Before service persons serve an item or set a table, they should look for certain items. If they find any of the following examples of visible soil, the utensils should not be used.

1. *Adhering foodstuffs,* such as dried on eggs remaining from the previous meal. Employees should check both the bottom and the top of plates. Sometimes, when dirty plates sit on top of each other, foodstuffs remain dried on the bottom of the plate.
2. *Stains.* No coffee, tea, or vegetable stains that classify the utensils as rejects.
3. *Physical damage,* such as cracks, or chips. A chipped or cracked dish is one that can never be completely cleaned because soils penetrate these areas. The crack or chip harbors bacteria and renders the dish unfit for use. The dish should be discarded.

If guests see any of the above problems, they will interpret the restaurant to be dirty. Visible soil indicates a lack of cleanliness.

Cleanliness of Banquet Rooms

Management must make certain that the banquet rooms are attractive and beautiful. There should be a maintenance program of regular cleaning, just as in the dining room. In addition, there are certain peculiarities regarding banquet rooms that the banquet manager must attend to in order to give the appearance of a clean and spotless establishment.

Details are extremely important in a banquet room. The banquet room guests will sometimes have to circulate around the room, setting their drinks on window ledges and running their hands over these ledges. Before every banquet, an employee should be assigned to wipe down the ledges with a damp cloth to remove the dust. Another place that dust always is found is on the lectern. Guest speakers place their hands on the lectern. If it is dusty or feels dirty, they will perceive that the banquet facility is dirty. That cleaning job should also be assigned to the employee. To check on the cleanliness of the banquet room, do what Ellsworth M. Statler used to do whenever he visited one of his hotels. He would enter one of the guest rooms, walk into the bathroom, and lie down in the bathtub. The reason?—another example of consumer orientation. He wanted to see exactly what a guest would see when the guest took a bath. Was the ceiling paint peeling? Were there any cobwebs on the ceiling? Do the same with your banquet room. Sit in a seat. Look around the room for cobwebs on the light fixtures or for any lights that are burnt out. Taking care of details makes a favorable impression on the guests.

Extra Tables and Chairs

In the regular a la carte dining room, extra tables and chairs are not a problem. They should always be set with the type of cover and place setting that the establishment uses for its business. However, the banquet rooms are different. Extra chairs and tables in view while parties are in progress is not appealing to the eye. In fact, it takes away from the appearance of the room. Some banquet houses stack the chairs and put them in the corner of the room with the unused tables. Put yourself in your guests shoes. You probably would not like to see extra tables and chairs in the room if you were paying for a banquet. Any extra tables and chairs should be stored in another room, or, if there is no other room available, a partition should be purchased to put in front of them.

Chapter Summary

1. Sanitation means keeping the restaurant free from dirt. A clean establishment is important in order to have a successful business.
2. A manager should know which health department has jurisdiction over the establishment, and how to find the health regulations that affect the business.
3. Managers should set acceptable appearance standards for grooming for their own particular operation.
4. Employees should be taught the method and the reason for handling utensils correctly.
5. Employees should know what constitutes "freedom from soil."
6. For health reasons, utensils cannot be set up the day before a party.
7. A clean establishment adds to the comfort and security of the guest.

Review Questions

1. Define the term sanitation. Explain its importance as it relates to you, the manager of the restaurant.
2. How would you discover the correct sanitation procedures for your establishment?
3. What makes the appearance of an employee acceptable? Describe the acceptable standards for your establishment and your reasons for them.
4. Why should utensils, glasses, and plates be handled by their bases or rims?
5. What are the four "freedoms from soil"? What should a manager do when the establishment does not meet the standards?
6. What are the reasons tables cannot be set in advance? Is there any exception to this rule?
7. Why is it important to have a clean-looking establishment in the hospitality business? Include information about extra tables and chairs, light fixtures, and dirty ledges.
8. Where should extra chairs and tables be stored during a banquet? Why should they not be stored in the same room that is having a function? Would there ever be an exception to this rule?
9. Should all restaurants have the same grooming guidelines? Explain your answer, giving examples to support your ideas.
10. What are the minimum standards that all service people must meet in order to serve guests?

How Do You Solve the Problem?

One of your best employees has Acquired Immunodeficiency Syndrome (AIDS). He has been employed with you for over five years. You have been receiving crank calls about members of your staff having this disease. The callers say they will not come to your restaurant. Do you keep this employee on or fire him? Take into consideration whatever laws are in effect in your community. Also, consider how the negative word of mouth campaign will impact the business.

References

1. Jess Stein, ed. in chief, *The Random House Dictionary* (New York: Ballantine Books, 1978), 793.
2. National Institute for the Foodservice Industry, *Applied Foodservice Sanitation*, 2nd ed. (Dubuque, Iowa: WCB, 1978), 7.
3. John Love, *McDonald's behind the Arches*, (Toronto: Bantam Books, 1986), 142.
4. Ibid.
5. Ibid, 143.
6. Walt Disney Company, *The Disney Look* (Burbank, California, 1987), 3.
7. Michael Bartlett, ed. in chief, "Owners Define Perfect Waiter." *Restaurants and Institutions,* 28 October 1987, 26.
8. Leon Gottlieb, *The Best of Gottlieb's Bottom Line* (New York: Lebhar-Friedman, 1980), 117.
9. Ibid, 123.
10. Edith A. Wilkin, "Cleanliness Training Important," *Nation's Restaurant News,* 12 October 1987, 7.

Chapter 3
Styles of Service & Place Settings

Chapter Objectives:

At the completion of this chapter, the student will be able to:

1. explain how service evolved historically;
2. describe the characteristics of French, Russian, and American a la carte services;
3. identify the advantages and disadvantages of the three a la carte services;
4. lay the correct place settings for French, Russian, and American a la carte service;
5. describe American, Russian, and Buffet banquet styles;
6. identify the advantages and disadvantages of the three banquet services;
7. lay the place settings for American, Russian, and Buffet banquet services;
8. give the definition of cover and the history of eating utensils; and
9. explain the uses of tablecloths and how to change the cloths during the busy times.

Confusion Over Names of Service

Throughout the United States and Canada, there is no definitive type of service. Each restaurant has its own style of service. There are three basic kinds of service used in a la carte restaurants. These are American, French and Russian. Most restaurants use a combination of all three to serve their guests. Many restaurant personnel have a basic understanding of the three types of service. However, they are not certain about the advantages and disadvantages of each particular service. Likewise, many people are confused concerning the difference between Russian Banquet service and French service. In addition, buffet style service includes three other types of service, which adds to the confusion. Overall, there is a lot of misinformation about the origins and the definition of the exact types of service.

Why the Confusion?

For many years service just happened. There were no textbooks written that taught proper service. In the search of literature for this text, only a few service books published before 1950 were found. What was discovered was that service was taught through a "pass it down system." It was learned only by men, who participated in apprentice programs at the great hotels and restaurants of the time. Little was ever written or recorded about proper service methods. The great hotels and restaurants that had excellent maître d'hôtels demanded proper service and had strict rules concerning service. Waiters learned how to serve guests properly, and service remained consistent. Once waiters ceased employment at the restaurants where they were trained and became transient, styles of service began to blend together.

Everyone took the best parts of a particular service and adapted it to their restaurant. Many ideas about service were passed down correctly, but others were passed down incorrectly.

Only in the past few years have textbooks and articles been written concerning service. Service is now beginning to take on as much importance as cooking.

First Textbook for Waitresses

The first books written for waitresses and hostesses were in the late 1800s and early 1900s. These books were not written for the hostesses and waitresses of today, but for the wife who entertained her husband's guests and the female who worked as a domestic in a private home. The preface of

TYPES OF SERVICE COMMONLY USED IN AMERICAN ESTABLISHMENTS

A la Carte	Banquet	Buffet
1. American	American	Simple Buffet
2. French	Russian	Modified Deluxe
3. Russian		Deluxe

Figure 3–1. The different names of service types. A la carte can be French, American, or Russian. Banquets can be either American or Russian. Buffets can be Buffet, Modified Deluxe, and Deluxe.

The Up-to-Date Waitress, written in 1906 by Janet M. Hill, states: "The manner in which we advocate that the duties of a waitress should be carried out has been evolved from a study and comparison of the methods of many housekeepers."[1] The book concentrates on the duties of the waitress serving her employer on a daily basis in his home, as opposed to working in a restaurant. Another book, entitled *The Modern Hostess,* written in 1904, concentrated on the duties of the woman serving at home. However, the beginning of the book does have a description and illustrations of a formal ten-course hotel dinner. Oscar, the great maître d'hôtel of the Waldorf Astoria in New York City, describes how service should occur throughout the ten courses. But Oscar did not explain from what side to serve or clear dirty dishes. The author, R.J. Bodmer, did say that serving the formal dinner would be the hardest part of entertaining, and it would be advised to obtain a professional butler "who understands service" and another waiter to serve the meal.[2]

The Beginnings of Service

The job of waiting on people evolved from early times, when individuals owned slaves. These slaves, called servants, had to serve their masters food and drink. Unfortunately, many people still perceive the service person of today as a servant rather than as a professional. The first jobs were not as demanding as they are today. Most meals were eaten at home. The only time a wealthy person ate meals outside of the home were at other wealthy individuals' homes. The servants accompanied their masters to serve them their meals.

The first banquets took place in classical Rome. These banquets were attended by wealthy Romans and were restricted to men. At this time, there were no restaurants or banquet houses. But these wealthy Romans did have Banquet Halls in their houses. The service given was not the type of service we think of today. The servant did not have to set the table with forks, spoons, or knives because the only utensil put on the table were spoons. There were no napkins to fold and put on the table, since each guest was required to bring his own cloth to wipe his hands.

The servants' job was not without danger. In addition to their usual duties of obtaining food and drink for their masters and peeling their grapes, one of their tasks involved tasting food. The purpose of tasting the food and drink was to make certain that they did not have poison in them. If the taster ate the food and lived, then the master ate it.

Early Superstitions and Facts

The Roman people were very superstitious. Guests were seated at a single couch with as few as three or as many as thirty people. The key was to have a multiple of three because that number held divine significance. All guests made certain to enter the banquet hall with their right foot first. This assured them that favorable things would happen to them.

Emperor Augustus, the founder of the Roman Empire, gave women official status in Roman society. This occurred around 27 B.C. He allowed women to accompany their husbands to banquets. Because there was a great amount of gossip at banquets, anything that was said at the table was not repeated if the host put a rose on the table. This led to the term *subrosa*, which means confidentially.

The First Commercial Establishments

In the years 1000–1500 A.D., travelers would stop for food and lodging at the inns and taverns in France and England. Everyone had the same meal served to them. This one choice, a complete meal, was called and is still referred to as table d'hôte.

In 1533, La Tour d'Argent opened in Paris, France. This was the first restaurant open to the public in the Western world. Guests at La Tour could order their own individual meals from a menu for the first time.

French Service

The first meals served in France were done so with considerable flourish and show. The meal was divided into three separate services. Hor d'oeuvres were served first. Then came the first service. Everything that the guests ate was placed in the dining room on tables and warmers (like today's buffet). Each guest was waited on by a server (called a valet) or two. The valet assisted the guests by obtaining the food for them. Guests, while seated, could serve themselves from the offered dish, but more often the valet would serve them. This sounds very similar to the buffet style of today and was called **Served Buffet Service of Ancient France.** Food and cooking became the rage in France. Any French person who wanted to be considered knowledgeable in the ways of the world learned about cooking. The French palate was becoming sophisticated. Under the reigns of King Louis XIV and Louis XV, it became stylish to own a famous chef. Families, like Bechamel, became proud to have a new sauce named after them. French people started to entertain more and service became an important element of the meal. Since so many people were becoming knowledgeable about food, service had to become creative to keep up with the new foods. Instead of food being prepared solely in the kitchen, it was prepared in front of the guests with a flourish. And as the guests were now civilized, they had utensils to eat their food with besides their fingers.

The Basic Place Setting

In homes and restaurants, the standard placement of flatware (spoons, forks, knives) generally follows the same pattern. It has not changed

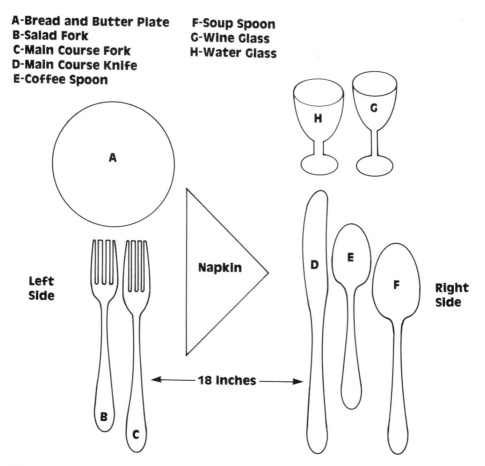

A-Bread and Butter Plate   **F-Soup Spoon**
B-Salad Fork   **G-Wine Glass**
C-Main Course Fork   **H-Water Glass**
D-Main Course Knife
E-Coffee Spoon

Figure 3–2. The traditional American Place Setting that includes a soup and salad course. Forks are on the left side of the guest; knives and spoons on the right side of the guest. Water and wine glasses are placed at the tip of the knife and tip of the spoon.

substantially from the original place setting begun in the homes and restaurants of France. To the left side of the guest is placed the bread and butter dish, and forks. The knives, spoons, glasses, and cups are to the right. A napkin is placed in the center of the place setting. A diagram of the basic place setting is illustrated in figure 3-2.

History of Knives

In the medieval times, knives were used for hunting and protection. Every man carried with him a knife. One of the uses for the knife, discovered by early man, was to spear his food with the pointed end of his knife. He could then transport the food to his mouth without using his hands. The inns and taverns in Europe that served food and drink to their guests did not provide the guests with any type of utensils, because everyone had their own. In addition, the medieval times were dangerous; the patron of the inn was in a strange place, never knowing who might attack him. When the patron ate, if he had to lay his knife down on the table, he would put it on his right-hand side. According to Sandy Rose, former Senior Vice President of Harry M. Stevens Corporation, this was in case of being attacked. The knife was in a perfect position, ready to be grabbed for protection. Because most people were right-handed, the knife went on the right side of the guest.

By the 1600s, knives were being placed on the tables at the restaurants. These knives were still pointed at the end. A French statesman, Cardinal Richelieu, a very powerful figure in the time of King Louis XIV, was eating at one of these restaurants. As he was eating his meal, he looked over at another table and saw an individual sitting there picking his teeth with his pointed knife! He immediately ordered all knives be rounded off at the edges instead of being pointed.

Exact and Correct Way to Set the Table

Needless to say, both the managers and the staff must know how to set the table. Then the manager must be a stickler on details by inspecting all tables and correcting mistakes before the banquet begins or the dining room opens. A manager will be able to walk into any room and know immediately what is correct and incorrect about the place settings. In time, the service staff will not even think about the proper way to set the table. It will become habit forming. Figures 3-3 and 3-4 illustrate the proper and improper way to set the table.

Generally, the utensil that will be used to eat the first course is placed the

Figure 3–3.   A table set up in the proper manner for a banquet. Forks are on the left side of the napkin; a knife and spoon to the right side of the napkin. Bread and butter plate are above the forks. Water glass is above the knife and coffee cup is turned upright (only because it is for American Banquet Service). (Photo courtesy of Peter Houghton)

Figure 3–4.   An improperly set table for a banquet. The ashtray is dirty. There are four glasses on the table (the maximum number is three). The coffee cup is turned upside down. The utensils are all mixed up. In addition, they are on the napkin. (Photo courtesy of Peter Houghton)

farthest from the guest. If soup was served first, the soup spoon would be the farthest spoon away from the guest's right hand. Next to the spoons are the knives. All blades are pointed toward the forks or center of the place setting. Figure 3-5 illustrates the basic place setting.

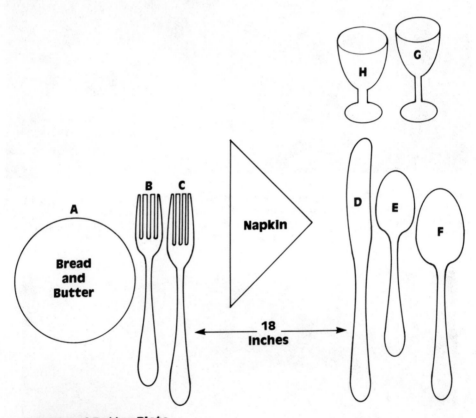

A—Bread and Butter Plate
B—Salad Fork
C—Main Course Fork
D—Dinner Knife
E—Teaspoon
F—Soup Spoon
G—Wine Glass
H—Water Glass

Figure 3–5. The proper diagram for a basic place setting. On the left side of the napkin is the bread and butter plate, the salad fork, and the main course fork. In the center of the place setting is the napkin. To the right of the napkin is the dinner knife (with the edge pointed toward the napkin), coffee spoon, and water glass above the tip of the knife. Notice there is no cup and saucer in this basic setting. However, there is a wine glass that is placed right next to the water glass.

Reason for Location of Utensils

Europeans cut their food with their knife held in their right hand. They eat their food holding the fork in their left hand. Americans have the habit of cutting the food the same way and then transferring the fork to their right hand before eating the food. Because of this European tradition, place settings continue to follow this general pattern.

Above the tip of the dinner knife is the water glass. Next to the water glass is the wine glass. The wine glass is located to make it easy for the service person to pour wine during the meal. Because wine is considered a food in Europe and because it complements the meal, and in some countries water was not fit for human consumption, it was an important part of the meal. Because guests drank more wine than water (if it was served), the placement of the wine glass made it easy for the service person to pour the wine.

On the left side of the place setting are the dinner and salad forks. Immediately above or to the left of the forks is the bread and butter plate.

The distance between the forks and knives should be twelve inches at a banquet, eighteen inches at an a la carte establishment. Most service staff, after setting a table for a few days, are able to place the utensils perfectly on the table. There is an easy way for a service person to determine this distance at banquets. The service person should stand facing the table, with a knife in the right hand and a fork in the left hand. These utensils should be placed on the table in direct line with the shoulders. Most adults have shoulders approximately twelve inches wide. The utensils should be placed one inch from the edge of the table. Whether they are put in a straight line or in a staggered up-and-down pattern, as shown in Figure 3-6, is up to the individual management of the restaurant.

Each restaurant can adapt its place settings to its menu, adding or subtracting utensils. For instance, if all guests are served soup with their meal, then a soup spoon is added to the place setting. Notice that there is no coffee cup or saucer at the place setting. These are brought with the dessert course or when the guest orders coffee. They are placed to the right of the spoons. The handle on the coffee cup should be located in a position that would be the same as the hour hand on a clock pointing to the number five. This position is called "cup at five o'clock." This is strictly for guest comfort. When the guest reaches for the coffee cup, the handle of the cup will not have to be moved. The guest's fingers will fit perfectly into the

Staggered Pattern of Setting Utensils

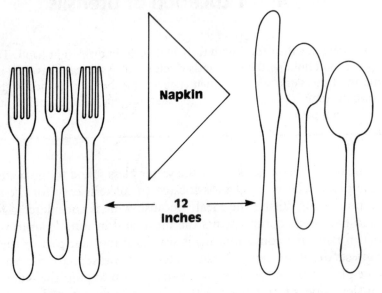

Figure 3–6. Flatware placed in a staggered pattern makes for a more attractive place setting.

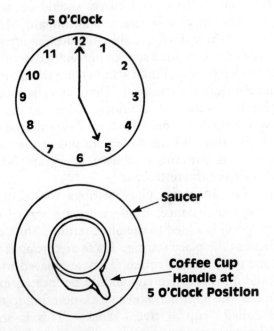

Figure 3–7. The handle on a coffee cup should be placed at a position that corresponds to five o'clock on a watch.

handle. This is just another detail that will make your restaurant stand out from your competitors. Everything in the restaurant should be for the benefit and comfort of the guest. Unfortunately, if the guests are left-handed they will be inconvenienced, because the placement of the utensils is a direct result of a right-handed society and European etiquette. When a service person notices (being ubiquitous) that the guest has moved the beverage glass to the left side, the coffee cup should be placed to the guest's left, with the handle at seven o'clock. These are the details that makes a guest leave a restaurant satisfied, even though nothing appeared to be done exceptionally. All that the restaurant did was to take care of the smallest details to make the guest's dining experience complete.

French Service Today

During the period when kings were in power and the wealthy aristocrats were influential in France, all the skilled cooks, chefs, and valets were employed by these individuals. In 1787, a revolution took place; the royalty was overthrown and removed.

As Napoleon gained power, it appeared that France's great culinary development would stop. This was a blessing in disguise for service. Because there was no more royalty, there was very little employment for the great cooks in the homes of wealthy people. The cooks had to find a new place to earn a living. Restaurants gave these cooks an opportunity for employment. Either the cooks worked for someone or opened up their own establishment. From 1765 until 1800, the number of restaurants increased from one to five hundred in Paris. The cooks introduced a new type of service to the French people. They used their culinary skills to prepare meals in front of the guest. French service as we know it today was born!

Today's French service is characterized by a service person finishing off (cooking, carving, flaming, and so on) the food in front of the guest. The food is partially prepared in the kitchen and brought to the table on a cart, called a *gueridon*. On the gueridon is a small heating utensil, called a *rechaud*. The food will be prepared on this gueridon, using the rechaud for last-minute cooking in full view of the guests.

Because the people doing the cooking at the table (after the French Revolution) were chefs, the job title of this service person is *chef de rang*. This person must be highly skilled in order to prepare foods in front of the guest. The French look upon food service as a profession; therefore, many talented individuals made a career as a chef de rang. Soon, going out to a restaurant became part of the culture of France. A career in the dining room or front of the house became a proud and acceptable profession. Having the skill to be able to prepare a meal in front of the guests was soon expected by the French public. Even today, food that is not prepared at the table, but served from the kitchen on a plate, is looked down upon. The person who assists the chef de rang is called the *commis de rang*. The main jobs of the commis are to place the food orders in the kitchen, bring the food to the chef de rang, and clear the dirty dishes from the guest's table.

French service has some excellent advantages.

1. The main advantage is for the guest. They get a high degree of personal attention.
2. The service is showy and elegant. Food is prepared with showmanship.
3. It may be possible to decrease the labor cost, because the chef and commis de rang are partially compensated with gratuities. Therefore, a fully staffed, highly paid kitchen crew may not be needed.

However, there are more disadvantages than advantages for a restaurant in using French service.

1. The restaurant must employ a highly skilled service staff, knowledgeable in cooking as well as service. They must know how to bone fish and

ADVANTAGES AND DISADVANTAGES OF FRENCH SERVICE

Advantages

1. Guest obtains high degree of personal attention.
2. Service is showy and elegant.
3. Food is prepared with flourish and showmanship.
4. It may be possible to decrease kitchen labor cost.

Disadvantages

1. Highly skilled waitstaff is required.
2. Quality standards are difficult to enforce.
3. Dining room fills with smell of cooked food.
4. Much more physical space is required than in American Service.
5. More and costlier equipment is needed.
6. Residence time is greatly increased, resulting in less turnover.
7. Menu prices are highest in restaurants that use French service.

Figure 3–8.

poultry, carve meats, dress salads, and prepare *flambé* items. The chef de rang must be knowledgeable of ingredients and must have the personality to perform constantly. These individuals might be impossible to find in some areas of the country. Therefore, a well-planned training program must be instituted and maintained.

2. If your restaurant does not have a good training program, and even if it does, there could be a problem with consistent quality of food prepared by all the chef de rangs at all the tables. It becomes difficult to enforce standardized recipes and to correct mistakes. Thus, the guests may get different quality food at different visits.

3. Because cooking is done in the dining room, the air may become stale with the odor of cooking unless the dining room has a good ventilation system.

4. Because gueridons must be used, a restaurant using French service will have less space for tables. French service requires eighteen square feet per guest, while other services only require fifteen.

5. It will cost more to buy and maintain the gueridons and rechauds. Other equipment must also be purchased which may not have to be purchased using American or Russian service.

6. It takes longer to serve guests using French service. A restaurant can not serve as many guests in an evening. Generally, restaurants with this type of service have only one sitting a night. Or they have an early and late sitting, if the demand is great.

7. The cost of the meal must be high enough to cover all the above costs. Therefore, restaurants that use French service have to charge considerably more for a meal than in any other type of service.

Russian Service

The cuisine of Russia was greatly influenced by the French. Catherine the Great (1762–1796), one of the rulers of Russia, imported French chefs and corresponded regularly with Voltaire. She was a great Francophile. In turn, the service in French restaurants was influenced by the Russians.

Because the Russians did not have many skilled chefs, the food served to the wealthy aristocrats was prepared in the kitchen, rather than in front of the guests. To make the food look as appealing as possible, it was being served soon on royalty's best serving pieces: silver trays. As the rulers of the two countries became allies (Peter II, Catherine's son, and Napoleon planned to invade Egypt together), the influence of each country was felt by the other. When the French returned home from Russia, the author believes they brought with them an idea for a new type of service to be used in restaurants. This new style of service in France was referred to as Silver Service.

When this new type of service was introduced to French restaurants, it revolutionized the industry. It became popular in the mid 1800s. No longer did restaurants have to find talented chefs to prepare food at the table; nor did they need gueridons. Now food could be served more quickly to more guests. Russian service is characterized by food being cooked and pre-portioned in the kitchen, and presented to the guests on silver trays. The service person then serves the food to the guests' plate from the tray. In the United States and Germany this service is called Russian. In France, because it originated in French restaurants, it is called French or Silver Service.

Russian service has many more advantages than French service for a restaurant owner or manager. It is best used for banquets rather than for a la carte service.

1. Food portioned and arranged on a silver platter looks eye-appealing and impressive.

ADVANTAGES AND DISADVANTAGES OF RUSSIAN SERVICE

Advantages

1. Ideal to use for banquet service.
2. Food looks impressive when served.
3. Guests have more space for comfort.
4. Faster service than in French service.
5. Waitstaff does not have to be a skilled as French service waitstaff.
6. Quality control of food is maintained.

Disadvantages

1. Service person has to be skilled in serving from platter to plate.
2. Tables must be positioned so they are easy to serve.
3. Different entrees require different silver platters, resulting in cold food for first guest.
4. High initial cost for purchasing equipment. Theft of silver is a possibility.
5. Last guest to be served is presented with an unappetizing platter.

Figure 3–9.

2. Less space is required than for French service, because gueridons are not needed; therefore, more tables can be placed in the dining room, resulting in more meals being served.
3. Guests will be more comfortable at the table, because thirty inches of linear space are needed for Russian service, as opposed to twenty-four inches for other services.
4. Guests can be served quicker, which allows for more turnovers than does French service.
5. The service staff does not have to be skilled in food preparation.
6. The quality control can be better maintained than with French service, because all food is cooked and put on platters in the kitchen.

Russian service does have some disadvantages.

1. A service person has to be skillful in manipulating a fork and spoon to transfer food from the platter to the guest's plate.
2. All tables must be located so that they can be easily served. If a table is located too close to a wall, it becomes impossible to serve a guest.
3. When guests order different entrees it will require bringing different platters to the table. This will be time consuming. The first guest served will end up with cold food to eat if he or she waits for all of the guests to be served.
4. There will be a high initial cost for purchasing the silver platters. A larger problem will be controlling the inventory of silver and preventing theft.
5. If all guests order the same entree, the last person served could find the look of the food picked over and unappealing.

Russian and French Place Settings

Because the two types of service are so similar, the place settings are identical. In both services, the place settings are as shown in Figure 3-10.

The difference between this setting and the basic setting is that the dessert fork and spoon are already on the table. One other difference is that the knife is on the bread and butter plate. Figure 3-11 shows the proper placement of a knife on a bread and butter plate at Victoria and Albert's at The Grand Floridian Beach Resort at Walt Disney World. Notice the placement of the glasses. There should never be more than three glasses at a place setting.

RUSSIAN/FRENCH PLACE SETTING

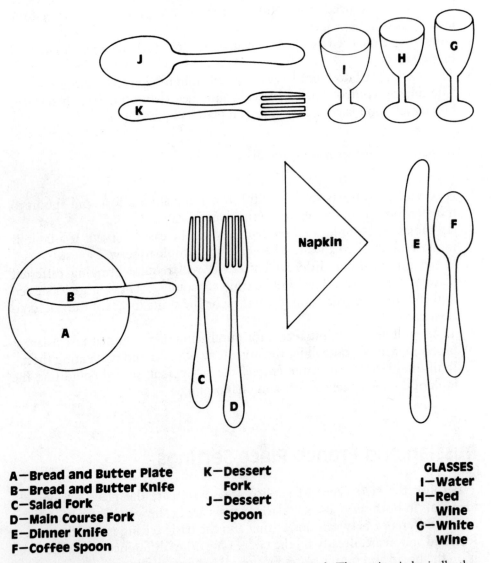

A—Bread and Butter Plate
B—Bread and Butter Knife
C—Salad Fork
D—Main Course Fork
E—Dinner Knife
F—Coffee Spoon

K—Dessert
    Fork
J—Dessert
    Spoon

GLASSES
I—Water
H—Red
    Wine
G—White
    Wine

Figure 3–10. Russian and French place settings are identical. The setting is basically the same as American style, except for a dessert spoon and dessert fork above the center of the place setting.

Figure 3–11. Place setting at Victoria and Albert's at The Grand Floridian Beach Resort at Walt Disney World. This shows the proper placement of a butter knife on the bread and butter plate. (© 1988 The Walt Disney Company)

 # History of Spoons

T he spoon is the oldest of all eating utensils. It is also the simplest. The earliest ones were made out of wood. The Egyptian spoons were carved from ivory and wood or various metals. Elaborately shaped handles were designed, and often decorated with lotus blossoms.

The spoon was a mark of class in medieval society. Each person brought his or her own set of utensils to dinner. Children were given their own set when they were old enough to eat with company. The expression "to be born with a silver spoon in your mouth" came about because wealthy families started the practice of giving a set of spoons to their children at birth. This phrase meant that the children came from a well-to-do- family.

Cesar Ritz

French cooking was becoming more popular and common in the 1800s. More restaurants were being opened. Russian service, as well as French, was being experienced by more guests. More restaurants were finding that Russian service was more economical to use. Waiters did not get as much respect as the talented chef de rangs of French service. Cesar Ritz is credited with making serving guests a profession.

Cesar lived from 1850 to 1918. His great learning took place when he worked as a commis de rang (assistant waiter) at the most famous restaurant in Paris, the Voisin. He took the job at Voisin so he could learn the best methods in serving techniques. He learned to deal well with people, and was so responsive to their wishes that before long guests were insisting on being served by him. He was a master at details. Soon he was in demand to manage restaurants and hotels all over Europe.

The following incident was typical of his quick thinking mind and obsession for details. He was working at a mountain top hotel in Switzerland called the Rigi-Kulm. A group of forty Americans were arriving for lunch. The temperature was eight degrees below zero and the heating system broke down. He had no way to cancel the party.

Ritz changed the setting of the party and the menu to give the guests the impression of warmth. The forty-seat table was moved into a small room and covered with a red tablecloth. Four large copper bowls were filled with methylated spirits; when the guest arrived it was lit. For each guest a hot brick was wrapped in a flannel cloth and placed under his or her feet. The guests began the meal with a hot consommeé and ended with crêpes flambées. Because of this obsession to details, the guests had no complaints about the temperature and the luncheon was a success.

Ritz's name and fame soon spread. His treatment of guests and his staff's service was legendary. He and Escoffier (the great French chef) began working together. Ritz would be in charge of the service, Escoffier of the kitchen. Escoffier created new dishes and named them for a favored few of their customers. Ritz chose the customers. Peach Melba, Melba toast, and Sauce Melba were created and named for the great Australian opera singer Dame Nellie Melba. His waiters were taught to give dignified service. They served in silence but were always at hand when needed. The dining room was always planned to be elegant and attractive enough to attract the most elegant of ladies.

In 1887, at age thirty-seven, he married a London hotelkeeper's daughter. While in London, he was asked to take over the management of the Savoy Hotel. This is the place where he made the biggest impact on the restaurant industry. He revolutionized dining out and even changed the habits of society. Restaurants were required by law to close at 11:00 P.M. He got Parliament to change the hour, and soon the Savoy's restaurant was open until 12:30 A.M.

Sunday dining become a feature of the week. The Savoy became known as the place to go and to be seen. He hired orchestras to play dinner music; the first one was led by Johann Strauss. He made evening dress compulsory and banned unaccompanied ladies from the dining room. He was accused of breaking up home life by making dining out fashionable. Because of him men's clubs suffered a loss of business. Men now took their wives out to dine at the Savoy instead of going to dinner at their men-only clubs. The common people could now go to a fashionable restaurant and dine with the aristocrats. In short, the common people could now "Put on the Ritz."

Setting the Cover

As Ritz made it a policy to have elegant surroundings for his restaurants, modern restaurant managers should also have standards for their establishment. Every restaurant and banquet house has a place setting on the table before the guests eat their meal. Our place settings are different from those of Ancient Rome and of medieval times. Some establishments have opulent linens, silver, and crystal; while others have only the bare essentials to do the job. The area or space for all utensils (including salt, pepper, and ashtrays) for each guest is defined as the *cover*. Many people refer to this as the place setting. However, note that the place setting includes *only* the utensils for the guest to eat the meal, while the cover includes all the space for each guest. A restaurant manager should make sure that each cover is set consistently. This is another factor that distinguishes an award-winning restaurant from others. At the Cross Keys Inn in Doylestown, Pennsylvania, owner Walter Conti (a Nation's Restaurant News Hall of Fame Winner) is a stickler for details. He inspects everything. At his restaurant each sugar bowl sits on the table facing the customer with its handles to the sides. It is in the same spot on every table to hide the ashtray from view.

With any style of service enough space must be allowed so that your guests are not crowded and your service staff can serve them safely. French and American services require twenty-four linear (straight line) inches of space for guest comfort; Russian service requires thirty inches. All should have an area fifteen inches deep. Therefore, in American banquet service, a table that is eight feet long by three feet wide can seat four guests on each side of the table, for a total of eight guests (as is illustrated in figure 3-12).

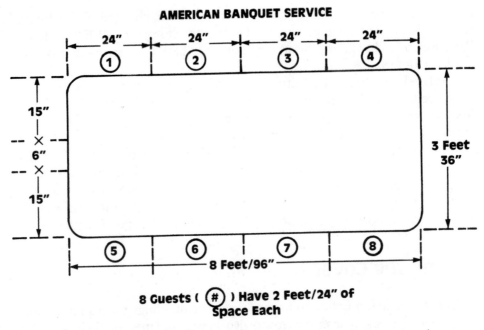

Figure 3–12. Space requirements for American banquet service. Each guest needs twenty-four linear inches. This table is eight feet long by three feet wide. It can seat four guests on each side of the table.

Regardless of the size of the table, the manager must make sure that both the guests and service staff have enough room so the guest can be comfortable and the service staff can serve properly.

Placemats and Tablecloths

The choice of what to put under the cover is up to the individual establishments. Some restaurants will use a placemat to cover the area for the place setting; others will use a tablecloth; still others use a tablecloth covered by a glass top.

Originally, restaurants that used placemats were low-priced coffee shops. Today, more and more restaurants (regardless of the type or the price of the meal) are choosing placemats rather than cloth because they are less expensive. The placemats can range in quality from paper to plastic or cloth. The placemat should be set about two inches from the edge of the table. The utensils go on the placemat.

Tablecloths are used for most banquets and, generally, in restaurants that have a high check average. Tablecloths should be placed on tables in banquet rooms by two people. The service persons stand on either side of the table while unfolding the tablecloth and laying it on the table. Tablecloths should be hung even with the seat of the chair. In an a la carte restaurant one person can place the cloth on the table, because the tables are smaller. In an a la carte restaurant it may become necessary to change the tablecloths during the meal period. All staff should know how to change the cloth without exposing the bare tabletop to the guests. Changing a cloth should be done discreetly, without a flourish that would distract the guests.

How to Change a Tablecloth

1. Remove all dirty plates and napkins from the table and place them on a tray (which is set on the tray stand, not on the table).
2. Move to one side of the dirty tablecloth all salt shakers, pepper shakers, flower vases, sugar bowls, and any other items that are part of the cover and which must remain on the table.
3. Fold back one edge of the dirty cloth and place the clean cloth on the bare part of the table.
4. Unfold the clean cloth to the center of the table, so it is almost touching the cloth to be changed.
5. Return all the items that are part of the cover to the clean tablecloth.
6. Complete unfolding the tablecloth.
7. Set the cover in the proper way, as required by management.

When service persons change cloths, they should never expose the bare table or place anything (clean or dirty items) on the chair. All personnel should know how to change a tablecloth and reset the cover. **No guests should ever be allowed to sit at a dirty table.**

Glass Tops

Some restaurants have discovered a new way to cut costs while still using tablecloths to make the restaurant look nice. The table is covered with a tablecloth, then a glass top (which has been specially made for each table) is placed over the cloth. The cover may be set directly on top of the glass. The one disadvantage is that the glass has to be cleaned with a glass cleaner after every meal. The smell of the cleaner might be offensive to some guests.

Completing the Cover

To complete the cover the table is finally set with a napkin, either cloth or paper. The napkin should be the last item to be placed on the table. Before the service person places the napkin on the table, the cover must be correct. The napkin can go in the center of the place setting, in a water or wine glass, or in the center of the starter plate (for establishments that use a starter plate). Figure 3-13 shows a fan-folded napkin in the center of the cover. The napkins should not go under the forks. Depending upon the policies of the restaurant, management may have the napkins folded in an artistic manner. The appendix of this book has a section on how to fold napkins.

Napkins

T he use of table linen began when the very rich started to cover their dining room tables with expensive decorated linen or silken drapes. The dining tables of that time were long and narrow. The cloths were generally square. To make the dining room look as attractive as possible, the cloths were set diagonally along the table. A corner of the cloth would hang over the edge of the table in front of each guest.

The eating habits and table manners of the guests were not good. It was common practice for the guests to wipe their greasy hands upon their clothes and spill food and drink on the cloths. It was not long before guests realized that there was no need to wipe their hands on their clothing and get their fine clothes dirty. They quickly figured out that this linen would be a great convenience for wiping their hands. Because of the way the cloth was situated on the table, they began to tuck the corner of the cloth under their chins to prevent the food from falling into their laps. And, of course, they wiped their face with the linen at the end of the meal. Hostesses soon (as early as the fifteenth century) had their servants make square pieces of cloths to match their tablecloths. That is how napkins were discovered.

Attention to details, especially in regard to table settings, is critical for a guest's first impression of your establishment. Tablecloths should be draped evenly at all tables. The proper length is fourteen inches. When the drape of the tablecloth is longer or shorter than fourteen inches the dining or banquet room looks unappealing.

Regardless of the type of tablecloths, placemats, and napkins that you decide to use in your restaurant, make certain that they are attractive, clean, and fit the style of your restaurant.

Figure 3–13.   Fan-folded napkin in the center of the cover. (Photo courtesy of The Old Journey's End)

The History of American Service

Dining in America was affected by the Puritan influence. There was only one purpose for eating: to refuel the body. To dine or enjoy the meal was thought to be bad.

The restaurant business in America got its start in the 1800s at taverns and road houses. Service at the beginning of this century was terrible. American service was and is still characterized by "Food on the plate, no wait." This was the American custom. All food was put on one plate and served to the guest, as opposed to French service, where separate plates for vegetables were used. All guests sat in a common room and ordered from a very limited menu. Too much food was served to the guest. The eating hours were set for the convenience of management.

During the 1830s, a great influx of French exiles entered America. These exiles brought to America their way to serve food. At about the same time, many German and Italian waiters and cooks came to the United States, because they had heard that the streets were paved with gold. They also brought with them a better style of service than was available in America. As they found employment in America, they introduced their methods of service in the places where they worked. Eventually, service got better and a style of service began to develop.

Another reason that service got better was that employers went to Europe and got entire kitchen and dining room staffs to come to America. The owners paid for the workers' trip over. This was a way to get to those gold-paved streets. The owners would offer to pay wages to the cooks, but told the service staff they could work only for tips. Restaurant owners did this to cut down on their labor costs. It worked; many people were looking to go to the new world, and they were pleased to have the opportunity. America had always been tipless. When the owners returned from Europe with their new staffs, they introduced tipping into America—claiming it was an established European practice.

At the same time that the great influx of immigrants were arriving in the United States, Delmonico's opened in New York City (in 1832). This restaurant gets the credit for teaching the American public how to enjoy fine dining. It also set the standard for elegance that all other restaurants in the United States tried to match. Delmonico's offered the first a la carte menu, courteous service, private dining rooms, flowers, music, and fine wines to its guests.

Oscar Tschirky, when he was employed as the maître d'hôtel at the Waldorf-Astoria, worked exclusively in the dining room. He elevated service to the highest standards in America. No waiter was allowed to have chin whiskers, or a mustache, as he considered facial hair to be unsanitary. He also got American restaurants to cut down on the abundance of food.

Thanks to Delmonico's, Oscar Tschirky, and the immigrants, America now had its own unique type of service developing which took the best parts of French and Russian service and combined it with American ingenuity.

American Service

American service is characterized by portioning all the food on the dinner plate in the kitchen. It is also referred to as plate service or German service. The service is the fastest of all types, and requires the least amount of skill to wait on guests. One service person generally works a station (a group of tables in an area of the room) containing between fourteen to eighteen seats. The main difference in serving food in American service, as opposed to French and Russian service, is that all food is served from the guest's left side with the service person's left hand, and all beverages are served from the guest's right side with the service person's right hand. Raymond J. Goodman theorizes in his book *The Management of Service* that the practice of serving food from the guest's left side occurred because Americans consume more beverages and more varieties of beverages than Europeans. Because the glasses are positioned on the right of the place setting, it was easier to serve the food from the left side, so as not to disturb the guest when he was drinking or reaching for his glass.

The advantages of American service far outweigh the disadvantages.

1. It is a simple service to teach and learn. The staff only has to put a plate in front of the guest. They do not have to know how to cook, carve, or flambé.
2. A skilled staff is not necessary. Almost anyone can be trained to serve American style.
3. The cost of equipment is small, as there are no gueridons or silver trays to purchase.
4. Service is extremely fast.
5. Less dining room space is required for each guest.
6. Because service is fast and less space is required per guest, more guests can be served during the meal period.
7. Menu prices can be lower for the same meals compared to other services.
8. Portion and quality control are excellent, as all foods are plated in the kitchen.

ADVANTAGES AND DISADVANTAGES OF AMERICAN SERVICE

Advantages

1. A simple service to teach and learn.
2. A skilled service staff is not necessary.
3. Cost of equipment is small.
4. Service is the fastest of all three methods.
5. Less dining room space is required for guests.
6. More guests can be served.
7. Menu prices can be lower than in other services.
8. Quality control can be excellent.

Disadvantages

Service is not as elaborate as in French or Russian style service.

Figure 3–14.   Advantages and disadvantages of American service

There is just one main disadvantage in using American service: the service is not as elaborate as are the other two.

American service is widely used in restaurants around the world today because the advantages far outweigh the disadvantages. Most restaurant managers will borrow parts of French and Russian service and incorporate it into their particular service style. For example, many restaurants in the United States offer salads made tableside (French); or they may serve a dish like lobster newburg, portioning it out in front of the guests (Russian). American service is the best type of service to use for most restaurants.

Banquet Service

A banquet is a meal where all the food has been preselected by the host before the guests enter the room. Banquets are served using American, Russian, or Buffet Style. All have advantages and disadvantages. The key factor in serving banquets is that the service person have as much needed equipment on the guests' table before they enter the room. The purpose of banquets is to serve guests faster than in a la carte dining. This is because most banquets are arranged for a special purpose—a dance, testimonial or awards presentation—not just to eat. A brief description of all types of banquets are given below.

 ## Origin of the Word Banquet

At large dinners in medieval times the seating arrangements were precise. The feudal lord and lady sat on a raised dais at one end of the room. The children and relatives sat on removable benches along the walls. The term banquet comes from the French word for bench, which is *banc.* Servants stood behind the chairs of the wealthy lords to help serve them food and drink. As in Roman times, tasters were employed by the wealthy couples to make certain that the food was not poisoned. At medieval and Roman banquets there were not many spoons, so the diners used their fingers or short, pointed daggers to bring the food to their mouth. There were no forks or napkins or place settings.

American Banquet Service

Like American Service, this is an easy service to serve. One waiter can usually serve from sixteen to twenty-four guests. The service is the same as American, the only difference is the place setting.

American Banquet Service Place Setting

The place setting for American banquet service is similar to American a la carte service. However, the place setting changes with every banquet. A separate utensil is needed for each course. Because the purpose of the banquet is to serve guests as quickly as possible, the utensils should be preset.

Therefore, the meal illustrated in figure 3-15 needs, two forks, three spoons, and two knives. The place setting appears in Figure 3-16. Note that the coffee cup and saucer is preset with the cup up and the handle in the correct position.

Figure 3-16 is the correct place setting for the menu as it appears in Figure 3-15. However, a banquet house may not have enough spoons to place three at each setting. Therefore, the banquet manager might be forced to use only two spoons.

However, if a restaurant is going to be in the banquet business, it is strongly recommended that the establishment purchase enough equipment to do the job properly.

TYPICAL BANQUET MENU

Item	Utensil Needed
Fresh Fruit Cup	Teaspoon
Salad, House Dressing	Fork
Prime Ribs	Knife to cut, fork to eat
Baked Potato, Green Broccoli	
Rolls and Butter	Butter spreader
Chocolate Mousse	Teaspoon
Coffee	Teaspoon

Figure 3-15.   The menu for a typical banquet, with the utensils needed to serve one guest. Needed are two forks, three spoons, and two knives. A bread and butter plate, cup and saucer, napkin and water glass are needed also.

AMERICAN BANQUET PLACE SETTING

A—Coffee Cup
B—Fruit Spoon
C—Coffee Spoon
D—Dessert Spoon
E—Dinner Knife

F—Main Course Fork
G—Salad Fork
H—Bread and Butter Plate
I—Water Glass

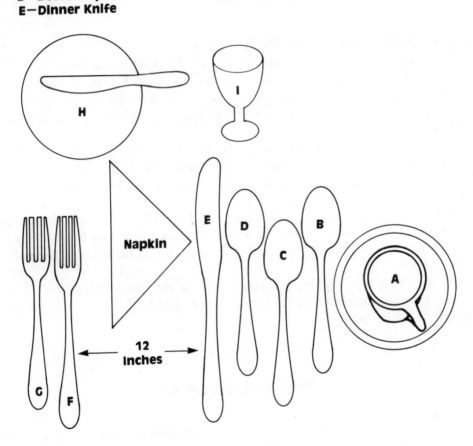

Figure 3–16.

History of Forks

The first types of forks had two prongs. They were used to hold sacrificial meat, not for eating. People ate by picking the food up with their fingers or the pointed end of their knife. Two people are credited with introducing the fork to modern society. A byzantine princess introduced the fork in the eleventh century to the people of Venice, Italy. Queen Catherine de Medicis was the second person. She introduced it to the aristocrats of France after returning from Italy in the mid 1500s. At first, it was used more as an amusement than as a serious eating utensil. By the 1600s forks became fashionable and were more acceptable than using one's fingers to eat with.

Like spoons, forks became very elaborate. These forks sometimes were as elaborate as a piece of jewelry. When people were invited to dinner, they carried their precious forks with them in special cases. Forks were introduced to England by Tomas Coryate, who brought back samples of them from Italy, where he first used them.

Governor John Winthrop of Massachusetts brought the fork to America. When he came to the colonies in 1630, he brought it along with his personal knife in his personal case.

By the 1800s forks had became acceptable throughout the Western world. Soon restaurants started to provide all utensils for guests.

Russian Banquet Service

This is the most elegant of banquet services. Two service people are generally assigned to work in pairs, serving a total of twenty guests. Food is served from platter to plate. One server serves the main course, while the other follows with the potatoes and vegetables. A skilled staff is needed for this type of service.

Russian Place Setting

Like the American setting, all utensils are put on the table. However, each guest has his own set of salt and pepper shakers. The dessert fork and spoon are set above the place setting. As in American banquet service, the amount of silverware needed is changed with each banquet, depending on the menu.

Buffet Service

Buffet service is characterized by the guests obtaining either their whole meal or parts of the meal from food that is displayed in the dining room. One service person can be assigned as many as thirty-five guests. The place settings for banquets have only enough utensils set to do the job.

There are three types of buffets. The first is simply called **buffet.** In this service, guests obtain all their own food and drinks. The service person has only one job: to clean up dirty dishes.

The second is called **modified deluxe buffet.** Tables are set with utensils and guests are served coffee, and perhaps dessert, by the service person.

The third is the most elegant, called **deluxe buffet.** The guests are served the first and second course, as well as their beverages and dessert. They obtain their main course from an elegant buffet. The service person must serve and clear many courses. They must have all the dirty plates cleared before the guest returns from the buffet table. One service person is needed for twenty guests in this style of buffet service.

Because it is a banquet, the place setting of the buffet is determined by what food is offered on the buffet. However, the manager must use common sense in determining how many utensils to set.

Chapter Summary

1. There are many styles in which to serve food and beverages to guests.
2. No one style is correct for all establishments.
3. Each restaurant and banquet house will have to decide the type of service it will give.
4. The style of service provided will depend on the restaurant's menu, decor, and pricing.
5. Some establishments will serve their food on silver platters, while others will serve their food on paper plates. You will have to choose which is best for your operation.

Review Questions

1. How did American service first begin, and how did it evolve?
2. Describe the differences in the three types of a la carte services.
3. Compare the advantages and disadvantages of the three types of a la carte services.
4. Diagram correctly the place settings for French, Russian, and American a la carte service.
5. Describe the different banquet styles: American, Russian, and Buffet.
6. What are the advantages and disadvantages of the three buffet services?
7. What must a manager know before he or she can diagram the place setting for American, Russian, or Buffet banquet services?
8. What is a cover, and how were eating utensils introduced?
9. Explain how to change tablecloths during a busy period.
10. How many guests is a service person expected to serve in each of the following services: American, French, and Russian a la carte; American and Russian banquet; buffet, modified deluxe buffet, and deluxe buffet?
11. How would you as the banquet manager for a party solve this equipment shortage problem? Each person should have three forks at his or her cover: one

for salad, one for main course, and one for dessert. You need six hundred forks, but have only four hundred. In addition, the rental company sent you only two hundred bread and butter plates, while you need six hundred: two hundred for the first course (melon), two hundred for the place setting, and two hundred for the last course (pie).

References

1. Janet McKenzie Hill, The Up-to-Date Waitress (Boston: Little, Brown, and Co, 1906), vi.
2. Christine Terhunne Herrick, ed. in chief, *Consolidated Library of Modern Cooking and Household Recipes* (New York: Bodmer, 1904), 25.

Chapter 4
Proper Guidelines for Service

Chapter Objectives:

At the completion of this chapter, the student will be able to:

1. define competency as it relates to proper service;
2. properly pick up, load, carry, and put down a tray;
3. define a sidetowel and explain its purpose;
4. recite and properly use the seven guidelines for providing competent service;
5. properly serve coffee and tea, and change ashtrays;
6. explain the different ways in which food is served in American, French, and Russian service; and
7. explain the proper method of serving guests at tables and booths.

Excellent Service

All restaurants and banquet halls strive to give their guests excellent service. Some of them succeed; but most of them fail miserably. It is a known fact that one of the major causes of restaurant failure is poor service. As was stated in Chapter One, survey after survey has shown that the American public values good service and despises poor service.

Many people, including restaurant reviewers, restaurant owners, and guests, have stated that excellent service can compensate for average food; but great food cannot compensate for bad service. Excellent service is the result of the two factors, competency and friendliness. Competency is defined as serving food and drinks to the guest in the correct manner. Friendliness is a characteristic that the dining room and/or banquet manager must encourage in service staff. At times, the manager has to be concerned if the service staff becomes too friendly with the guests. This friendliness leads to informality and then sloppiness. Friendliness, if done correctly, is an extremely important aspect of excellent service. However, the service staff must also be competent in order to provide excellent service.

Importance of Competency

The manager must teach and reinforce correct serving methods to the service staff so that these methods become second nature. The *Random House Dictionary* defines competent as "having suitable skill, experience, etc., for some purpose."[1] Competent service in a restaurant has one main purpose: the guest will leave the establishment pleased with the dining experience. Competency in a restaurant can best be described in the following way: Competency occurs when the customers do not have to ask the service person for any item during a meal. The water glasses are refilled. The meals are served without the service person asking which guest receives which menu item. In short, the guests know they have had a great dining experience, because they have not had to ask the service person for any item. The service person brought all items to the guests before they could think of asking for it.

How to Obtain Competency

Great restaurants instill competency in their staff through great attention to details, training, and follow-up of serving methods. The **success** of a **restaurant** depends on the **manager.** If the manager overlooks the little details, the service staff will also overlook the little details. However, if the manager pays attention to details, the service staff will consistently follow the lead of the manager.

Competency comes from management. Management must teach their staff the proper way to serve their guests. As previously stated, training at Walt Disney World concentrates on the competent service methods. In addition, management continuously monitors their service. The staff must be reminded about what they are doing correctly and incorrectly. Anything being done incorrectly must be corrected immediately. Managers are taught to be coaches, and to coach cast members in the correct way to serve. The key to competent service is training. A customer will immediately notice things that are right and wrong about the establishment. Restaurants that have all details in place usually are excellent at service. Places that look disorganized usually give merely adequate or even poor service.

A How-Not-To Story

A wedding reception was held at a country club in one of the richest and most elegant communities in America. The first thing that was noticed when entering the dining room was that all the tables and covers were set in a haphazard manner. Some coffee cups had their handles at the four o'clock position, some at the five o'clock. The cups were placed at the top of the place setting, mixed in with the bread and butter plates. It appeared that there was a problem with taking care of details. Sure enough, the concerns were justified. After being served an adequate meal (nothing outstanding, nothing poor), the wedding cake was served. However, the tables had not been totally cleared of the dishes from the main course. Nevertheless, the service staff brought the cake to the table and pushed the dirty dinner plates to the center of the table. What was an adequate meal turned into a disappointment for the guests as they had to eat their wedding cake while staring into leftover broccoli, stuffed baked potato skins, and fried chicken.

The Key to Competency

In the February 1979 issue of *Connecticut Magazine* is a story about the Copper Beach Inn in Ivoryton. This restaurant, voted best in the state of Connecticut by the readers of the magazine, was owned by Jo and Bob McKenzie. One reason for their success was their training methods. They did not just hire someone and call him or her a service person. The owners set policies for their staff and trained them thoroughly.

All new service staff and bartenders were required to study a sixty-page service manual and to pass a written test on the McKenzie method. Included in the manual were all the minute details that stress how service is to be accomplished. For example, the placement of tomatoes on the salad dish was explained, as well as how to remove dishes. Even the proper way to stand in the dining room, upright and with hands behind the back, was covered.

But their key to excellent service was the constant supervision and implementation of their policies. All the manuals and training are worthless if the manager does not enforce the guidelines set forth in those books. Colleen Sherman has worked in four different types of restaurants. In an interview with the author, she compared the type of training and follow-up methods she has received. She noted that all of the restaurants varied in their training. At the family restaurant, she was told she was a waitress. That was the extent of her training. Her next job was at a chain restaurant. She had to study and memorize menus and policies, and was then assigned tables to serve. When she worked at a franchise chain restaurant she had to pass three written tests before being assigned as a waitress. However, at all these places there was no follow-up to her training. She considers her most successful training to have been at Walt Disney World, because of the follow-up training she received.

Walter Conti at Cross Keys Inn also uses follow-up. He notes the errors made by staffers and corrects them, thus maintaining excellent service. The key to a competent serving staff is good training plus excellent and consistent follow-up training. As in all learning, repetition is the key to

THE KEY TO COMPETENCY

Training by management
plus
consistent observation of the service staff
plus
coaching and complimenting
and
repetition
by
the manager

Figure 4–1.

success. The dining room and banquet manager must stress and reinforce the competent way to serve the guest.

The Sidetowel

All professional service persons must have with them a napkin to use as a sidetowel. As the veteran waiter Sam Bubonia at The DeWitt Clinton Hotel in Albany, New York, used to say, "You are not a professional waiter unless you have a sidetowel with you."[2] The sidetowel has two purposes.

First, it can be used as an insulator; the service person can pick up and serve dinners with the sidetowel rather than risking getting burned from handling hot plates.

Second, if there is any type of spill, the service person has a cloth to clean up the spill. There is no need to waste valuable time running back to the kitchen to obtain cloths to clean up the mess. Therefore, the sidetowel becomes a time-saver.

When the sidetowel is not used for any of the above purposes, it should be placed over the service person's left arm, not stuck in the back pocket like a handkerchief. It must always be clean. If the service person is not using the sidetowel to serve food, it goes on the opposite arm. Figure 4-2 shows three service staff ready to greet guests.

Trays

A wonderful invention was made for waitpeople. This invention was the tray. Two basic types of trays are used in the restaurant industry. Large

Figure 4–2.   A service staff ready to greet guests. The first server has no sidetowel. The second has the sidetowel properly positioned over his arm. The third has the sidetowel improperly positioned on her shoulder. Also, the waiter is wearing a hat, which may or may not be improper. (Photo courtesy of Peter Houghton)

trays, called hotel ovals, are used to carry food and plates to and from the guest. The other type are small, round, rectangular or oval trays (called tea trays) which are generally used to serve drinks.

Large-sized trays enable the service person to carry many items at once, as opposed to delivering food as they do in diners and coffee shops, item by item. It may be impressive to see a service person carrying eight dinners stacked up on both arms. However, using a tray is much more professional looking, efficient, safe and sanitary than using the style called arm service.

Many of the best establishments (for example, Walt Disney World) insist that waitpeople must use a tray to carry all items. The server must use a tray even if it is to carry a water pitcher or one coffee cup. Waitpeople should not be allowed to serve guests directly from the tray without putting the tray on a traystand, as it creates a safety hazard.

Easter Dinner

As the family approached the restaurant for their Easter dinner, they saw an ambulance at the entrance. Entering the restaurant, they heard a child screaming.

Once the child was taken to the hospital, they were told what had happened. After the child's family (grandparents, parents, and children) had finished their meal, the mother asked for coffee. The service person carried the hot, steaming cup of coffee to the table without a tray. The mother swung around in her chair, hit the server's hand, and the hot coffee spilled on the child, causing second-degree burns.

Not a pleasant way to celebrate a holiday! All because the server did not use a tray.

Dining room and banquet managers who insist that the service staff use trays will have a much more competent service staff than managers who do not. Once the service staff forms the habit of using the trays, it becomes second nature. Soon their service improves, because they are carrying more items on each trip between the dining room and the kitchen. As a result, they make fewer trips and save themselves a most valuable commodity: time.

Besides being able to carry more food and beverages to tables using a tray, another advantage is that it is safer and more sanitary than using arm service. The tray is bigger than a plate. Therefore, anyone walking past will most likely see the tray and there will be less chance of an accident occurring. Using a tray is more sanitary because the plates do not slide down the server's arm into one another. When this happens, one guest's gravy ends up on the other guest's plate. Using a tray is more eye-appealing and pleasing to the guest because the plates do not slide down the server's arm into one another.

However, the greatest reason for using a tray is that all the food can be delivered to the guests' table at the same time. This makes the guests' meal more enjoyable, and the restaurant more efficient.

The small trays are used to bring drinks from the bar or one or two items from the kitchen. Some establishments will allow their servers to serve the guest directly from the tray, but that may create a safety hazard. Other establishments, like Walt Disney World, insist that the servers place the tray on a sidestand and serve from the sidestand to the guest.

Whatever the policies of the establishment, using a tray to serve food is much more efficient than using arm service.

Traystands and/or Sidestands

There must be a place for the waitpeople to place their tray. Trays can be set down on a permanent table in the dining room called a sideboard or service station. Or they can be placed on lightweight devices called traystands.

Traystands are excellent for use in a restaurant or at banquets because they are light enough to be carried by the server in one hand, while carrying a tray of food with the other hand. Therefore, the service person can carry the stand right to the guest table. This saves the service person time and extra steps, because the tray is right next to the table instead of being located a distance from the table. Traystands open easily and are secure, so they are easy to use and safe. Using trays and having traystands located near the guests' table is the most efficient way to deliver food to the guests.

The Correct Way to Lift and Put Down a Tray

There is a correct way to lift and put down a tray on the traystand. First, when training the staff, they should be taught the parts of the traystand. Make certain that they know all the parts and how they operate.

There are two legs which open up and have cloth supports which hold the traystand together. The service person's body must be lined up parallel with the cloth supports. If the waitpeople line up correctly, their hands will not get tangled with the metal supports when they put down or pick up the tray. Figure 4-3 shows the proper way to line up to pick up a tray from the traystand.

Proper Way to Lift a Tray

Waitpeople should be taught to line their body up even with the traystand. The opening of the tray stand should be at a right angle with the server's body. They should bend down at the knee, as if they are genuflecting, as illustrated in Figure 4-3. Figures 4-4 and 4-5 illustrate the proper and improper way to pick up a tray. In order to protect their clean shirts from the dirty tray, it is recommended that service persons place a clean napkin or cloth on their shoulder. The tray is then slid onto the service person's shoulder. Most waitpeople slide it onto their left shoulder because they are right-handed. However, it does not matter which shoulder the tray is carried on as long as it is carried properly.

The service person's hand (if the tray is going on the right shoulder, it should be the right hand, as is shown in Figure 4-4) should be placed under the tray. The larger tray or hotel oval is usually carried while it is resting and balanced on the palm of the server's hand. More experienced waitpeople will

Figure 4–3. The proper body position to pick up a tray from the sidestand. The server's body is parallel with the cloth supports. This position makes it easy to slide the tray onto her shoulder without getting her hands tangled up with the metal supports. The server is squatting, not bending over to pick up her tray. (Photo courtesy of Peter Houghton)

balance the tray on their fingertips. The inexperienced server should grasp the front of the tray with the free hand (as shown in Figure 4-4) for stability. The service person lifts the tray by using leg muscles, not back muscles. A tray should never be carried as illustrated in Figure 4-5. This is too dangerous and may result in injury to the server.

How to Put Down a Tray

The procedure is the opposite of that for lifting a tray. The server must align his or her body so that the tray can easily be slid onto the cloth supports. The server should then bend down at the knee and slide the tray onto the traystand. Employees should be taught never to bend over at the

Figure 4–4.   The proper manner in which to pick up a tray. The tray is balanced correctly with dirty dishes neatly stacked. On the server's shoulder is her sidetowel which protects her blouse from getting soiled. The tray has been slid to her right shoulder, and she is lifting the tray with her leg strength. (Photo courtesy of Peter Houghton)

waist. If they do, they may injure themselves because they are using their back instead of leg muscles. Once the tray is on the stand, the server takes the sidetowel off the shoulder and places it in the proper position (either over the arm or used as an insulator for the hot plates).

The smaller tray or tea tray is carried waist high. Because this tray is so light, the service person can place it on a sideboard without bending down. If the dining room manager allows drinks and food to be served directly

Figure 4–5. The improper way to carry a tray. Positioned in front of the server. Tray is poorly balanced with dirty dishes. An injury may result to the server. In addition, the server has no sidetowel. (Photo courtesy of Peter Houghton)

from the tray, it must be held in the correct hand. With drinks, hold it in the left hand; with food, the right hand.

Loading a Tray

The first thing a server must do is to check that the tray is clean on both the top and bottom surfaces.

Trays are designed with either a non-slip surface of cork or without it. If the tray does not have a non-slip material, the staff should be taught to take a damp, clean cloth, and put it on the tray. Even if the tray is made with a non-slip material, a clean cloth placed on the tray will make the service look more professional.

In loading a tray, the heaviest items should be placed on the side of the tray that will be closest to the server's body. This will allow the server's shoulder to bear the brunt of the weight and allow the server to have more control over the tray. When more experienced servers carry the tray by balancing it on their fingertips, they place the heaviest items in the center of the tray.

The lighter items and glasses are placed to the outside of the tray or away from the service person's shoulder. Items with spouts and handles should have their spouts and handles facing the center of the tray.

When serving food, the servers should be instructed to keep all hot items together. If it is necessary to carry both hot and cold food on the same tray, instruct the servers to separate the cold food from the hot food. Plates should never be stacked on top of each other unless plate covers are used. When serving soup, the cups should be placed around a stack of saucers. The soup should not be placed on the saucers until the server places the tray on the traystand.

When removing dirty dishes, the establishment should have an organized system for loading trays so that all plates are stacked neatly. This means all bread and butter plates are stacked on each other, instead of having a dinner plate on top of a bread and butter plate, with forks, knives, and spoons stuck in between them. Figures 4-6 and 4-7 illustrate the proper and improper method of loading dirty dishes onto a tray.

It must be emphasized that the only way the staff will load their trays properly is if they are taught correctly by the manager. Once the training is complete, there must be consistent reinforcement by the manager; that is, correction and reinstruction if done incorrectly, and praise if done correctly.

Guidelines for American a la Carte and Banquet Service

For a restaurant to have competent service there are standards that must be met by all servers. The following guidelines have evolved over many years of serving. Originally, they were thought of as rules, but they should be renamed guidelines because rules are too rigid for the dining room business. Perhaps that is why they were not and are not enforced consistently. Often, because of circumstances beyond the server's control, common sense must prevail when serving guests. The server will often have to serve from the "wrong side" because of the physical constraints of the room or for the

Figure 4–6. The proper way to load a tray of dirty dishes. The silverware is separated from the plates. The top plate has all of the leftover food on it. When the server brings the food into the kitchen, it will be easy to unload the tray. (Photo courtesy of Peter Houghton)

guest's comfort. However, these guidelines should be enforced whenever possible.

The Seven Guidelines Explained

1. Ladies are served before men.

Yes, this does mean that if there is a party of two couples (two men and two women), the service person serves one woman and then the next woman. The service person serves in this order; woman #1, woman #2, man #1, man #2. If the server can easily determine who is the older woman at the table, she should be served first.

There are instances when the server would break this guideline. Children should be served before adults. Then serve the females, then the men.

People always wonder if this can be done. Does it make any sense? When guests dine at The Publick House in Sturbridge, Massachusetts, they indeed

Figure 4–7. The improper way to stack dirty dishes. The dishes are placed on the tray with no specific method. This makes for a dangerous and hard to carry tray of dirty dishes for the service person. (Photo courtesy of Peter Houghton)

THE SEVEN GUIDELINES OF SERVICE

1. Ladies are served before men, (if children are present, they should be served first, then ladies, then men).
2. Food is served from the guest's left side, with the service person's left hand.
3. Beverages are served from the guest's right side, with the service person's right hand.
4. All guests' food must be brought to the table at the same time.
5. Do not remove guest plates from the table until all guests are finished eating their meal.
6. Never stack or scrape dirty plates on the guests' table.
7. Dirty dishes are cleared from the guest's right side with the service person's right hand.

Figure 4–8.

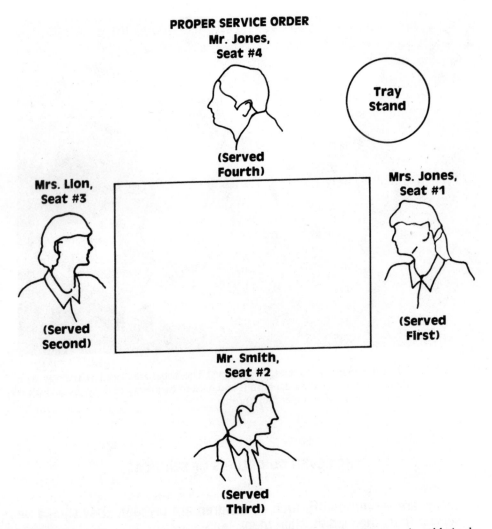

PROPER SERVICE ORDER

Mr. Jones, Seat #4 — (Served Fourth)

Tray Stand

Mrs. Lion, Seat #3 — (Served Second)

Mrs. Jones, Seat #1 — (Served First)

Mr. Smith, Seat #2 — (Served Third)

Figure 4–9. The proper sequence to serve a table. The server should serve the table in the order 1, 3, 2, 4. The women are served first and then the men are served.

see that it is possible to serve the children first. The server first took the order for drinks. She returned and served the youngest child his cola. Then she walked past the mother to serve the older son his soda. She returned to their mother to serve her drink. And finally, the father was served his drink. It did not take that long to serve all four guests. She served all drinks from the guests' right side with her right hand. Throughout the meal, service was performed quickly and competently. The dining room (which seated over

100) was filled and the service was superb. It added to the great food and pleasant atmosphere of the restaurant.

Another exception to this guideline is when serving a banquet, where the room is set up with long banquet tables seating more than ten people. With long banquet tables it makes little sense to skip over the men because there are so many guests at the table. If a server is working at a banquet where the banquet table has ten or more people on each side of the table, it is more logical to serve the guests in sequential order.

2. Food is served from the guest's left side with the service person's left hand.

There is a logical and practical reason for this guideline. If the service person served with the right hand from the left side of the guests it would create a dangerous situation. The service person is putting his or her arm right in the faces of the guests. This could be most unappetizing if the waiter has body odor. Also, the guests would have to back away in order to prevent the service person from brushing or hitting them with his arm. It is also dangerous for the service person. Figures 4-10 and 4-11 illustrate the proper and improper way to serve food in American service. There are times when a guest will not pay attention to the service person and may move unexpectedly. When the service person sees the guest moving quickly, the server's arm can be swung out and away from the guest if the service is being done correctly. The chance of an accident occurring is reduced by proper service.

Because the service person is serving with the left hand, service should proceed in a clockwise direction. Many people have trouble with the concept of clockwise and counterclockwise; a simple way to remember the correct direction is "to follow your nose." Proceed in the direction that your nose is pointing. Serve food from the guest's left side with your left hand and follow your nose. Figure 4-12 illustrates the proper direction in serving a party of four.

There are a couple of exceptions to this guideline also. Serving food to guests seated at a booth or a table positioned against a wall requires a different set of procedures. The service person must serve and pick up with the same hand. Look at figure 4-13. The server should serve the guest in seat A, using the left hand. The guest in seat C is served using the right hand. Removing dirty dishes, the service person would use the same hand that was used to serve the meal. This allows the server to keep his or her arm out of the face of the guest. The same rules of serving women before men apply.

When two guests are talking to each other, the service person does not interrupt their conversation by serving the food properly. Instead, serve one

Figure 4–10. The waiter is serving food properly to the guest. He is serving from the guest's left side with his left hand. His sidetowel is used as an insulator between his left hand and the hot plate. His right hand is behind him. (Photo courtesy of Peter Houghton)

guest from the left side, the other from the right side. Remember, when serving from the right side, the right hand should be used. If there is a physical item in the way (like a pole) or the table is positioned in such a way that makes it impossible to serve the guests from their left, serve them from their right side.

Figure 4–11.   The waitress is serving the food incorrectly to the guest. She is serving with her right hand from the guest's left side. Her sidetowel is on her shoulder. (Photo courtesy of Peter Houghton)

3. Beverages are served from the guest's right side with the service person's right hand.

Because a large majority of people are right handed, the glasses and cups for beverages are put on the right side of the guest. It is logical that the service person would pour beverages from the right side of the guest. Therefore, to be consistent, all beverages are served from the right side.

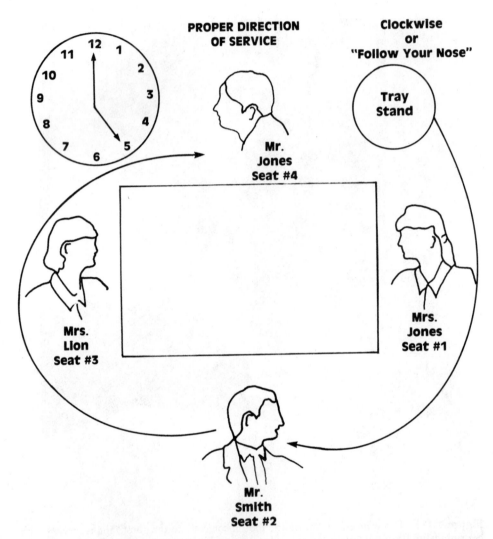

Figure 4–12. The proper direction of serving a meal. The service person would serve guest #1, then #3 going in a clockwise direction. Returning to the tray, guest #2 would be served followed by guest #4.

When serving an alcoholic beverage, a cocktail napkin should be placed in front of the guest. The beverage should then be placed on the cocktail napkin. If there is a meal in front of the guest, the service person will place the beverage above the spoons and knives on the right side of the guest.

When service persons have to pour water, wine, or coffee into a glass or

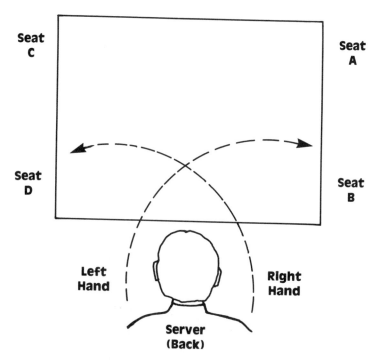

Figure 4–13.   Service at a booth. The server serves and picks up with the same hand. Guests in seat A and B will be served and dirty dishes picked up with the left hand. Guests in seats C and D will be served and dirty dishes picked up with the right hand. The same rules concerning serving women before men apply.

cup already on the table they **must not** pick up the glass or cup, unless leaving the glass or cup on the table would create a safety hazard.

The proper way to pour water is to pour with the right hand, keeping the left hand folded behind the back. Some establishments prefer that the service person hold the sidetowel (with the left hand) under the lip of the glass to catch any drips or spills. Water glasses should be filled three-quarters to the top of the glass. Figures 4-14 and 4-15 show the proper and improper way to pour water.

Coffee should be poured with the right hand while the left hand holds a coffee shield. This shield (bread and butter plate) is placed at an angle between the coffee pot and the guest to protect the guest from coffee spills and steam from the hot pot. Figure 4-16 illustrates the correct way to pour coffee.

Tea should be brought to the guest in a small pot and be placed above the coffee cup. The teabag should be in the pot, steeping.

Figure 4–14. The waiter is pouring water the correct way, from the guest's right side with his right hand. The glass is not removed from the table. However, his sidetowel is in his back pocket, which is incorrect. It should either be over his left arm or under the lip of the glass to catch the drips from the water pitcher. (Photo courtesy of Peter Houghton)

However, a good service person is always aware of guest's needs. If a guest is left-handed, he or she will switch the water glass or coffee cup to the left side. When this occurs, the server should serve from the guest's left side with the left hand. One important **rule** is **never to reach in front of the guest.** For example, when the service person is pouring coffee and the guest has moved the cup to the left side, the service person would **never pour**

Figure 4–15. This waitress is pouring water the incorrect way. She is pouring from the guest's left side with her right hand. Her elbow is right in the guest's face. The water glass is lifted off of the table, and she has no sidetowel. (Photo courtesy of Peter Houghton)

coffee from the right side. This would mean he or she would have to reach across the guest to pour coffee into the cup on the left side of the guest.

Generally, all beverages are served from the right side with the right hand.

4. All guests' food must be brought to the table at the same time.

One of the most annoying situations for a guest is to be served first and then have to wait for others at the table to be served their food. This creates

Figure 4–16. This waitress is pouring coffee the correct way. Served with a coffee shield, from the guest's right side with the service person's right hand. Her sidetowel is on her right arm. (Photo courtesy of Peter Houghton)

two problems for the guests. Guests with proper manners will wait for the whole table to be served before they begin to eat their meal. Most likely their food will get cold, as the service person has to return to the kitchen to obtain the rest of the food. Colleen Sherman says that "the supervisors at Walt

Disney World never let a service person go to a table without the complete order."[3] It is also embarrassing and annoying for the guests.

The manager should insist that all food reach the table at the same time. This is especially true at banquets when the guests have their choice of two main entrees. All guests must be served the meal at the same time even if half of them are eating chicken and the other half beef. The manager must devise a system (which is explained in Chapter twelve) by which all guests are served at the same time.

5. Do not remove any guest's plates from the table until all guests are finished eating their meal.

This guideline means exactly what it says. It is a mystery why waitpeople remove plates from guests before all the guests at the table are finished eating their meal. This implies to the guests who have not finished their meal that they are taking too long to eat. Therefore, they must hurry and finish their meal. Of course, if a guest is done and pushes the plate to be cleared away, then take the plate away.

Another part of this guideline is that a new course must never be served until the dishes from the previous course have been removed from the table. This is another of the strict competency rules that are enforced at Walt Disney World: A server must remove the soup course before being allowed to serve the salad course.

The only exception to this guideline may occur during a banquet. Because most banquets are on a strict time schedule, if the banquet manager waited for all guests to complete every course it could put the banquet behind schedule. If a guest has not finished with the salad course and the main course is ready to be served, the banquet manager could instruct the service staff to do the following: Have the service staff remove all the finished salad plates. If the guest is finished eating his or her salad when the service person brings out the entree, the service person should remove the dirty dish before serving any of the main entrees. If the guest is still not finished with the previous course, the service person should ask permission to move the plate. The server should move the dish above and to the left of where the entree will be placed.

6. Never stack or scrape dirty plates on the guests' table.

This is the most irritating and unappetizing habit a service person can have. Some waitpeople take the dirty dishes and stack them—one on top of another—right in front of the guests, as is illustrated in figure 4-17. It is even worse if the service person scrapes all the leftovers onto one plate in the center of the table. Some of them will even dump the cigarette and cigar

Figure 4–17. The improper way to clear a table. The waiter has the guest's dishes stacked in front of the guest and is dumping the ashes from the ashtray into the leftover food. In addition, the waiter is picking up from the guest's left side and has his sidetowel over his shoulder. (Photo courtesy of Peter Houghton)

ashes from the dirty ashtray into the leftover mashed potatoes, as the waiter is doing in figure 4-17. This is not an enjoyable way for the guests to end their meal.

If the restaurant or banquet establishment allows smoking, there is a proper way to change the ashtrays. The service person should bring to the table a clean ashtray. The clean ashtray should be turned upside down and placed over the dirty (capped) ashtray. This will act as a cover, so when the service person removes the ashtrays no ashes will spill onto the guests' table

Figure 4–18. The waitress is preparing to change a dirty ashtray. She is changing it with the hand that is farthest from the guest; in this case, her right hand, because she is on the guest's right side. She is capping the ashtray with a clean ashtray. (Photo courtesy of Peter Houghton)

Figure 4–19. A closeup shot of how to cap an ashtray. The clean ashtray is being placed over the dirty ashtray. The waitress will remove the dirty ashtray using the clean ashtray to stop the ashes from flying out of the ashtray and into the guest's food. (Photo courtesy of Peter Houghton)

or into their food. The server places the capped ashtray behind his back and with his free hand places the clean ashtray (the cap) back on the table. Figures 4–18 and 4–19 illustrate the proper way to cap an ashtray.

7. Dirty dishes are cleared from the guest's right side with the service person's right hand.

The guest's dirty dishes must be cleared with the service person's right hand, except when it makes more sense to clear from the left side (then it should be done with the service person's left hand). Figure 4–20 illustrates how the waitress uses common sense by removing the bread and butter plate with her left hand from the guest's left side. She does so because if she removed the bread and butter plate from the guest's right side, she would have to reach in front of him. A service person should never reach in front of the guest, as is being done in Figure 4–21.

Figure 4–20. This waitress is using common sense to remove the dirty bread and butter dish from the guest. She is removing it with her left hand from the guest's left side. (Photo courtesy of Peter Houghton)

The correct and efficient way to remove dishes from the table is as follows: From each guest, the service person will first remove the silverware with the right hand and transfer it to the left hand. Next, the dirty plate will be removed, and it will be transferred to the left hand. "Following your nose" (going counter clockwise), the service person will remove the next guest's silverware and dirty plate. The server will step back, out of view of the guests. The leftover food will be scraped from the plate just removed onto the first one removed. The new plate will be shuffled to the bottom of

Figure 4–21. This waitress is clearing the dirty dishes incorrectly from the guest's left side with her right hand. (Photo courtesy of Peter Houghton)

the stack held with the left hand. The silverware should be held in the fingers of the left hand and laid across the top plate with the food scraps. The dirty plates should be placed on a tray in the neat organized manner that was discussed in the tray loading section. This procedure takes practice to master, but it is the most efficient way to clear a table.

Before serving the dessert course, the server must "crumb the table." The server would take either the sidetowel or a crumbing device and brush the crumbs from the table into a bread and butter dish, as illustrated in Figure 4-22.

Other Helpful Hints for Serving

Whichever hand you are using to serve or pick up, place that foot forward for balance. For example, if serving food with your left hand, place your left food forward.

Figure 4–22.   The correct way to crumb a table. The waitress, using her sidetowel, brushes the crumbs off the table into a bread and butter plate held in her right hand. She is crumbing from the guest's left side using her left hand. (Photo courtesy of Peter Houghton)

If a guest places a dirty dish on his or her left side (to the left of the fork), the service person should remove the dish from the guest's left side with his left hand.

Keep in mind that the above are guidelines, not rules. The most important criteria is the comfort and safety of the guest. If you have to serve from "the wrong side" for the guest's comfort, do it.

Guidelines for French and Russian Style Service

The guidelines are basically the same as for American service, with the exception of guideline number two.

1. Ladies are served before men.
2. In French service, food is served from the guest's **right side** with the

service persons **right hand;** in Russian service, food is served from the guest's **left side** with the platter in the service person's **left hand,** while serving with the **right hand.**

3. Beverages are served from the guest's right side with the service person's right hand.
4. All guests' food must be brought to the table at the same time.
5. Do not remove guest plates from the table until all guests are finished eating their meals.
6. Never stack or scrape dirty plates on the guest's table.
7. Dirty dishes are cleared from the guest's right side with the service person's right hand.

Guideline Number Two Explained

In French service, food is served from the guest's right side with the service person's right hand.

In French a la carte service, the service person has to transfer food from a pan at the gueridon to the plate. The plate is then served to the guest from the guest's right side with the waiter using his right hand.

In Russian service, food is served from the guest's left side with the platter in the service person's left hand, while serving with the right hand.

This is the most confusing and contradictory of all the guidelines. In Russian service, clean plates are put down from the guest's right side with the service person's right hand. The food is then brought out on a silver platter. After the food has been presented to the guest, the service person transfers the food from the tray to the plate. This is accomplished by holding the tray in the left hand. The service person should serve the guest from the left side with the right hand. Even though this method will not prevent the service person from putting the arm in front of the guest and making the guest back away, this is the method that has been taught since the beginning of Russian service.

It is the author's belief that it is done because it is easier for the service person to transfer food from the platter to the plate. At times it can be difficult to manipulate the serving fork and spoon. There is a chance that the food may slip out of the fork and spoon. So instead of the service person having to swing his or her arm around with the food, the plate is a lot closer to the tray. It is easier for the service person to serve the guests in this manner.

Chapter Summary

1. The dining room and/or banquet manager who learns and insists that the guidelines of competency be followed will have an establishment with excellent service.

2. If the manager can combine this competency with the staff's friendliness, the establishment will be successful from a service standpoint.
3. Competency in a restaurant means that the guest does not have to ask the service person for anything.
4. Following the seven guidelines for serving guests will ensure competent service.
5. Proper methods for using traystands and trays are necessary for both efficiency and safety.

Review Questions

1. Define competency as it relates to the service staff.
2. Can excellent service compensate for average food? Explain your answer by giving examples to justify your position.
3. What problems must the manager foresee regarding the friendliness of the staff with the guests?
4. How does the dining room manager obtain competency from his staff in regard to proper service?
5. What is a sidetowel, and what is its purpose for a service person? How should it be carried when it is not in use?
6. Describe the proper manner in which a tray should be loaded with dirty dishes. What is a traystand, and how should a tray be picked up from the traystand?
7. Why should trays be used to carry food or beverages?
8. List and explain the seven guidelines of service.
9. Are there any differences between the American and the other types of a la carte service in regard to the guidelines of service?
10. Why are the guidelines of service called guidelines, not rules? Is there any part of the guidelines that is a rule?
11. You, as the manager, have an excellent waiter. Guests like him; they always tell you he is an asset to your establishment. He constantly outsells all the other staff in desserts and wines. However, he breaks all the guidelines of service. He serves from the wrong side, picks the glasses off the table to pour water, etc. In short, he ignores proper guidelines of service. How would you get him to adhere to the guidelines? Or, do you think it is not necessary for him to adhere to the guidelines since he is such a great waiter?

References

1. Jess Stein, ed. in chief, *The Random House Dictionary* (New York: Ballantine Books, 1978), 187.
2. Sam Bubonia, interview with the author in Albany, New York.
3. Colleen Sherman, interview with the author in Schenectady, New York, 2 April 1987.

Chapter 5
The Styles of Service

Chapter Objectives:

At the completion of this chapter, the reader will be able to:

1. give the names and responsibilities of the four typical service positions in a dining room for a restaurant that provides American service;
2. describe and explain the three service options in a restaurant that provides American service;
3. define the term *station,* and demonstrate the proper method of setting up stations;
4. explain the importance of and how to assign sidework in order to have a smooth-running operation;
5. describe and organize a dining room using the team method of service for the service staff;
6. explain the advantages and disadvantages of the three types of service (team, individual stations, and captain) in the American restaurant;
7. teach the service staff the proper sequence of serving a meal; and
8. describe how to serve wine to guests.

American Dining Room Service Styles

The American dining room is unique in the world of service. In other countries, such as France, there are clear rules that each restaurant follows to provide its guests standard service. A standard has been set and all restaurants follow the same standards concerning service.

America is different. Because the United States is a melting pot of cultures and different types of service, there is no one style used by all restaurants. One restaurant may have a captain to take orders and service people to serve the meal, while another just a block away eliminates the position of captain and has the service person do all the service. A third, a few doors further on has three people waiting on one table of two guests. All three restaurants are successful, yet all use different styles of service.

Dining Room Service Personnel

In American restaurants, there are four traditional job titles for individuals who serve the guests. They are: the service person, the busperson, the captain, and the wine steward.

Because there are no firm standards followed by American restaurants, establishments may call their employees by one title and have them doing another job. Or they may eliminate certain job titles and combine them in other job descriptions. Therefore, in each restaurant job titles and responsibilities change. In some restaurants, a captain will be assigned to take food and wine orders. Another restaurant will have a wine steward to take and serve the wine selections.

All restaurants must have people, called the service staff, who will actually serve the meal. Many restaurants have a person, called a busperson, to assist the service staff. In some types of services, the jobs of captain, wine steward, busperson, and service person are combined into the service person's job. In other restaurants, a team of either two or three members works together to give the guests service.

The following sections will give a description of the responsibilities of each job and the qualities needed by dining room personnel.

Qualities of Successful Dining Room Personnel

Certain qualities are needed that will make the dining room personnel successful in dealing with the guests. The manager must be aware of these qualifications when hiring service personnel.

The personal appearance of the applicants must be excellent. This was clearly stated in Chapter Two.

They must have excellent communication skills, both verbally (through clear speech) and written.

Dining room personnel must be sensitive to their guests' and fellow employees' feelings and needs.

The personnel must be able to work well under pressure. Being a service person is an extremely stressful job. They will have to be able to gather a variety of information, understand it, and make correct decisions. Many times, this must be done in a split second.

In addition, they must be organized and efficient.

Captain

The job of captain is usually found in a restaurant that has a high-priced menu. The surroundings are generally nicer than in an average restaurant and the clientele is usually willing to spend a great deal of money for a meal. One establishment that uses the captain system is the New York Racing Association at their Aqueduct, Belmont, and Saratoga racetracks. The captain is usually responsible for an area of the dining room (called a station) that has as many as sixty seats and four service persons. Because the tables are only used for one meal period (called a seating) and time is not a factor, the station at the racetracks is larger than normal. A more typical station has between thirty-five and forty seats, a captain, and two service persons.

The captain has the following responsibilities and duties:

- supervision of the service staff and buspersons in their station;
- greeting the guests who have been seated at the tables in the station;
- merchandising (selling) and taking all drink and food orders;
- tableside preparation, if called for;
- sometimes serves the meal (but more often the service person does the serving);
- ensures that the service staff and buspersons clear the dirty dishes and reset the tables.

The captain has been a service person and has been promoted to this position after demonstrating proficiency in selling and serving. This job is a selling job. As the captain is the first person that the guest will talk to about the meal, the captain must be personable. Also, he or she must be able to manage employees, because this position also is a supervisory one.

Wine Steward

As the name implies, this person is responsible for suggesting and serving wines to all guests in a restaurant. This job requires a personable individual with a knowledge of wines. The wine steward must know which wine will complement which food on the menu. It is the responsibility of the steward to suggest, sell, and serve wines to the guests. Usually, one wine steward is sufficient for a restaurant. If there is no wine steward, this job becomes the responsibility of the captain or the service staff.

Busperson or Dining Room Attendant

This job called busperson or dining room attendant is basically an assistant to the service staff. For many years, this job was thought to be filled by an individual who was unskilled and/or illiterate. It was unfortunate, because many managers placed individuals in this position who had no idea of how critical the job was in the successful operation of the dining room.

The specific jobs of the busperson seem easy enough. They are:

- setting the place settings on the table;
- clearing the dirty dishes from the dining room and bringing them into the kitchen;
- assisting the service person whenever necessary in clearing away dirty plates from a table and restocking the service area with condiments, plates, glasses, and other items needed for the smooth running of the dining room.

Because the above jobs seem so straightforward and easy to do, managers usually assigned one busperson to work with two or as many as four service staff.

The busperson was usually poorly trained, if trained at all. That is when the so-called easy job turned into a problem for the manager, service staff, and guests. The busperson could not keep up with the pace of a busy dining room. In the middle of the rush hour, the service staff would find themselves with dirty tables and not enough clean linens or plates or condiments.

The busperson should not be an unskilled worker, but a person who is training to become a service person. The busperson must be as organized and efficient as a service person. If the busperson is not organized, then the whole dining room will suffer and the guests will receive poor service.

The Service Person

Service persons are the eyes and ears of the dining room manager. They interact directly with the customers. The guests are more likely to tell them what is good or bad about the restaurant than tell the manager. In the eyes of the guests, the person who waits on them **is the restaurant.** The chef of the restaurant could have been awarded four stars by the Michelin guide; the restaurant could have won an award for interior design; the manager can have excellent financial and managerial skills; but if the service staff does not perform up to the guests expectations, the restaurant is bad. The guests are the ultimate critic. If they leave dissatisfied, they will tell many of their friends. The number one reason for trying a new restaurant is the recommendation of friends. Therefore, the manager's number one priority must be hiring, training, and supervising the service staff with excellence. It has been proven over and over again that proper service can make a restaurant successful. Even more so, poor service can ruin a restaurant.

What do You Think?

A couple had an eight o'clock reservation for dinner. They were seated right at 8 P.M. As they looked around the beautifully designed room, they noticed the fresh flowers on the white-clothed tables. Classical music was being played in the restaurant by talented musicians. The food being served to the tables around them was attractive and plentiful. It was obvious by the looks on the faces of the other guests that the food was excellent and many people were enjoying themselves. However, it was ten minutes before anyone approached their table to take their drink order. Finally, an order was taken and delivered. The service person put it down and disappeared for fifteen more minutes. At 8:32 the service person came back and took the order. The wait between the courses seemed like an eternity for the couple. Finally, the main course was served at 10:03. It was served to them in a very formal, non-caring manner by the service person. The food was excellent and plentiful. What do you think the couple told their friends about the dining experience? Will they ever return to this restaurant for another meal?

The service persons have very specific duties. They are responsible for the total service of the meal. In most American restaurants, the service persons work alone. They have no one else to assist them in serving the meal. If the host seats too many people at their tables at once, or if there is a complaint about the food, they find themselves unable to serve and attend to all their guests needs, or they are (as it is known in restaurant slang), "in the weeds." They have no one else to rely on. They must greet the guests and from that point serve the guests flawlessly through the end of service. Their only assistance comes from the untrained, unskilled busperson that you have read about previously. They generally have a station that has anywhere from four to seven tables seating between sixteen and twenty-four guests.

Specific responsibilities of the service person are:

- obtaining any specific instructions about reservations and policies for the meal period;
- preparing the station, checking chairs and place settings for cleanliness, and making certain all tables are set corerctly;
- greeting customers;
- suggesting menu items;
- serving food and drinks;
- inquiring about the guests' satisfaction with the meal;
- clearing dirty dishes;

- suggesting desserts;
- serving dessert;
- preparing and collecting bill;
- offering to the guests a closing remark;
- doing preparation work for the next day.

Each restaurant has its own specific tasks for the service person. The tasks should be outlined in an employees' manual. The Barnsider Restaurant chain requires its employees to know all the facts covered in their 228-page training manual. The chain tests the employees for proficiency. Their training program is an extensive one that may last up to one year. There is a constant reinforcement of the policies by veteran service staff employees.

The manager must know all the job tasks of the service person. Once the manager knows and understands the tasks of the service person, another task is at hand: understanding how implementing and assigning stations makes a dining room run smoothly.

Stations

All restaurants should divide their dining room up into small sections called *stations*. Each station has between sixteen and twenty-four seats in the section. This depends on the size of the tables and other factors. By using this method, the manager and service staff know who is responsible for each table. The end result is excellent service for the guests. Using the station method, the service people are responsible for one part of the restaurant rather than for the whole dining room.

Many restaurants assign one service person to one station. Other restaurants assign a captain and two or four service people to a station that may have up to sixty seats. Still other restaurants use a system that has a three-person team responsible for up to sixty seats.

A manager should organize the stations to maximize excellent guest service. For example, a dining room has four tables of four seats and two tables of two seats with a view of the ocean. Even though this is only a total of twenty seats, it should *not* be one station. These tables will be requested by the guests first, so it is best for the manager to split up these tables into two or three stations. But the tables in the station must be together. Look at figures 5-1 and 5-2. If you were a manager, which plan would give your guests the best service?

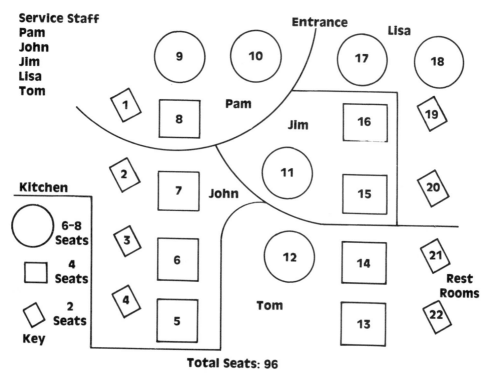

Total Seats: 96

Figure 5–1. Stations set up for a ninety-six-seat dining room. Five servers all have their tables close to one another. John has the most tables because his station is closest to the kitchen door. Jim is an inexperienced service person. Tom is the best service person, so his station has more tables; but his area also has the rest rooms, which are not a desirable location. Pam and Lisa both have twenty-two seats to serve. This is the correct manner in which to set up stations.

Several factors must be taken into consideration when the manager divides the room into stations. These factors are:

1. the distance of the guest tables from the kitchen;
2. the number of guests that are seated at each table;
3. the physical attractiveness of the station;
4. the amount of food preparation required at the table;
5. the union contract requirements; and
6. the competency of the staff.

Distance of the Guest Tables from the Kitchen

The station that has the fewest number of tables should be the one farthest from the kitchen. Because of its location, it will take the service person

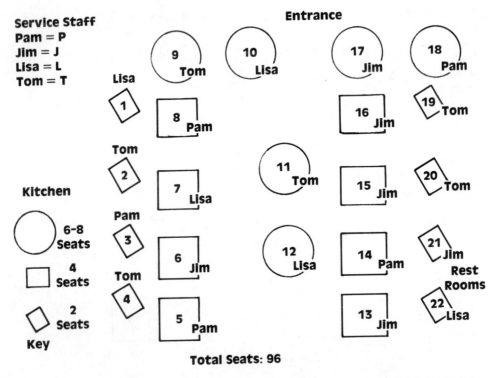

Figure 5–2. This dining room also has ninety-six seats. Each service person should have twenty-four seats to serve, because there are only four of them. All four have their table scattered all over the dining room. The service in this restaurant will be poor, mainly because of poor station assignment by the manager. This type of station assignment is incorrect.

longer to obtain the food. Therefore, the number of guests that can be accommodated in this station will be less than in the other stations.

Number of Guests Seated at Each Table

A mixture of small tables that seat two (called deuces) and larger tables (called tops—four people, 4-top; six people, 6-top) is ideal for organizing a station. There should be a maximum of twenty-four seats in a station for one service person to serve. But the twenty-four seats should not be made up of twelve deuces. That would be almost impossible for a service person to serve, because that is too many parties to wait on at once. Ideally, the station should consist of a 6-top, three 4-tops, and three deuces. Of course, this station must be close to the kitchen area. All stations should be designed with a variety of tables that seat different numbers of guests.

Physical Attractiveness of the Station

In every restaurant, there are tables that are more desirable to the guests than others. Traditionally, tables by the kitchen or rest rooms have been designated as the poorest tables. Tables by the windows, with a view of nice scenery, have been the best. If there is entertainment in the restaurant, tables closest to the entertainment will be the most popular. The popular station should be smaller than the one by the kitchen door, because many guests will request the popular tables.

Amount of Food Preparation Done at the Table

If the menu of the restaurant has a lot of items that will be prepared or finished off at guest tables, the number of seats at the station should be fewer than twenty-four. Because the service staff has to do a lot of tableside cooking and tossing of salads, they will spend more time at the guest tables. However, if the restaurant has a set menu (as often is the case on holidays), the number of seats in the station can be increased.

Union Contract Requirements

A union contract generally states the number of guests a service person can serve at a station. If that number is exceeded, a per-person bonus must be paid to the service person who has served the extra guests. One of the purposes of a union is to provide jobs for their members. It is in the best interests of the union (and management) to keep the size of the stations reasonable. Therefore, this bonus fee discourages management from making the stations too large, as the fee will generally be more expensive to the restaurant than employing another service person.

Competency of the Staff

Every manager will realize that some service persons are more competent than others. These service persons can serve more guests than others. A manager must take this fact into consideration when assigning stations to his or her staff.

Assigning Stations

There are two methods of assigning stations after all the above factors have been considered. The first one is called the seniority method. The second is referred to as the rotation method.

Seniority Method

In the seniority method, service people with the most seniority are assigned permanent stations. The station truly becomes their little restaurant. On their day off they are replaced with a relief service person, usually one with little seniority. Normally, in this system, the best stations are assigned to the service staff who have been employed at the restaurant for the longest time. This system is used in restaurants where guests "lunch" daily at the same restaurant. The guest has a standard reservation for the same table and wants the same service person to serve him or her every day. Once this method is put into place it is almost impossible to change.

Rotation Method

This method is favored by many restaurant managers and employees. The service staff is rotated among all the stations on a daily basis. Mary, our service person is responsible for station one on Monday, station two on Tuesday, and so on throughout the week. This system allows the manager to close off the poorer stations when business is forecasted to be bad. It requires more planning and organization than the Seniority Method, but it allows all service staff to have the better as well as the poorer stations.

Whichever method is chosen for a restaurant, guest satisfaction must be the determining factor. Because much of guest satisfaction depends on the attitude of the service staff, the method selected must satisfy the needs of the restaurant, guests, and service staff. Once the decision concerning stations has been made, the next problem that managers have to deal with is that of sidework.

Sidework

Sidework is one of the necessary jobs that must be done by the service staff. It is a job that is not well liked, because it does not produce tips directly. However, the manager should explain to the staff that sidework is a positive factor in making the restaurant a success. For instance, if the salt and pepper shakers are filled before the guests enter the restaurant, the service persons will not have to interrupt service to fill up the shakers during the restaurant's busy time. Therefore, the service persons can serve more guests, and the amount of income for both the restaurant and the service persons will increase. In addition, the restaurant is displaying competency. Another benefit is that the service persons will be less pressured and be able to spend more time talking or suggestive selling with their guest. Sidework can be defined as all the extra jobs that service persons must do to get the restaurant ready to serve the guests. Sidework can be assigned before the shift or after the shift. Examples of sidework are filling salt and pepper shakers, restocking condiments, cleaning the coffee stations, and folding napkins.

Sidework can create many problems for a restaurant if the manager does not establish a policy. If a restaurant manager has to staff for more than one meal period (breakfast and dinner), many times there are disagreements between the two shifts over which one is doing more sidework. The restaurant's policy must define the exact duties and responsibilities of the service staff concerning sidework. Employees must be taught about the importance and need for doing sidework and the reason why it contributes to the success of the restaurant. They must understand that the tasks must be completed, but that the guest is still their most important responsibility.

 How do You Solve this Problem?

O ne evening a couple went out for dinner at a local diner. The food was served quickly and correctly by an efficient waitress. Because it was near closing time, as soon as the food was served, the waitress went to an area where there was a lot of stainless steel equipment. She proceeded to wipe it down and make sure it was clean for the next day. She was a master at doing this sidework. The stainless steel was shining and the condiments were replaced. However, she did not return to the guest's table to see how the meal was or to offer dessert. It took a long time for her to bring the check. But her sidework was completed.

Scheduling Sidework

The manager must plan out the specific tasks needed in the restaurant and decide how many people are required to do the tasks. Sidework should be scheduled on a daily basis. All assignments concerning sidework, just like stations, have to be posted for all the employees to see. The sidework can be rotated, just like the stations are rotated. In some establishments, the sidework becomes a part of a certain station. For example, the service people assigned stations one and two have to fan fold 100 napkins each day. Therefore, if Pam is scheduled for station one today, she knows that she must fold the 50 napkins. This method creates accountability for both the manager and employees.

SIDEWORK DUTIES

Station	Daily Duties
1 & 2	Fan fold 50 napkins
3	Refill salts & peppers, sugar bowls
4	Wipe down all stainless steel
5	Flowers
6	Dust woodwork and window sills

Note: On days when there are fewer employees, sidework duties will be combined.

Figure 5–3. The sidework chart that has been designed for a restaurant with stations. By organizing the sidework duties in this manner, all employees know exactly what their responsibilities are concerning sidework.

Each restaurant will have its own specific jobs for sidework. The key is that the manager must be organized and follow up to make certain that the sidework is completed. When the manager does this, sidework will become an integral part of the success of the dining room.

Restaurant Success

By now the reader knows that one of the main reasons for the success or lack of success of a restaurant is the service that the guest receives. The dining room manager is the key person to ensure that the guests receive this level of successful service. The manager is responsible for hiring and training the service staff. The training should not be a one-time session, but continuous. The manager must follow-up on the training through observation and evaluation. Service standards must be explained and maintained. As repetition is the best teacher, let us review the seven guidelines of service.

1. Ladies are served before men (if children are present, they should be served first, then ladies, then men);
2. Food is served from the guest's left side with the service person's left hand;
3. Beverages are served from the guest's right side with the service person's right hand;
4. All guests' food must be brought to the table at the same time;
5. Do not remove guest plates from the table until all guests are finished eating their meal;

6. Never stack or scrape dirty plates on the guests table; and
7. Dirty dishes are cleared from the guest's right side with the service person's right hand.

Serving the Meal

The sequence of serving a meal is relatively the same from restaurant to restaurant. It generally is served in the following sequence:

- Drinks
- Appetizer
- Rolls and Butter
- Salad
- Entree
- Coffee/tea
- Dessert
- Wine is served when requested (if with dinner) or immediately when ordered.

In some restaurants, the salad course is served in the European tradition, after the entree.

Special instructions should be given by the manager to the staff concerning substitutions; furthermore, menu items should be clearly explained and the service staff should know them.

However, people occasionally do not learn the material unless they know they will use it. More and more restaurants have tests as part of their training program. Passing a test is one of the criteria for obtaining a job with the restaurant. This makes the applicant and the employees realize that the restaurant is serious about providing proper service.

Methods of Service

Staffing in an American dining room depends on the management of the restaurant. There are three ways in which the dining room can be organized for service. The most common method has one person waiting on a specified number of tables, being aided by a busperson. The second is borrowed from the French system, which has a captain responsible for an area of the restaurant. The captain is assisted by service persons and buspersons. The third method is a relatively new system, referred to as a team system. As the name implies, a great amount of teamwork is needed to make this system succeed.

It becomes necessary for the manager to know how each of the above systems works, in addition to their advantages and disadvantages. It is then up to the restaurant manager to decide what type of system will work best in the restaurant. The critical part of making any system work is training and follow-up. All of the systems explained below will work if the manager trains and reinforces the policy constantly.

Regardless of the method of service your restaurant will use, all follow the general sequence stated above. The advantages and disadvantages of each system are as follows.

Individual Service Person Method

The service person is assigned a small area of the restaurant called a station. It is the sole responsibility of that service person to provide expert service to all the guests at the station. The service person must be extremely organized. If any mistakes are made or if the service person cannot handle all the problems in the station, the guests will receive poor service. The station generally has between sixteen and twenty-four seats. Many restaurants provide buspersons (one for every two to three service staff) to assist in clearing the dirty plates. Figure 5-4 shows a service person and his responsibilities.

The advantages of the individual service person method are as follows.

1. It is an easy method to teach and learn.
2. The guests know their service person.
3. The manager knows who is responsible for service.
4. The service person gets to keep all of the tips.
5. The service person knows that he or she is responsible for the serving and guest satisfaction of the total meal.

However, this method has disadvantages as well.

1. If there is a problem; the service person can become overwhelmed and the result will be to provide poor service.
2. Service people have no one to rely on if there is a problem.
3. Because training is so simple, employees can easily move from job to job. This system does not encourage loyalty to the restaurant.
4. The service person is responsible for serving the entire meal. If the service person is performing poorly, the guest will have a poor dining experience.

Figure 5–4. The individual service person. He is responsible for presenting the menu, taking the order, and serving the meal and beverage. (Photo courtesy of Peter Houghton)

Captain Method

This system is characterized by having a captain responsible for a double or triple station. The captain has been promoted from a service person. The service staff assist the captain in serving the station. There may even be a busperson to assist the service staff and captain. The captain is usually in a supervisory position, and acts as a sort of public relations person. Captains generally stay in the dining room, while the service staff obtain and serve food from the kitchen.

The advantages of the captain method are:

1. The restaurant has other supervisors besides the host or manager in the dining room.
2. The guests will have more than one person to serve them.
3. If a problem develops, the captain can assist the other service staff in the station.

4. The guest will have the benefit of having an experienced—and, most likely, a personable—individual to take their order.

The disadvantages are:

1. A restaurant must have an individual experienced in both supervision and waiting to fill this position.
2. The job descriptions and roles are clearly defined; thus, not much flexibility is built into this system.
3. The guest is expected to leave a larger tip because it must cover both the captain and service staff.

Team System

A new system that was characterized as an idea whose time has come was highlighted in *Nation's Restaurant News:* the team system.

Ross Sponder owns the 48-seat dinner restaurant called The Palace Cafe in Santa Barbara, California. His system employs a method wherein a service person takes the initial order and informs the customers that any of the twelve waiters or waitresses can help them with whatever they want. Each table has a pamphlet which states: "Our staff works as a team in order to better serve you. You need not look for the person who initially took your order for additional service. Just ask anyone! This system of service is designed to help you enjoy your time here by making everyone on our staff available to take care of your table."[1]

Sponder has virtually no employee turnover. His biggest challenge was breaking the service staff of the habit of sticking to their individual territories or stations. But the problem was overcome by requiring dining room servers to pass an intense practical examination.

The teamwork concept has turned out to be a highly efficient style that makes jobs easier, provides better service, and results in higher gratuities.

SIZE OF STATIONS

Type of Service	Number of Seats at Station
Individual Service Person	16-24
Captain	48-72
Team	40-45

Figure 5-5. The typical number of guests a service staff should be responsible for at a station.

Another restaurant that uses a similar system is La Paloma in North Miami, Florida. This system provides for a service person to take the orders and give them to the kitchen staff. Speed runners bring food to the tables, while the service staff answers customer questions. The result is speedier and more efficient service.

How the Team System Operates

The team is divided up into three positions, an Aid, a Lead, and a Follow-up. The two critical jobs are the Lead and the Follow-up. Normally, a team is responsible for a station which has between twelve and fourteen tables and forty to forty-five seats. A restaurant of 150 seats usually has three teams serving the guests. It generally takes five months to master the concept of team service. Because of the long training period, this reduces the normally high turnover of service people.

The Aid

The first job that is learned is that of the Aid. Of the three positions, the Aid training takes the longest to master; about three to four weeks. This is because the new employee must learn the policies, menu, and organization of the restaurant. The Aid has the following responsibilities:

1. The normal duties of the busperson.
2. Picking dinners up from the kitchen and delivering them to the guests (this is the only part of the meal in which the Aid participates).
3. Taking entrees from the guest table, if the Lead requests.

The Lead

The Lead is the first member of the team that the guest comes in contact with in this system. The Lead should be personable and a suggestive salesperson. The two main duties that the Lead is responsible for is suggestive selling and the timing of placing dinner orders into the kitchen. The duties of the lead are as follows:

1. Suggestive selling for drinks and appetizers.
2. Serving drink orders.
3. Taking the guest's drink and dinner orders.
4. Obtaining additional drinks for the guest.
5. Selling and serving wine.
6. Setting the pace of service for the other two team members.
7. Turning the dinner order into the kitchen and timing the dinners.

The Follow-up

The Follow-up is the quarterback of the section, making sure the station runs smoothly. This is the most mentally demanding of the three jobs. This person must run the section, making sure the guests are satisfied and solving problems. The Follow-up is the one member of the team that should never leave the station. If it is necessary to leave the station, the Follow-up should have the Aid and Lead assume the duties. The Follow-up has the following responsibilities:

1. Checking the guest satisfaction with the meals.
2. Conversing with the guests about their meals.
3. Assisting the other two members of the team in taking orders (Lead) or serving meals (Aid), if necessary.
4. Solving any problems concerning the meals.
5. Clearing dirty dishes from the guest's table.
6. Suggesting and selling dessert.
7. Totaling up and presenting the check to guest.
8. Collecting the money for the guest check.

Figure 5–6. The team system. The Lead presents the menu and takes the order. The Follow-Up is holding the tray and the aid is holding the water pitcher. Only the Follow-up has his sidetowel positioned properly. (Photo courtesy of Peter Houghton)

Advantages and Disadvantages of the Team System

The team service, if done properly, provides the guest with the best service. The reason for this is that there is always a service person available if the guest has a problem. One member of the team is on the floor of the restaurant at all times. The team members are always available but they are not hovering over the guest, as is the case with the individual service person.

The biggest problem for the guests is that they often get confused because they are being waited on by three people. Guests don't understand how the team system works and are confused over who is getting the tip.

The advantages of this system are:

1. There are three people to take care of guests' needs.
2. A professional service staff is obtained through a thorough training program.
3. It provides an organized system for anticipating guests needs.
4. There is consistent peer evaluation of service.
5. Jobs are clearly defined, but flexibility is built into the system.

Its disadvantages include:

1. An extensive training period is needed.
2. The system may be difficult for experienced service staff to accept.
3. Guests become confused about who is serving them.

The team system has nontraditional job titles and names. But the job descriptions resemble the traditional jobs found in restaurants that provide their guests with American dining room service. Once the team system is mastered, restaurants are reluctant to go back to the old method of service.

Wine Service

Regardless of the type of service a restaurant uses, the staff should be instructed in the proper method of serving wine. Knowledge of wine and wine service by the service staff is essential for guest enjoyment.

Restaurant patrons should be encouraged to enjoy wine with their meal by the service staff. In order to do this, the service staff must be knowledgeable about wine. For instance, the staff must know what wine best complements what food, and how to present and serve wine properly. This section will not cover what wine complements what food, but it will discuss wine service. It is recommended that service people take courses on wine, and that they sample wine with foods to become confident and knowledgeable on the subject.

As a general guideline, red wines complement foods that are hearty, like prime ribs and steak. White wines are generally served with lighter dishes, like poultry or fish. Sparkling wines are served with lighter dishes, but are used mostly for celebration. If a guest asks for the "wrong type of wine" with a meal, the service person should not challenge the guest's choice of wine. There are some white wines that complement a hearty dish, or the guest may have a favorite wine that is drunk with every meal. The service person may suggest a selection that complements the food, but this depends on the service person's feeling about the guest. After determining that the guest indeed wants the particular wine requested, it should be brought to the guest.

Presenting Wine

Once the guest has selected a wine, the server should bring it to the table and present it to the guest for inspection, as illustrated in Figure 5-7. The bottle should be presented with the label facing the guest, so the guest can ascertain that the bottle is exactly what was ordered. The server should present the bottle resting on the sidetowel for two reasons. One, if the bottle is wet, the sidetowel will keep the bottle from slipping from the servers hands. Two, the sidetowel acts as an insulator and will not transmit as much of the server's body heat to the wine. Serving wine at the correct temperature adds to the enjoyment of wine.

As soon as the guest approves of the bottle, the server should open the bottle—at the service stand, not on the guest's table. The cork should be presented to the person who has ordered the wine, and a small tasting should be poured into the glass. The guest samples the wine and either approves of it or tells the service person it is not acceptable.

You First!

The purpose of having the host taste wine first is steeped in history. In ancient times, the way to eliminate your enemy was to invite him or her to your dwelling to share a bottle of wine. The guest was offered the wine first, drank it, and died. This is because the wine was often laced with poison. It was easy to hide the poison in the wine. Before long, guests demanded that their host sample the wine first, reasoning that if the host drank first, the wine would be safe to drink. The tradition carries on today.

Figure 5–7. The correct way to present a bottle of wine. The bottle is held with the sidetowel, with the label facing the guest. (Photo courtesy of Peter Houghton)

Unacceptable Wine

If the wine is not acceptable, the service person should ask if the guest would care for another bottle of wine. The service person should not challenge the integrity of the guest, but should inquire what is wrong with the wine. Depending on the policy of the restaurant, the guest may or may not be charged for the wine.

Many restaurants that have expensive bottles of wines employ a different method of handling wine service. When a guest orders an expensive bottle of wine, the manager is called to the guest's table. The guest is told the conditions of the purchase. For instance, the manager may say the following:

"You have made an excellent choice on the 1898 Chateau Lafite Rothschild. However, because the wine is so old the restaurant can not guarantee the quality of the wine. If we open the wine for you, you must pay for it." The guest then has the option of accepting or refusing the wine.

Serving Wine

When the guest approves the wine, the server should pour the wine into the guests' glasses using the guidelines for serving beverages. Red wine glasses should be half filled. White and sparkling wines should be poured three-quarters to the top of the glass. Sparkling wines should be served in two steps. The service person should pour an amount into the glass so the bubbles and foam will not overflow the glass. Then the other glasses are poured in the same manner. The service person should then go back to the first glass that was poured and continue to fill up that glass so the guest receives a glass that is three-quarters filled. When the service person pours any type of wine, the bottle should be twisted to the right to stop the wine from dripping.

Red wines should be placed on the guest's table. The sparkling and white wines are placed in a container to keep them at their proper temperature. This container is either an ice bucket that is placed near the guest's table or a container that retains the cold temperature and sits on the table. Throughout the meal, the service person should return to the table and refill the guests' wine glasses when needed.

Proper Serving Temperature of Wine

Serving wines at the proper temperature are essential for guest enjoyment. When wines are served correctly they offer incredible perfumes and bouquets. Proper temperature balances the sweetness and acidity in wine.

White, rosé, and sparkling wines should be served chilled. Sparkling and sweet dessert wines should be served at 35°F to 45°F. Rosés and dry white wines should be served at 45°F to 55°F. These wines should be stored in a cooler for at least two hours. If they are not, and the guest orders a wine that should be served chilled, the service person can put it in a bucket with ice and water. It will be at the proper temperature in about fifteen or thirty minutes. However, any restaurant that sells wine should have proper refrigeration.

Red wines should be served at the old European room temperature of 55°F to 65°F. A red wine served too warm becomes out of balance and overwhelming. Particularly robust reds that contain more than 13% alcohol begin to smell like ether. It also causes a slight warm sensation in the wine drinker's throat. If red wines are served too cold, they lose their aroma and bouquet. Coldness brings out the astringency from the tannin and makes the

Name of Wine	Serving Temperature (Fahrenheit°)
Wine coolers, Rosés, Beaujolais, White wines	45 to 55
Red wines	55-65
Sparkling, Sweet White Dessert	35-45

Figure 5–8.   The proper serving temperatures of wine.

wine taste harsh. If it is possible, a red wine should be opened up for half an hour before serving to let it breathe. This breathing makes the wine taste smoother.

Serving wine with a meal adds to the pleasure of the dining experience. Restaurants that have service staffs that are knowledgeable concerning wines and wine service offer their guests an additional benefit.

Chapter Summary

1. There are four typical service positions in American service: captain, wine steward, busperson, and service person.
2. There are three methods of service: the individual service person, captain, and team methods.
3. Six important factors are taken into consideration when a room is divided into stations.
4. Sidework is essential for a smooth-running operation.
5. The proper serving sequence of a meal and the proper method of wine service are of the utmost importance for the maximum enjoyment of the guests.

Review Questions

1. What is the best system for your restaurant? Now that you have read and know about the three systems, which one would you choose for your restaurant? Give specific reasons why you would choose one system over the others.
2. What are the four traditional job titles for dining room service personnel? Explain the job duties of these employees.
3. List and explain five qualities that applicants must have to be successful as dining room service personnel.
4. What is the main difference between the captain system and the team system in dining room operations?
5. Explain the jobs of the wine steward and dining room attendant.
6. What are stations? What factors contribute to assigning stations?
7. What are the two methods for assigning stations. In your opinion, which is the better method. Explain your answer.

8. What is sidework? Why is it necessary in a restaurant? What are its benefits for the service staff?
9. Explain and list the seven guidelines of service.
10. What is the sequence of courses in a typical American a la carte restaurant? Is there ever any change in the sequence of courses? If so, explain when and why there may be a change.
11. What are the three positions in the team service, and what are the individual responsibilities.
12. What should a service person know about wine service? What are the proper temperatures at which wine should be served to guests?

Reference

1. Charles Bernstein, "Teamwork Service: An Idea Whose Time Has Come," *Nation's Restaurant News*, 10 August 1987, 13.

Part 2

Dining Room Management

Chapter 6

Training the Service Staff to Serve the Meal

Chapter Objectives:

At the completion of this chapter, the reader will be able to:

1. write an essay stating the importance of thorough knowledge of the menu;
2. state the importance of a service person knowing the ingredients of all menu items;
3. write down and organize food and beverage orders so that there will be no question of who gets what;
4. explain the importance of cooking times;
5. understand the importance of suggestive selling and merchandising;
6. define the term *86*, and tell how to avoid problems with 86 items;
7. order food from the kitchen;
8. give the serving sequence of a meal;
9. explain the importance of training, testing, and evaluating employees; and
10. explain the purpose of having a substitution or no substitution policy.

The Manager's Role

The dining room manager is the key to a successful restaurant. It is the manager who sets the tone and the pace of the establishment. The success or failure of the restaurant is determined by the manager. The manager should not be at the restaurant twenty-four hours a day, or even eighteen; but the restaurant should run as if the manager were there that many hours.

How do successful restaurant managers make their businesses run effectively, even when they are not present? By proper selection, teaching, training, and continuous evaluation of all employees. A dining room manager is like an orchestra leader. The orchestra leader does not play an instrument; the dining room manager does not serve food; but both of them are responsible for their guests' enjoyment. They both have to select, teach, train, and evaluate their talented employees, so the guests will receive an enjoyable experience.

The importance of competency and friendliness have been emphasized in the previous chapters. There are many types of service available for the restaurant manager to choose. But all this does not make good service. The final important element in providing excellent service occurs because the staff *knows* and *communicates* information that adds to the guests enjoyable dining experience.

Parts of the Meal

All dining experiences can be broken into three parts, as it relates to service. The first part is getting prepared to serve the guests. The next part is merchandising and taking the meal order. Finally, the actual service of the meal.

It does not matter if a restaurant offers French, American, or Russian service to the guests; nor does it matter what the style of service (team, individual service person, or captain) is. The following information will apply in all settings.

Learning the Menu

The dining room manager should insist that all employees know all the information about items on the menu. Employees should know which foods or beverages are offered, their pronunciation, and their ingredients. It is the responsibility of the manager to prepare this information for the employees. The information must be clearly written in a manual and given to all of the employees. Many restaurants, such as Specialty Restaurants and Casa Lupita Mexican Restaurants, are using this type of training method.

In order to make certain that the employees become knowledgeable, they are tested on the material. Casa Lupita stresses to its employees that customers have no idea about what it is like to open up a restaurant. Guests don't think about the problems of a restaurant; they simply want good food and service. Applicants should be told when hired that knowledge of the material in the training manual is a requirement to start and keep the job. The Barnsider Restaurant chain manual states clearly the purpose for knowing the information. They inform their applicants that they must know the material before they are allowed to work on the floor of the dining room, because they do not use their guests as guinea pigs for training the service staff. Therefore, before any person becomes a service person he or she must know the material required by the chain. The appendix of the manual contains a series of tests that may be asked of the applicants. The applicants are required to know 90% of the answers to the questions before they are allowed to work on the dining room floor. All managers should set up a policy of testing employees on materials. There should be a test covering all the items that the manager feels is important to make the guests' meal an enjoyable experience.

Lack of Knowledge

A couple went out for dinner in an area noted as a summer vacation resort. The waiter approached the table to inquire if the guests wanted a before-dinner drink. The woman ordered a whisky sour and the man asked "What kind of ale do you have?" The waiter thought for a moment and then blurted out "Ginger, sir." The man had to explain to the waiter that he was inquiring about an alcoholic beverage, not a soft drink! Obviously, this service person had very little or no training. He certainly did not know all the items on the menu.

The training manual must cover areas such as general policies, food prices and descriptions, beverage prices and descriptions, and specific information about the restaurant. Is it hard to set up a training manual? Is it hard to evaluate employees? Does it take a lot of the manager's time? Of course, it does. But it pays off in guest satisfaction, return business, and—in the long run—profits!

Dining Out: What Went Wrong?

The party of six guests had dinner at one of the new Yuppie, fern bar type restaurants. The restaurant seats about 150 on several levels. There is a large rectangular bar with tables surrounding it. About four tables were occupied, with a total of fifteen guests in the restaurant. One bartender, a hostess, and six service persons appeared to be staffing the restaurant.

The guests were seated at an 8-top. Next to the table were two round tables, both 6-tops. One of the guests asked the hostess if the group could move to one of the 6-tops, and the hostess instructed the waitress to move the party.

The waitress moved the menus and place settings to the new table. She then asked for their orders. They ordered salad and asked her what the salad dressing choices were. She said she didn't know because that was her first night on the job. She added that she had worked at the restaurant during the summer, before she went away to college. She asked the waitress next to her for the choices of salad dressings and then repeated them back to the guests. One of the guests was reading her menu and did not hear the choices. When she ordered her salad, the whole process had to be repeated, with the waitress again asking the other waitress the choice of salad dressings.

It was now time to order the main course. Companion A ordered a burger without a bun and a diet coke (she had asked for her dressing to be served in a separate dish for her salad). The other guests order their main courses also.

Five of the six meals were delivered to the table. The order for Companion A (the hamburger) was served on a bun. There were three other meals, besides the hamburger, which were to receive French fries as an accompaniment. Each meal had on the plate, the sandwich, an orange garnish, and a sprig of parsley, plus a large area of white space left on the plate. Five minutes later, the waitress brought a community basket of French fries to the table, explaining that they had not been ready when she had brought out the other food. By the way, the sixth meal (cajun-style shrimp) was finally brought to the table with the French fries.

Coffee was asked for and brought. The coffee was served with a napkin between the cup and the saucer. The coffee spilled all over the napkin. The waitress asked the customer if she wanted a new napkin. The customer felt like saying "No, I'd rather slop it over my dress."

Who is responsible for this mess, and what is wrong with this restaurant?

What Should the Service Person Know?

Before a manager allows employees to wait on guests, there are many facts they should know. The first group of facts deals with specific policies about the restaurant. Acceptable standards of appearance, dress, and attendance should be explained **before** the service person has been hired. Additional items, such as what time to report to work, food and drink policies concerning consumption both on and off the job, and serving hours, should also be explained to the employees. These facts must be reinforced in a training booklet.

The next set of facts should deal with the establishment. The purpose of having these facts known is so the service people can answer any and all questions that guests ask. It will create a positive feeling toward the service person by the guest if the service person is able to answer questions intelligently and confidently.

A third group of facts should be concerned with the physical layout of the restaurant. It should also explain how to order and pick up food and beverages. There should be an area which explains how to write and read guest dinner checks. The list is long but important for a successfully run restaurant.

Knowledge about the Restaurant

Guests perceive service persons in two ways: Are they nice, and can they answer questions? Guests will ask many questions. Most of them are legitimate, but others may seem silly. However, they are not silly to the guest.

All of the employees must know the history of the business. For example, questions will be asked concerning the ownership of the restaurant; how long has it been in existence; and the names and locations of other restaurants in the chain. All new employees at Walt Disney World, as part of their Traditions Orientation Session, have to know the names of the seven dwarfs and many other bits of trivia. Another type of question that could be asked is, "What restaurants are in the The Grand Floridian Beach Resort?"

Other facts employees should know are the days and hours of operation of the restaurant in which they are employed. If there are any other restaurants

Figure 6–1.   The Grand Floridian Beach Resort, home of many excellent restaurants. (© 1988 The Walt Disney Company)

on the premises or in the hotel, the employees should know their hours of operation, type of foods served, and the general price range.

There should be an area in the manual which outlines trivial and historical bits of information about the community and the restaurant. For instance, room 1140 of the DeWitt Clinton Hotel in Albany, New York, was where Thomas Dewey spent election night in 1948. When he went to bed that November evening all the pollsters had predicted that he had won the presidential election in a landslide. When he awoke, Harry S. Truman was the new president of the United States.

There should be a daily listing stating what events are occurring in the restaurant, hotel, and community.

All of this information is vital for the service person to be able to answer questions intelligently and to converse with the guests. This knowledge demonstrated by the service person will make the guest feel comfortable and confident in the server's competence.

Physical Layout of the Restaurant

In order for the service staff to take orders and deliver food correctly to the guest tables, all employees should receive a floor plan of the dining room. The floor plan should have the size and number of each table in the dining room. The diagram should be planned so that the employees will be able to understand it. Confusion should be kept to a minimum. For example, instead of numbering the tables in a haphazard manner, all tables in the first row would be labeled from 10 to 19, the second row from 20 to 29, and so on. As most dining room tables remain in the same location day after day, the staff will know the location of each table. It is much simpler for a manager to say "Check table 21 for a problem," than to say "The guy over at the table by the window has a problem." All employees will know exactly where table 21 is located by memorizing the floor plan.

It is also important in the floor plan to label the size of the tables. However, most service people are not concerned with the size of the table (e.g., 60″ in diameter); instead they are concerned with how many guests each table would seat. The diagram must state the number of seats at each table. An easy method for diagramming the size and numbers of the tables is illustrated in figure 6-2. Notice that all tables are numbered in the manner described above. Some of the table numbers have a circle around them, others have a rectangle, while still others are drawn at an angle. In addition, some tables are drawn larger in size than the other tables—another helpful visual reminder. By designing the floor plan carefully and making the employees memorize it, service will run smoothly.

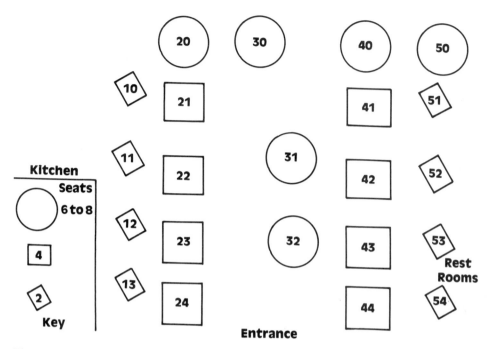

Figure 6–2. A numbered floor plan diagram. The tables are numbered in a logical pattern to make it easier for the service staff to do their job efficiently. Tables illustrated with a circle (such as #20) seat from six to eight guests; those with a rectangle (#21), four guests; and those drawn at an angle (#10), two guests.

Writing and Reading the Order

The manager should stress to the employees the correct way to write and read a guest check. The manager must translate all the menu items into *standard abbreviations*. Each item must have its own abbreviation.

All employees (including kitchen staff) are required to know and use the abbreviations when ordering food from the kitchen or serving food. This is to prevent any confusion in the restaurant. For example, what does *SS* on the check mean? Would the guest receive shrimp scampi, sirloin steak, or swiss steak. Abbreviations are used for all menu items, including accompaniments. For example, *BAK* would mean a baked potato, while *BAKy* means that the guest has requested sour cream with the baked potato.

Many times restaurants offer a children's menu. The child's portion would be abbreviated with the letter *C* in front of it. For example, if *SS* means sirloin steak, a *CSS* is a child's portion of sirloin steak.

Knowledge of the Menu

Many times guests are not familiar with your menu, so they ask the service person about the entrees. For example, a guest will ask "What is the shrimp scampi?" The service person should know the names of all items, how to pronounce them, and be able to describe them. The training manual should have a description of all menu items. Shrimp scampi is as follows:

Shrimp Scampi

P ronounced like Shrimp Skamp-ee   Abbreviation SKP
Five sized 15/18 shrimp, sautéd in garlic butter and served over a bed of wild and white rice.

All items on the menu should be described in this manner and the staff must know all of them before they are allowed to wait on guests.

Ingredients

In today's society there are many people who are allergic to certain spices and foods. In the description about the shrimp scampi, the ingredient garlic is mentioned. The manager should list any spices or ingredients that are predominant in the recipe. For example, when a guest asks if there are any sulfates in a food item, they are asking for a specific reason. In addition, the manager should also instruct the service persons to ask the chef about the ingredients in the food if they do not know them. The service person should not guess about ingredients in food. Many guests have gotten ill from a service person guessing instead of knowing the correct information.

Many people have severe allergic reactions to some types of food, spices, additives and other ingredients. It has been reported that allergies have resulted in the deaths of individuals who unknowingly or accidentally ate that particular food item or ingredient.

Figure 6-3 shows a variety of food presented on a buffet aboard a cruise ship. The service staff should know the names and ingredients of all the food.

Garnishes and Substitutions

In the manual, there should be an area that explains how each food item should be garnished. A diagram or picture of where the garnish is placed and how it looks is helpful. For instance, the manual would state that all hamburger plates are garnished with a leaf of romaine lettuce and with an

Figure 6–3.   An awesome display of food prepared for a buffet aboard a cruise ship. The service staff must know the names of the items and the ingredients used to make them. (Photo courtesy of Royal Caribbean Cruise Lines, Inc)

orange slice at the three o'clock position on the plate, as is shown in Figure 6-4.

At the end of the food item section there should be an explanation of what each guest receives in the form of accompaniments with their meal. For example, all beef items will be served with *BAK*. It is a good idea to use the abbreviations in the manual so that the employees will realize the importance of learning and using them.

Finally, in this section there should be an area that states what (if any) the substitutions are for each item. For example, *RIC* (rice) can be substituted for any *BAK*. It is important to have a clearly stated policy for substitutions. Some of the people who patronize restaurants will have a legitimate reason for asking for the substitution; others will only do it to get more food for their money. If the service persons have a question about what items may be substituted, they should be instructed to inquire from the person in charge of the restaurant.

No matter how large or small the restaurant is, if the manager writes out the policies, the guest will receive the same meal and the same answers to the questions, regardless of the service person. Most likely, the restaurant will be more profitable, because guests will feel comfortable knowing there is consistency everytime they dine at the restaurant. They will not be frustrated because one time they are allowed to substitute *RIC* for *BAK* and the next time they are not.

Cooking Methods

Guests often inquire about terms on the menu that are unfamiliar to them. For instance, a guest may ask the meaning of sauté. Each employee should

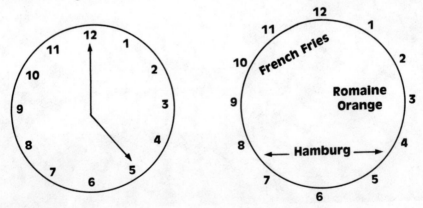

Figure 6-4. Diagram of the positions of items on a plate, using a clock as a guide. The hamburger is placed from 4 to 8 o'clock; the French fries from 9 to 1 o'clock; and the romaine and orange at 2 and 3 o'clock, respectively. When served to the guest, the orange is placed at the three o'clock position.

know the more common preparation methods of cooking foods. There are at least twelve methods. This information is also needed in the manual. An example of two cooking methods: *Baked*—cooked by dry, continous heat in an oven; *sautéd*—browned or cooked in a small amount of hot fat.

Preparation Time and Cooking Doneness

This is a critical part of the service person's training. Knowing how long it takes to cook an item and knowing what medium or pittsburgh means is important for ordering and picking up food from the kitchen.

A chart of the cooking time of all menu items should be listed. The chart should range from pittsburgh to well done, with the normal cooking time for each item.

In addition, there should be a description of what the terms for cooking doneness mean. A diagram of all the types of cooking doneness that the chef can prepare is most helpful. For example, a steak ordered medium would be described as having a pink hot center. One unusual way to cook meat is referred to as a pittsburgh. A steak done in this manner is raw on the inside and black on the outside. It is cooked by having the cook drop fat onto the fire. This causes a big flame to rise through the grill. The cook chars the outside until it is black; the inside is raw and cold to touch.

Alcoholic Beverages

As with the food, there should be a description of every item the restaurant has available to its guests. In addition, there should be a description of how the drinks are made, the glass the drink is served in, and the proper garnish. The brand names of all wines and beverages must also be included in the section on alcoholic beverages. Here is an example of a drink description:

Margarita

P ronounced like Marg a rita   Abbreviation MARG
Made with tequila, triple sec, lemon and lime. Served in a fiesta grande, straight up (^), or on the rocks (v). Garnished with salt around the rim of the glass and served with a lime wheel.

Glasses

There should be a diagram or a picture of all the glasses that are used for drinks. Underneath the picture should be the name of the drink that is served in the glass. There should also be a description of the glass. For example, a *fiesta grande* glass would be described as a $16\frac{3}{4}$ ounce glass used for all frozen margaritas.

Pricing

Because menus are constantly being changed, a separate price sheet should be distributed with the current prices. Owing to the fluctuation of prices, putting prices into the manual would be a waste of time and money. The prices will most likely change more often than any other information in the manual. When done on a separate sheet, the manager only has to print the new prices instead of the entire manual.

Tasting the Food and Beverage

This is another part of the training for the service staff that must be continuous. However, many restaurant managers refuse to let their staff taste the food. Instead, they serve them an employee meal each evening. The feeling is that it is too expensive to serve to the staff. In reality it is too expensive *not* to serve it to the staff. The guests are going to ask the service person how the food tastes. If they have never been allowed to sample the food, how will your service staff know what to tell the guests? The service staff should taste all food and beverage items as soon as it is practical. This does not mean that each night, the service staff should have a gourmet meal; but they must taste the food that they will be recommending and serving to their guests. One way of accomplishing this is by having meetings where the service staff samples the menu items. Or management could encourage the service staff to entertain their families at the restaurant and purchase their meals at a discount.

Once the service staff have mastered the knowledge concerning the restaurant and menu by the testing criteria set up, it is time for them to move on to the second part of serving the meal.

Merchandising and Taking the Order
Has this ever happened to you?

A t a restaurant, you are asked by the service person if you want a salad. You reply, "Yes." The service person says, "And what would you like on your salad?" That's it; that's all they say. They figure you must be a mind reader. The next time someone says that to you, reply "Poppy seed vinaigrette," or some other made-up salad dressing, and watch the expression on the person's face!

Merchandising Food and Beverage

Merchandising food and beverage is simply another term for selling. Selling occurs because the guest likes and is confident in the service person's ability. This part of the training program should concentrate on getting the guests to like your staff.

This should be done by placing the service staff in common situations that occur daily in the restaurant. This is called role playing. For instance, have the service staff ask the "guests" what type of salad dressing they want, using the example of the problem stated on the preceeding page.

The service person should assess the mood of the guests as they approach the table. Are they celebrating and in a festive mood or do they appear somber, as if they have just returned from a funeral? Once the service person has assessed the situation, the behavior should be appropriate for the situation.

Each guest deserves and expects a warm, sincere greeting. If the staff person knows the guest, the guest should be addressed by name. Furthermore, the staff should acknowledge the presence of the guest immediately and take care of any requests as soon as possible. This will make the guest feel as if the restaurant appreciates the patronage and will add to making the dining experience a positive one.

Assisting the Guest with the Order

Many times guests will know exactly what food they wish to order; but at other times they can not make up their minds. There is a trick that experienced service persons use to sell items and help guests make up their minds. If the guests are asked for their order and they do not give it quickly or are hesitating, count backwards from seven. If the guests have not made up their minds by the time the server reaches zero, then they will need help. And that opens it up for the service staff to sell suggestively.

Suggestive Selling

The first step in suggestive selling is having the guests like the service person. Once this happens, the guests will be responsive to the service person's suggestions. The guests now trust the service person's knowledge and judgement. He or she has answered all the guests' questions about the restaurant, told them what is happening in the area, and is perceived as knowledgeable.

The next question, the guests usually ask is, "What's good on the menu?" "Everything," is a poor response. Instead, train your staff to turn the question around and ask the guests what type of food they like, fish or beef? The service person may then describe a meal that tastes and looks great based upon their preference. This is the main reason why employees should be required to taste all items on the menu. They are then able to describe how the food tastes and can base their recommendations on what the guest desires.

The key to suggestive selling is for the service person to do the thinking of the guest and to keep a positive attitude. The staff must put themselves in their guests' place, then use mouth-watering descriptions of the menu item for the purpose of selling the item. The service person shouldn't say, "Would anyone care for dessert?" Instead, he or she should describe the desserts available.

Chocolate, Anyone?

A typical suggestive selling job occurred when a veteran waiter was removing the dinner plates at the end of the meal. While he was crumbing the table, he said, "May I get you coffee?" As soon as the guests said "Yes," he added, "By the way, if you like chocolate, I tasted our great new decadent dessert, the triple chocolate cake. I'll be back with your coffee and a dessert menu." The service person had obtained the guests' trust; they liked him, and he put the idea of a specific desserts in their minds. They all ordered desserts.

If a service person does not suggest desserts, or merely asks the guests if they care to see a dessert menu, too often the answer is "No." By suggesting a specific dessert and using mouth-watering descriptions, the rate of success of selling desserts will be greatly enhanced.

Another technique used by experienced salespeople is to suggest last the item they wish to sell. This is because people usually remember the last thing said to them.

Suggestive selling can build the profits for the restaurant by encouraging guests to order extra items that they normally would not have ordered. It also builds up the check total; and as most guests tip on the total bill, the amount of tip for the service person increases.

The Special of the Day

What is a special of the day? If you are shopping in a supermarket or for clothes, a special means reduced prices for that item. Does a special in the restaurant mean reduced prices? Contrary to that, it usually means a special item prepared by the chef. The price is special, also—usually higher than a normal menu item.

A manager might do well to change the name of the special of the day to the *chef's creation*. Then the service staff can approach the table and explain the chef's creation to the guests.

The question: Should the service staff be instructed to inform the guests of the price of the chef's creation?

In an April 18, 1987 Ann Landers column, a reader wrote in for advice about etiquette in a restaurant. The reader stated that the service persons rattle off the specials of the day, and, while they all sound wonderful, they don't tell you the price. When the bill comes, it is a lot higher than if you had ordered from the menu. Would you buy a shirt or blouse without knowing the price?

No one has ever satisfactorily explained the reason why prices are not given when a special item is offered. In staying with the premise of this book, that our job is to please the guests, the service staff **must** recite the prices to the guests. This is another positive factor that builds up the trust of the guest. Another annoying custom is for restaurants to instruct their service staff to offer an item (such as blue cheese dressing), and state is is "a la carte." Most guests have no idea what a la carte means. The service staff should inform the guests the price of all items.

Wine, Dessert Tables, Gimmicks

There are other techniques that may be used to assist the service staff in selling additional items in a restaurant. These are usually associated with wine and dessert sales.

More and more restaurants include wine glasses at the place setting. Others sell a sample two-ounce portion of wine to the guests. Still others put a bottle of unopened wine on each table to encourage guests to order wine with their meal.

Desserts provide the opportunity to increase sales enormously. Even though the American public is becoming more nutrition conscious and eating lighter meals, survey after survey has found that guests will order desserts. Many restaurants display their desserts so the guests can view them before they begin their meal. This technique has been used successfully by many restaurants for merchandising desserts. If the desserts are kept attractive and eye-appealing, the guest will usually order dessert. However, if the cart or table becomes messy and unappetizing, it does the restaurant more harm than good.

Another excellent way to merchandise desserts is to bring out a sample tray of all desserts. The service person brings the tray to the guests' table and

Figure 6–5. The dessert display at Victoria and Albert's restaurant at Walt Disney World's Grand Floridian Beach Resort. (© 1988 The Walt Disney Company)

describes the desserts to them. This method eliminates the problem of the desserts looking unattractive, because the desserts on the tray are not served to the guests. Instead, the service person obtains the desserts from the kitchen. As soon as a dessert on the tray looks unappealing, it is replaced.

One of the best selling gimmicks that has been used for ages is initiated by the manager. If done properly, it can increase sales and repeat business dramatically. It involves the manager giving away an item that will call attention to that item. For example, a restaurant sells flaming coffee as an extra item. The manager should approach a table that is located in the center of the dining room, where other guests can see the coffee being prepared. The manager should introduce himself or herself to the guests, inquire about their meal, thank them for their business, and offer to buy them an after-dinner coffee. Once the coffee is being prepared, all the eyes in the dining room are attracted to the coffee presentation. This display will encourage other guests to order the coffee after their meals. This can be done with a fancy dessert, large glasses of beer, or any type of fancy entree. The cost of this to the restaurant is the cost of the item. In addition, the guest will feel special, because the manager gave away an item (back to Maslow's Hierarchy).

The manager must encourage the service staff to sell extra items. The guests have already made the decision to patronize the restaurant. With suggestive selling, the service staff can increase profits for the restaurant. However, one word of caution: the manager must make certain that the service staff do not push so hard that the guests will become upset with their selling aggressiveness and have negative thoughts about the dining experience.

Taking the Order

Training your staff in the correct way to take a guest's food and beverage order is critical. There are many correct methods to take the order. All of them should have one goal: to serve the meal to the guest without the service person having to ask who gets what.

The manager should teach the service staff how to talk to the guests and how to take meal orders. The staff should not be allowed to say to the guests, "Whadda ya want?" instead of, "May I take your order?" Avoid addressing guests by "hon," "doll," "fella," "madam," and other words that can be interpreted as derogatory. The staff should be encouraged to address people by their name; always by the last name, until the guests tell the service person to call them by their first name.

The manager must impress upon the service staff that they should treat the guests as if they had never dined at the restaurant before. They do not know how the specials are made or what the salad dressing is that evening. It must be impressed upon the service staff that this will be the first time the guest hears the specials. Even though the service staff may have repeated them 100 times that evening, employees should be taught to **explain every item to each guest.**

The manager must train the staff to explain in detail the chef's creation of the evening. When it is time to offer the guest the choice of salad dressings or vegetables, explain what they are. Rather than let the staff say, "And what would you like on your salad?" encourage them to say something like: "A salad is included in the meal. Our choice of dressings are: blue cheese; Russian; Italian; and our house dressing, which is a sweet and sour dressing made with mustard and honey." The same should be true for vegetables, potatoes, and chef creations, especially if the item is new or one that is not normally served in the geographical area where your restaurant is located. Included in the explanation can be the ingredients, how it is prepared, and the price.

Finally, the order should be repeated back to the guest. By doing this, your service staff will avoid any misunderstandings of guest orders.

However, the method used should not be annoying to the guests. For instance, a service person who echoes every single item that the guest orders will be annoying. It is much better to wait until the complete order is taken and then repeat the main course back to the guest.

The job of the service staff should not just be to serve the food, but to be the human link between the kitchen and the guest. This is why the importance of verbal communication between the service staff and the guest must be stressed. It gives the restaurant a personality.

Where to Stand

There are two opinions on where the service person should be standing when they take the guests' order. Both agree that order taking should follow the proper guidelines of service: children first, then women, then men. There is an exception, when one person is the host of the party and he or she is ordering for the entire table.

The first method states that the service person should stand to the left of the guest and take the order, then move to the next person, following the proper guidelines of service, and take the order. The problem that occurs using this method is that if the service person takes the order by following proper guidelines, it may be necessary to skip over one male guest to take the next female's order. The service person will then have to return to the man, and move back and forth, creating much unnecessary confusion.

The second method is to have the service person stand in one spot and take all the guests' orders from that spot, following the proper guidelines of service. This works well at a table with two to four guests. However for more than four guests, especially with rectangular-shaped tables, the service person may have to move to different spots in order to hear the order.

86 Items

The term *86* in the restaurant business means to be out of an item. When a restaurant sells all of its orders of prime ribs, the chef will tell the service staff, "Ribs are 86ed." Before a service person takes the dinner order from the guests, they should know what items are 86ed. Managers must set up a system that provides a list of 86ed items to the service staff, either through verbal communications or via a blackboard. The manager should train his chef and kitchen staff to inform the service staff when there are ten servings of a particular entree left. The service staff will then be able to inform the guest that they think that the dinner item is available, but will have to check with the kitchen. This will avoid embarrassment by the service person and annoyance to the guest. It is a bad situation to have the guest decide on shrimp scampi, have the service person take the order, and then come back to say, "I'm sorry we are out of the shrimp, what would you care for now?" It gets even more annoying to then have the guest decide on another item, only to find that the kitchen is out of that too. Who will make the third trip to the table to tell the guest?

Home Base

Many of you have experienced the auction game. The service person comes to the table with two dinners and asks "Who's the beef and who's the shrimp?" It does sound funny, but it can be embarrassing and insulting. This should never happen. The most common way of taking orders to avoid this is referred to as *home base*.

The home base system works in the following manner. The manager decides on one focal point in the restaurant as the home base. It may be a clock, the front door, or some other stationary item in the restaurant. The service staff use the home base as the starting off point to identify all the seats. The chair closest to home base is chair one. For example, in this party of two, with the clock as home base, the person in seat *A* is number one. The chairs are then numbered clockwise from chair one (as that is the direction in which the service person will be serving). Figures 6–6 and 6–7 illustrate home base at a four-top with only two guests at the table. In Figure 6–7, using the clock as home base, chair *A* would be the first chair if a guest were seated in that seat. Because the guests are seated in *B* and *C*, *B* becomes the first seat and *C* the second.

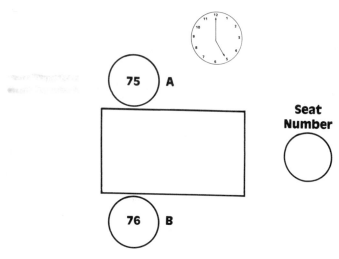

Figure 6–6.   Using the clock as home base, the seat closest to the clock is home base. Seat A is home base.

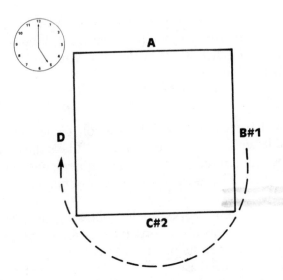

Figure 6–7.   Using the clock as home base, seat B becomes #1, as no guest is seating in the A seat.

Order Forms

Once the staff knows where the home base is, the next thing the manager must teach the staff is how to write the guest orders. The system must be explained simply enough so that any employee who picks up the food order can deliver it to the guests without having to ask who gets what.

Each service person should be provided with some sort of form with which to take orders. The service person must be organized; but more importantly, it is up to the manager to devise this policy in such a way that all employees will know who gets what item. Some managers, in addition to using the home base system, will have their staff put an X next to the seat number of the women. This is a variation on the system called *code order*.

Here is an example of a guest's order form.

Order Form

Table Number 49   **Time 7:02**

Seat	D	App	MC	Sal	Pot	Fig
				bc	b	gb
1	ws	sc	ss			
2 x	ws	os	NYS	it	m	c

In the above example, the woman is seated at seat 2. By putting an X next to her number, all employers will know that an X means a woman is seating there. Because all employees know the standard abbreviations, this form can be used by all staff. The time and table number are also on this form to tell the service person what time the order was taken. This form can be expanded to include desserts and after-dinner drinks; however, it would be preferable to use a new form for these items. Across the top of the form is *D* which stands for before dinner drink; *App* for appetizer; *MC* for main course; *Sal* for salad; *Pot* for potato; and *veg* for vegetable. Because more restaurants are using computerized systems to order food in the kitchen, the manager would be wise to institute this system. The computer system provides for the food order to be transmitted directly to the kitchen, without the service person entering the kitchen. The printer is programmed to print orders based upon cooking time priority (the longest item to cook is shown first). Even though the computer system relays the order to the kitchen, when it is ready, the restaurant has to have a system in place in order for the employees to know what guest gets what food item.

Ordering on the Guest Check

Some restaurants use a system that has the guest check remain at the table, in a slot provided in each table. The duplicate check (dupe) is brought into the kitchen to order the food. This guest check can have the system of "who gets what" directly written on the check. The service staff will write the check in the following manner: The seat immediately to the left of the slot is the number 1 seat. Going in a clockwise direction, the seats are numbered consecutively, 2, 3, 4. The management arranges the tables so that the slots are always in the same position relative to the home base.

On the bottom of the check the server writes in the table number and the last three digits of the check. This information appears on the dupe which is turned into the kitchen. An example of a check follows:

Sect 5   **245666**

Chair

				Food	Bar
1	NY	mr	Xs	14.95	
2	Rib	end m	BQ	15.95	
3	Smp +S	r	p	10.95	
4	F sOs	m	1p	16.95	
	Amarone 1 – 4 (3)				45.00
2	Bq 2,4			4.50	
1	mk 3			1.95	
2	c cho 1,3			2.50	
2	wit 2,4				4.50
1	vo w 1				2.25
1	jb v 3				2.25

26/666

An Explanation of the Check

This check combines many different techniques for taking orders. The service staff must know what all items and abbreviations on the check mean. Working from the bottom of the check up, the 26 represents the table number. As all staff know the layout of the restaurant, they will all know where table 26 is located.

The last three numbers of the check 245666 are represented by the 666. Any person who picks up the food in the kitchen will know that the food will be delivered to table 26. Once the food is placed at table 26, the staff member can verify that it is the same check by comparing the last three numbers on the dupe with the guest check in the slot at the table. If there is a problem at table 26, such as food not being served quickly enough, the manager can go into the kitchen and check on the status of the dupe.

The *1 jb v 3* for $2.25 means that there is one order of J & B scotch served with Vichy to the guest in seat number 3 for $2.25. The server can see that it is a drink because the price is listed under the bar column.

Reading up the check, the first food item is the *2 c cho 1,3* for $2.50. This means that there are two orders of clam chowder served to the guests at seats 1 and 3. The total price of $2.50 ($1.25 each) is placed under the food column.

Continuing up the check to the *Amarone 1–4 (3)*, the service staff knows that the table ordered one bottle of this red wine, with four glasses. The *(3)* means that the guest seated in seat 3 ordered the wine.

Above the line, the ordering is different. The chair numbers are written, and then the entrees are ordered. For instance, the guest seated in chair 1 is to receive a *NY mr Xs* for $14.95. Translated, this means a New York sirloin, cooked medium rare with baked potato (*x*) with sour cream (*s*).

These are two methods for writing guest orders and to determine who gets what order. There are other methods, but they all have one thing in common. They are set up in an organized manner that can be easily learned. The key is to have the manager decide on one system and have all of the staff use the same system.

Code Order

Another system for determining who gets what is the code order. This system is not recommended, because too much confusion and embarrassment can result. The code order system was used in the past when a single service person was responsible for the station. The service person would write next to the order a code which would identify the guest. The code would represent some distinguishing feature that made one guest stand out from the others, such as blue tie or red hair. This system can create problems because not all the service staff would understand the system. It also could be embarrassing if the service person uses a code order that was derogatory toward the guest—such as fat person, bald, or grey hair.

Placing Orders in the Kitchen

Correct ordering in the kitchen is a must for having the guests receive their dinner cooked and served to them properly. As the service staff knows the time it takes to cook every item, they should submit their orders based on the mood of the guests and on how long it will take to cook the meal. In most restaurants, the time to submit the order is when the service person picks up the guests' salad from the kitchen. In restaurants that have a salad bar, the service person is instructed to turn the order into the kitchen when the guests go to obtain their salads from the salad bar. However, each manager can determine what is best for his or her own individual unit.

Depending on the type of system, the service persons may be required to order all the entrees at the top of their check. They may put all the cold items at the bottom. Others may have a computerized system that prints all the orders in a priority based on cooking times. It does not matter how it is done, as long as all members of the staff use the common abbreviations and the same system.

Serving the Meal: Timing is Everything

This is the critical part of the meal. The meal can be progressing favorably, but if the meal is served incorrectly the evening can be ruined. The service staff has ordered the meal correctly. It has been cooked properly, and the kitchen is waiting for the service person to serve it to the guest in the dining room. But instead of being picked up and delivered to the guest, it sits in the kitchen, becoming colder and less appetizing. This now becomes the crucial part of the meal. The server has to deliver the correct meal to the guest. Timing is of the essence. The staff must get the meal to the table as soon as it is ready. If the dinners sit too long, the quality suffers, and the guests become impatient.

More and more restaurants are using electronic means to notify the service person that the meal is ready. Either through a light system or by using a public address system to call out the service person's name. As soon as the food is ready, the service person should pick it up and bring it to the table. But before doing so, the service person should take a few seconds to check that all the food items on the dupe match those that have been prepared by the kitchen. He or she must also check to see that all special instructions on the dupe have been followed. The tray will be loaded by placing the cold items first, then the hot items. (The hot items should be placed on the tray last, so they will not cool off as fast.) The food on the tray should be arranged to serve the guests in the most efficient manner. Any condiments and garnishes should be brought to the guests' table along with the entrees.

The sequence for serving a typical meal will be explained. Because the team system is the newest of all the systems, that system will be used. However, this typical meal will work in any system.

Sequence of a Typical Meal

1. All the sidework has been completed, the service staff is prepared to receive their guests. The service staff knows the chef features of the day; what items are 86ed. They have their guest checks and duplicate order forms to take orders.
2. Guests are seated by the host, presented with menus, both food and wine. Chef features are recited or given out using a printed daily chef feature menu.
3. The Lead approaches table, greets guests in a friendly manner; answers questions about the menu and offers to take drink or wine orders.
4. Drinks are written on the check and the order form, using the system that has been taught to all service staff. In the team system, the check never leaves the table. The check is placed back into the slot in the table.
5. Drinks are served on a cocktail napkin in the center of the setting. If the setting has a show or starter plate, the drink is placed on the center of the starter plate. All drinks are served from the right side of the guest with the service person's right hand.
6. The food order is taken by the Lead. The Lead attempts to merchandise the additional items. After the order is taken, the menus are collected by the Lead.
7. The order is placed on duplicate check; Lead holds it in his or her pocket until it is time to turn it into the kitchen to order food.
8. The Aid picks up appetizer (first course) from the kitchen and serves it to the guests. When an appetizer is served and there has not been a piece of flatware included in the cover for an appetizer, it is brought with the food. For example, if a bowl of soup is served, the soup is served from the left side with the left hand, and the soup spoon is placed on the right side of the guest. The staff should be instructed not to reach across the front of the guests but to walk behind them and put the spoon in its proper location.

9. Rolls and butter are served by the Aid, being placed in the center of the table.

10. The first course is removed from the guest's right with the Aid's right hand.

11. Salad is served, or the guests go to the salad bar. If a guest requests salad dressing on the side, place it in a separate container and serve it on a bread and butter plate, called an *underliner*. The salad is placed in the center of the place setting or on the starter plate.

12. When salads are served, the Lead turns the check into the kitchen for the food to be cooked.

13. Wine could be served at this point, or it could have been served as soon as it was requested. The Lead shows the label to the person who ordered the wine. Once the guest verifies that this is the wine desired, the Lead opens the wine and presents the cork to the guest. The guest should feel the cork (it should be wet) to determine if the wine was stored properly. The Lead then pours about an ounce into the glass of the guest. Once the guest approves of the wine, the Lead will pour the wine into the glasses of the guests, using proper serving techniques. Glasses of red wine should be filled 1/2 full; white, 3/4 full. The bottle of red wine is placed on the table, while the white wine should be placed in an ice bucket.

14. Salad plates are removed, as well as the starter plate. If guests tell the service staff they would like to finish their salad with the meal, the staff person should move it to the left of the place setting.

15. When food order is ready, kitchen informs the Aid to pick up food by calling out section 1. Other restaurants can develop a system for informing service staff when the food is cooked and ready to be served.

16. Entree is picked up in the kitchen. The plates are placed in the same order as written on the duplicate check. The Aid compares the food to the duplicate check. If any mistakes are found, they are corrected immediately. It is the responsibility of the person picking up the food to make certain that the plate is eye-appealing, attractive, and the proper temperature.

17. Before food is served to guests, service person makes certain that plates are proper temperature, attractive (no gravy or au jus (natural juices) slopped on the rim of the plate), and garnished correctly.

18. Entree is served without asking who gets what. If vegetables or potatoes are served in a side dish (called Monkey dishes), they are placed above and near the main entree dish. (Reminder: The staff should be instructed never to put one course in front of the guest before the previous course has been removed. For example, if a woman has not finished eating her

salad when the service person removes the other salad dishes, her salad dish should be removed before her entree is placed in front of her.)

19. Entrees are served without having to ask who gets what meal. Condiments that accompany the main courses (such as sour cream, catsup, and so on) are placed on the guests' table.

20. All entrees are brought to the table together. If the service person has more entrees than can fit on the tray, another service person should carry out the remaining food. This will ensure that all guests receive their food at approximately the same time; no one will have to wait while the service person returns to the kitchen to pick up the additional meals.

21. All meat items are placed in front of the guest with the meatiest part facing the guest (meat in front), so when the guest cuts the meat, they cut into the most tender part. If starch and vegetables are served on the same plate, they are the items furthest away from the guest.

22. As soon as all entrees are served to the guests, the service person checks the table to determine if more rolls and butter are needed or if more wine is to be poured, and inquires if there is anything else that the guests would like.

23. Throughout all the service, the Lead is constantly checking the tables to determine if guests need more drinks. In order to save time, the lead learns to take more than one table's order at once. Then the Lead can order ten or twelve drinks at once instead of having to make four separate trips back and forth.

24. Each manager should have their service staff check back to the table as soon as the guests sample their food to inquire if the food is done to their satisfaction. The question should *not* be, "Is everything OK here?" because that assumes that it is not. Instead, a better phrase would be, "Is the steak cooked the way you ordered it?" Any problems should be taken care of immediately. Food should be returned to the kitchen and recooked if it was not done well enough. If food was done too well, the staff should inform the guest that it will take extra time to cook the meal over. Offer an alternative, an item that is already prepared and can be served immediately (such as prime ribs).

25. Once the guests inform the Follow-Up that the food is done to their satisfaction, the guest check is flipped over so the other members of the team can see that the table has been checked.

26. The service staff should return to the table to pour extra wine and water throughout the meal. Water glasses should be filled as soon as they are half empty. Any time a service person performs any service at the table, he or she should converse with the guest.

27. As soon as all guests have finished eating their meals, (the staff can determine this as guests put their utensils across their dinner plates or push their dinner plates away from them) their plates should be removed.

28. If any guests have not finished their main course, an inquiry should be made to determine if the guests would like to have the remainder of the meal wrapped so they may take it home. If the answer is "Yes," the server should take one plate at a time to the sidestand to wrap the left over food, and bring it back to the guest. This eliminates having the guest question whether the food they have received is their own. The service persons should bring wrapping material with them when they are preparing to clear the dirty dishes.

29. Remove all the dirty dishes, including bread baskets, bread and butter plates, butter plates, dirty glasses, and wine glasses.

30. The service staff should crumb the table with either the sidetowel or a crumbing device. The crumbs should be swept into a bread and butter plate.

31. Inquire from the guests if they would like coffee or tea. The staff can merchandise dessert by using descriptive words, such as "our triple chocolate dessert."

32. Coffee is served by the service person, using a coffee shield. Tea is served by placing the tea pot above the coffee cup. Serve cream, sugar, and lemon with the tea and coffee.

33. Dessert is served to the guests. If one dessert is ordered for two people, bring two forks. If the dessert is gigantic, inform the guest, and bring extra plates for other guests to share the dessert.

34. Serve second and third cups of coffee and tea without having the guests have to ask for additional beverages. Remember that once the dirty entree dishes have been cleared and the coffee and dessert served, the meal is not over! The guests deserve as much attention at the end of the meal as they received at the beginning of the meal.

35. The check should be presented to the guests. If the staff can not determine who is the host of the party, they should place the check face down in the center of the table.

36. When the guests pay the bill, the guests should be thanked for their patronage and encouraged to return.

37. After the guests leave, the staff must reset the table for the next party of guests.

38. Throughout the meal the service staff should always be thinking of ways to save time. They are never to go into the kitchen empty-handed or come out empty-handed. They must be attuned to when and how to change the ashtrays if the guests are smoking tobacco.

The above illustrates a typical sequence of serving a meal. Depending upon the restaurant's menu, some of the steps may be changed to suit its needs.

Chapter Summary

1. The manager must select, train, and evaluate the employees.
2. Guests expect two qualities in service personnel: politeness and the ability to answer questions.
3. The service staff must know the physical layout of the restaurant, the menu, the ingredients in all food items (including garnishes and substitutions), cooking methods and cooking times, and all alcoholic beverages offered by the establishment.
4. The service staff must be well versed in suggestive selling, particularly of desserts and chef's specials.
5. In serving the meal, **timing is everything.**

Review Questions

1. A check for $15.97 was presented to a guest, who paid it with $20 bill. The service person brought three cents change back to the table, having kept the four one dollar bills without the guest offering the tip. Is there any problem here? And if there is, how would you as a manager handle the complaint from the guests and make certain that it never happens again?
2. What would you do as a manager if the guest refused to pay the bill because it is the policy of your restaurant not to tell the guests the "special prices?"
3. Why should the service person have a thorough knowledge of the menu?
4. Why is it important that a service person know all the ingredients of all menu items?
5. The cooking times of all menu items is important for a service person to know. Explain why you believe this is true or false.
6. What is suggestive selling, and what is its benefit for the restaurant?
7. What does the term 86 mean? How can servers avoid problems when an item is 86ed?
8. What is the home base system? Describe how it operates.
9. Should guests be allowed to substitute items on the menu?

Chapter 7
Organizing the Dining Room to Accept Guests

Chapter Objectives:

At the completion of this chapter, the reader will be able to:

1. give an historical background of the host's job;
2. list the qualities that make a good host;
3. explain the importance of stations and sidework as they relate to the host's job;
4. recite the five P's of management and know what the saying means.
5. discuss the factors that effect scheduling; and
6. organize a dining room to accept guests.

The Host

The key person in the dining room is the individual who greets the guests. This person may be called the maître d'hôtel, the director of service, or the host or hostess (called the host in this chapter). Regardless of the name, this job must be staffed by a competent individual. In most instances this is the first human contact the guest will have with the restaurant. Therefore, the host is identified as the restaurant to many patrons.

Guests often decide to patronize a restaurant based upon the greeting and attention they receive from the host. In addition to greeting the guests, the host is responsible for the operation of the dining room. This person is the one who must ensure that the guests have an enjoyable dining experience, and who must solve any problems that may arise in the dining room.

An Historical Overview
The job of the host has evolved from the classical restaurant. In this type of restaurant the job titles were as follows: *directeur du restaurant; maître d'*

Figure 7–1. A hostess at a restaurant. She is the first person that the guest comes into contact with in the restaurant.

hôtel; deuxième maître d'hôtel; and a *maître d'hôtel de carré.* This type of staffing had a host for each area of the restaurant.

The directeur du restaurant had complete charge of the restaurant, including the kitchen and dining room staff. He was responsible also for long-term planning, food and beverage cost controls, and service.

The maître d'hôtel was the host of all the dining rooms in the hotel. The operations may have been in many different restaurants. He was in charge of the dishwashers, cleanup crew, and linen service. If the hotel was large, there may have been a second (deuxième) maître d'hôtel, who was responsible for one dining room.

The maître d'hôtel de carré had the responsibility of a section of the dining room, similar to the captain of today.

Because of the high labor cost involved in employing many individuals in a restaurant, many restaurants have consolidated the above jobs into the position of host. However, there are some larger restaurants that still have a director of food and beverage, and also a host. Figure 7-2 compares the early job titles to the responsibilities of restaurant personnel today.

THE HOST'S POSITION

Early Days	Responsibility	Today
Directeur du Restaurant	Total Restaurant Operation	Food & Beverage Manager or Host
Maître d' Hôtel	All Dining Rooms	Food & Beverage Manager or Host
Deuxième Maître d' Hôtel	One Dining Room	Host
Maître d' Hôtel de Carré	One Section of the Dining Room	Host or Head Service Person (often called Captain)

Figure 7–2. The early job titles compared with the responsibilities of restaurant personnel of today.

Authority of the Host

The authority and respect of the host has deteriorated over the years. As service became more and more lax in America, the job of the host was considered an entry level position. Restaurant owners paid the host at the minimum wage rate because the owners felt that this person did not directly produce money as a service person. Consequently, the person who was given this job was poorly trained, if trained at all. This position changed from being a job of prestige, that had power and respect, into a job that restaurant owners felt anyone could do. Instead of having experienced waitpeople striving to become the host, they avoided it because it did not pay as much money as their tipped position. The restaurant industry as a whole, and especially service given to the guests, suffered tremendously.

Today, the pendulum has begun to swing back to the experienced and respected host. Restaurant owners are realizing the importance of having a well-trained host. A well-informed and personable individual holding the job of host will make the restaurant a success. Restaurant owners are now compensating their hosts at a higher pay rate than the minimum wage. As the laws regarding tip reporting and taxes become more stringent on restaurant owners, more and more are instituting a fixed gratuity. From this fixed gratuity, the host is being paid a much higher wage than minimum. Other restaurants, who still have a voluntary tipping policy, are making the service staff contribute part of their tips to the host.

Restaurant owners are, once again, realizing the importance of having a competent, personable host to greet their guests.

Host Selection

Selecting a person for the host's job is important and challenging for the manager or owner of the restaurant. This is because a major portion of the job is dependent upon the host to observe a situation or problem, weigh the positive versus the negative aspects, and make a decision—all in the time frame of a few seconds. Because the ability to think quickly and react to situations positively is a necessary qualification, the manager must try to select an individual who is personable and can work well under stress. The selection process should be structured in such a manner as to determine the personality and the ability to work under stress of the applicant. Figure 7-3 lists the criteria for selecting a host. In addition, the manager should look for some additional specific qualifications that have been identified with excellent hosts. These qualifications are discussed in the next section.

Qualifications of the Host

The qualifications for a host fall into two general categories: physical and behavioral (see Figure 7-4). The first relates to the appearance of the individual. The second refers to the manner in which a person interacts with people.

The host is the first person guests see when they walk into a restaurant, therefore the physical appearance of the host must be positive. Figure 7-5 shows a host outside his restaurant. This host makes a positive physical appearance. As with the service staff, cleanliness is essential. Any uniform (tuxedo or evening gown) must be neat and clean. These uniforms are a symbol of professionalism. The host should be proud of wearing the uniform.

The second qualification, behavioral, is the ability to deal with people. The host has to be able to meet the needs of the restaurant's guests and employees. Sometimes this is not easy. Many of the guests are not pleasant, because they may be having a bad day, are not used to waiting for a table, or for a myriad of reasons that the host has little, if any, control over. Employees provide another challenge. They will complain about the

CRITERIA FOR HOST SELECTION

Individual Selected to Be A Host Must:
1. be personable
2. work well under stress
3. be able to think quickly
4. be able to make decisions

Figure 7-3.

QUALIFICATIONS NEEDED TO BE A HOST

Physical

Deals with Host's
own appearance

Behavioral

Deals with Host's
behavior toward
guests and employees

Figure 7–4.

amount of tips that the guests have left and about their stations, for example. The host must have the ability to satisfy all the employee and guest complaints, whether they are legitimate or not.

Useful Behavioral Traits

For the host to do the job effectively, there are other behavioral traits that are needed. The book *The Professional Host* lists some of them as attentiveness, courteousness, dependability, economy, efficiency, honesty, knowledge,

Figure 7–5. A host outside of his restaurant. He makes a positive physical appearance.

loyalty, preparedness, productivity, quietness, sensitivity, tact, persuasiveness, and skill.[1] Even though it would appear that every person has the common sense to know and use these traits, many do not. The following information will give examples of the importance of the specific traits.

Attentiveness

Like the service staff, the host must be ubiquitous. He must know what is occurring in the dining room at all times, and must appear to have eyes in the back of his head. The host has to know the status of all tables at all times; whether table 3 has been served their main course; if table 5 needs more wine. An absentminded person or daydreamer does not belong in the position of host. This job requires a person who will be consistently alert to the guests' needs.

Courteousness

The host must treat the guests as though they were guests in his home. Words such as "please" and "thank you" are thought by many people to be magic words. Guests appreciate hearing these magic words, and the host is encouraged to use them whenever appropriate. Greeting the guests by name and addressing the guests by name throughout the dining experience is another positive thing the host can do to make the guest feel important. Throughout the guests' dining experience, the host should return to the table to show his genuine concern about their satisfaction. By using the magic words "please," "thank you," "excuse me," and especially the guest's name, the host will not only impress the guest by his courtesy but will provide a positive model for the service staff to follow.

Courteousness also includes assisting the guests with little things that show concern. These little things are not something that will make a person jump up and down and say, "Wow, did you see what the host did!" Instead, they are displays of courteousness that will make the guests feel that the restaurant really cares about them and is happy to receive their business. Examples of courteousness are: assisting the guests in removing or putting on their coats; pulling out the chairs for the guests as they are shown to their table; and checking back with the guests to determine if the table or temperature of the room is pleasing. Pulling the shades down so the sun will not shine in the guests eyes is another example. The difference between a great restaurant and a good restaurant is taking care of the details—and courteousness is a detail.

Dependability

Dependability is a trait that is valued highly by restaurant owners. It is a sign of maturity. Basically, it means that the employees will be responsible for their own actions. It also includes the fact that the employees will accomplish the goals that have been set, either by management or by the employees themselves. This trait is extremely critical for any person who will hold the responsible job of host.

Economy

Economy means to keep costs at a minimum. This will be the host's responsibilities. The dining room is an area where costs can rapidly get out of control because of improper scheduling, improper use of linen, and food waste. If the host schedules too many service staff, the labor cost will be a drain on the restaurant. If staff is allowed to use extra equipment (like extra sidetowels) when they are not needed, money is lost. Common sense is important in keeping waste to a minimum. An example of economy is to save and reuse individual packaged jellies if they have not been opened.

Efficiency

Efficiency means finding the quickest and easiest way to do a task without jeopardizing the guests' satisfaction. The ability to organize reservations in a systematic manner is an example of efficiency (see Figure 7-6). By having an efficient reservation system, the host can take reservations correctly. This will allow the host to spend more time in the dining room (or working the floor) instead of trying to straighten out a mess caused by an inefficient reservation system. The more organized the host is, the more time can be spent with the guests.

Honesty

A person who deals with the public, especially in the host's job, will have to make many decisions that will test his honesty. For example, a guest approaches the host and asks for a table. The host has all the tables reserved and informs the guest of this. The guest produces a $50 bill and asks, "Are you sure?" The host and the guest both know that the patron is buying the table. What should the host do?

Other opportunities will arise to deceive the customer as well as the employees. In all instances, if the host is dishonest and allows the staff to be dishonest, word will spread that the establishment is dishonest. This will result in negative word of mouth from both guests and employees, and the business will suffer.

Loyalty

Loyalty is another highly rated behavioral trait of a host. It can be defined as being (or giving the impression to the public of being) totally supportive of the ideas and philosophies of the restaurant. An example of not being

Figure 7–6.   A hostess checking her reservations for the evening meal. By planning ahead, she is demonstrating the quality of efficiency. (Photo courtesy of The Desmond Americana)

loyal is downgrading the establishment to the guests by such comments as, "Management has no idea of how to run this place."

Knowledge

As with the service staff, the host has to know all facets of the operation of the restaurant. In fact, he must know more about the operation than the service staff, because the guests perceive the host as the key figure in the restaurant. The host should know all the facts about the operation of the restaurant, including the preparation and service of food and beverage. In addition, the host has to be aware of the physical layout of the restaurant how to deal with credit card charges, and the accounting procedures of the restaurant. With today's ever changing technology, knowledge of computers and computer systems are critical.

Knowledge of community events is an important part of the host's concern. If a guest asks a question and the host doesn't know the answer, he will have to find out the answer and return to the guest with it.

Service, Indeed!

A couple invited two friends to dinner and a play one Saturday evening. A reservation was made at one of the couple's favorite restaurants; in addition, that restaurant provides the catering for the theater where the party of four were to attend the play. While driving to the restaurant, the host turned to the invited couple and said, "Well, we won't be late for the play, but we will be a little early, because our tickets are for next Saturday. I called and tried to exchange the tickets and get us seats for tonight; but as the theater only seats two hundred people they are sold out." When they arrived at the restaurant, the host/owner greeted them warmly and inquired whether they were going to the play or "were there for a leisurely dinner?" The guest explained the problem. The owner asked for the tickets and said, "Let me see what I can do." By the time the salad had arrived, the owner was back at the table to inform the group that he had secured tickets for that evening's performance.

Preparedness

Nothing is more frustrating for guests than to have to wait for something: a reservation, food, or drinks. The host has to be ready to accept guests into the dining room at its stated opening time. If a guest is promised a 3 P.M. reservation, then the table should be ready for them at 3 P.M. Preparedness is the act of planning and organizing all equipment and supplies so the guest will not have to wait for service.

Procrastinators do not belong in the hospitality industry. The host should have a plan for each situation and be considering alternative plans in case of a problem.

Quietness

A good host is a person who is always available when needed. However, the host has to be aware of the proper time to talk to guests and when to leave them alone. When talking to the guests, it is done in a nice manner, not in a loud or boisterous one. The host must act with dignity, and do the job quietly.

Sensitivity

Restaurants are the place where many special occasions are celebrated, such as engagements, wedding anniversaries, births, and job promotions. Unfortunately, it is also the place where many marriages and relationships are ended. People often choose a restaurant in which to tell their spouse or lover that the relationship is finished, because they think that the hurt party will not make a scene in so public a place. The host has to be sensitive to the needs of the guests and observe their actions to determine how much attention they want from the host. Sensitivity is a two-part trait: first to observe what is occurring between the guests or to the guests, then act appropriately. If the guests have just become engaged, congratulations should be offered. A dessert or drink may be offered, compliments of the restaurant. If the couple obviously is having a fight, then staying away from the table is best. Going to the table and asking how the food is would not be appropriate. That would show a lack of sensitivity.

Skill

A skillful host knows how to "work the floor." He knows how to obtain the most efficient or effective use of the tables in the shortest period of time. The skillful host knows how to keep the guests happy and how to motivate them to return. Skill also involves making salads tableside, carving meats and poultry, and pouring wine.

Tact

The ability to say the right phrase at the right time without offending the guest would be a definition of tact. Saying to a guest, "Where have you been, I haven't seen you in a long time," can be interpreted by many guests as untactful. A more tactful way of saying this would be, "It's nice to have you patronize the restaurant, we're glad to have you here again." This says the same thing, but it will not offend the guest.

Tact is also involved when inquiring about the guests or their families. The host has to be aware of what is happening in the community. Reading the local newspapers will give the host information needed to avoid embarrassment and appearing untactful. For example, in last week's newspaper the host read that John Smith had been cut from the professional baseball team. When Mr. and Mrs. Smith come to the restaurant, the host would not ask them, "How is your son's baseball career going?"

Productivity

Productivity is defined as the ability to get the maximum amount of tasks accomplished in the shortest period of time. There are times when the host must take reservations, greet guests, take their orders, and return to their table to see if the meal is to their satisfaction. In addition, the host must monitor the service staff's performance, seeing that the sidework is being done and that the dining room is operating to its maximum potential.

Persuasiveness

This is another important behavioral trait, especially when dealing with guests who have problems. Persuasiveness could be used to convince the guest to take a different table, or to take a different time because the restaurant is sold out (booked solid). Convincing the guest to change his or her mind about something is persuasiveness.

There are many more behavioral traits that the reader will be able to identify; however, an individual has to exhibit some, if not all, of the traits stated above in order to be an excellent host.

The Host's Responsibilities: The Five 5 P's of Management

In order for any restaurant to run efficiently, the host must be prepared. The key to having a successful restaurant or banquet are the five P's of management: *Prior Planning Prevents Poor Performance.*

This phrase and the meaning of it are important for all restaurant employees. However, this philosophy is especially critical in the host's job. The five P's of management mean is that if all tasks are planned in advance, problems will be kept to a minimum.

Therefore, a plan is needed to use before each meal period. This plan may be in the form of a checklist, as illustrated in Figure 7-8. Each restaurant may design one that fits the needs for that particular unit. By completing it, the host ensures that the restaurant is prepared to accept guests. The following are some examples of what items may be on the checklist and why they are important.

The list should include checking both men's and ladies' room for all paper products and for cleanliness. If the host does not do this task, it will have to

Key to Successful Restaurant and Banquet Management

PRIOR PLANNING PREVENTS POOR PERFORMANCE

Figure 7–7.   The five P's of management.

HOSTS DAILY CHECKLIST FOR OPENING THE DINING ROOM

1. Inspection of the service staff for proper grooming guidelines.
2. Men's room and Ladies room:
   Clean
   Paper products
3. Physical cleanliness of the dining room:
   Floors free of crumbs and lint
   Light fixtures clean and no burned out bulbs
4. Printers have enough paper to complete meal period
5. Menus are clean and chef's creations have been added
6. Reservations have been blocked
7. Computer system has been programmed with the chef's creations
8. Host is neat and clean, ready to accept guests

Figure 7–8.   A sample checklist for the host, to be done daily.

be attended to during a busy time, taking valuable time away from the guests.

Another important area to check is the physical cleanliness of the dining room. Are the floors free of crumbs or lint? If the floor is dirty, it will have to be cleaned or vacuumed before the guests arrive. All light fixtures are inspected for burned out bulbs or cobwebs. The host may think "It's not my job," but the host is responsible for the operation of the dining room. The guests want to feel that they are eating in a restaurant that is clean and safe. Burned out light bulbs, dirty floors, and cobwebs send a message to the guest that the restaurant does not care about cleanliness.

For restaurants that have a computer system, printers will have to be checked first thing to see if there is enough paper to last through the meal period. With some computer systems, if the paper runs out, the computer will not work. All prices and new items should be put into the memory of the computer before the staff take their first order.

The host may assign an employee to complete any task not completed. The first responsibility of the host is to prepare the dining room to accept guests. The host must have the dining room ready to accept guests when it is scheduled to open its doors. As has been said before, the difference between a good and a great restaurant is attention to details. A good host will anticipate and avoid problems. A great host will use the five P's of management to have an excellent restaurant.

Organization of the Dining Room

Knowledge of the menu, pricing, ingredients, and all facts that are essential to the smooth and profitable operation of a restaurant are as essential to the host as it is to the service staff. In addition, the host has to be the supervisor of the service staff.

The host is the person responsible for making the service excellent. Successful restaurants constantly evaluate service throughout an employee's career. The host is the person who is responsible for the training and performance of the service. In addition, the host will have to schedule employees and assign stations and sidework to make the dining room operate at its maximum efficiency.

Factors that Affect Scheduling

Have you ever been to a restaurant where you are served slowly because there are too many guests and not enough staff? It becomes apparent that there is an obvious shortage of service staff to serve the guests. For example, a restaurant has 120 seats that are filled and only has two service persons to tend to the guests. The person responsible for scheduling has not scheduled enough service staff to meet the demand of the business. It is imperative that the host schedule the correct amount of staff to meet the demands of business, while not overstaffing the restaurant. Overstaffing causes a loss of money and, at times, may even result in poor service. In order to schedule effectively, the host must take certain factors into consideration and then schedule the employees correctly. The first step begins with forecasting.

Forecasting

Forecasting is planning for anticipated business based upon previous history of the restaurant, reservations, and events that are planned for the community which will affect the business.

A formal written forecast of covers produced on a weekly basis is the most important aspect in scheduling.

Scheduling

There are many factors that will affect correct scheduling. The first has to do with the qualifications of the individual waitpeople. The next has to do with the type of menu and style of service that the restaurant offers. The third involves events that are occurring in the community in which the restaurant is located. If the restaurant is located in a hotel, expected occupancy rates of the hotel will play a major part in scheduling. Another factor is based upon the history from previous years' business. The final factor would be the number of reservations for the meal period. Scheduling is one place where the five P's of management are extremely important.

The first consideration is the qualifications of the individual waitpeople. For example, one service person may be able to work best waiting on a lot of small parties; another may work better with large parties. Knowing this information allows the host to compensate for the inadequacies of the staff.

Next, the host has to consider the type of menu and the style of service that is offered by the restaurant. If the restaurant uses American service, the number of guests that can be served efficiently by one service person is anywhere from sixteen to twenty-four. Individual restaurants determine how many guests a service person is required to serve. This depends on the menu, the meal period, and the atmosphere of the restaurant. The host can use this standard in forecasting and scheduling.

The third factor that affects scheduling is to determine what events are occurring in the community that will positively or negatively effect the restaurant's business. For example, if there is a parents' weekend at the local college, and the restaurant serves breakfast, then it should be staffed to accommodate the extra guests. If there is a youth sporting event scheduled in the community, and the restaurant appeals to that market, it will be busier than usual. The host, the service staff, and the cooks want to avoid surprises. No one likes to be swamped with business when they are not prepared to handle it.

The next factor is particular for those restaurants that are located in a lodging establishment. Almost all hotels send out a forecast of the prospective occupancy rate (this is the anticipated amount of guests who will be staying in the establishment on a certain night). If the rate is expected to be 100%, then the restaurant will be very busy for breakfast. It is amazing that when a hotel has 100% occupancy, the restaurant is not staffed properly for breakfast. That is the meal that will be eaten most often by the hotel's guests. Effective staffing in this category also means scheduling employees to work at the correct time. Having employees come in from 8 A.M. to 4 P.M. would be a mistake if the hotel's clientele are business people. They want to be out of the restaurant by 8 A.M. It is easy to obtain advance occupancy figures, thereby reducing the probability of an insufficiently staffed restaurant.

The next factor is determined by the history of the restaurant. Every restaurant needs a book at the host stand (some people call it a log book) for the purpose of recording the history of that day's business. Included should be the number of meals that were served for each meal period, the weather, and special events that were occurring in the community (such as conventions). The guest history also includes how much money was generated per hour and per meal period. This will assist the host in forecasting the staffing for the next year. In addition, it is recommended to have an area where the day shift host can leave messages for the night host concerning important items, such as, "Jane called in and she will be twenty minutes late tonight."

Finally, the manager reviews the number of reservations that are normally taken on that particular day. If the restaurant is booked up far in advance, all the reservations will be factored into the scheduling.

By no means is this a complete listing of the factors that the host must consider when staffing the restaurant; however, the above items will help the host in this regard. This planning allows the host to staff the restaurant properly for all types of business, including the least busy (slow) nights. For example, the night before Thanksgiving is traditionally not busy in a hotel dining room. However, the dining room must be open. Using the previous history, plus the expected occupancy rates, the host can schedule a skeleton crew. On the other hand, one of the biggest business days at a restaurant like Churchill Downs in Louisville, Kentucky, is Thanksgiving. At the racetrack, the restaurant must be staffed to accommodate the large group of guests. Taking into account all of the above factors, the host can now develop a schedule to satisfy the demands of both businesses.

Scheduling the Employees

Based upon the factors that were discussed above, the host can determine how many service people are needed for a certain time period. This time period is usually a week. It is most beneficial to both the host and employees when the schedule is completed and posted in advance, so everyone will know when they have to work.

The restaurant industry has a reputation for not treating their service staff decently. Many times, restaurant owners engage in day-to-day scheduling. When service persons ask for their schedules, they are told to call at 10 A.M. the next day. Then they are told to work or not to work. This type of scheduling is bad, because it negatively affects morale. Posting the schedule on the same day every week for the same period of time will alleviate the problem.

The busiest days in the restaurant business are the times when everyone else is enjoying themselves (weekends and holidays). Employees should be told when hired that they will have to work weekends and holidays. However, the host should strive to give his employees two days off in succession.

There is a system the author designed in order to improve scheduling, and that resulted in improved morale. First, the schedule was made every Wednesday and posted every Thursday. As an example, the schedule went from Friday, April 1, to Sunday, April 10. The employees would know a week in advance who had to work the following weekend. The next week's schedule went from Friday, April 8, to Sunday, April 17. Using this method, the host is planning for seven days, but always scheduling for ten days. An example of the two weeks' schedule are in Figures 7-9 and 7-10. Notice that the last weekend (April 8, 9, 10) of Figure 7-9, and the first weekend (April 8, 9, 10) of Figure 7-10 are the same.

This method improves morale and it will allow the employees to plan in advance if there is a special event they wish to attend. For instance, Pam knows that she has the weekend of the 16th and 17th off, when the schedule is posted on Wednesday, April 6.

In addition, if the employees wanted a special day or weekend off, they were allowed to switch with other employees, as long as the host was told. However, it was made clear to the employees who were scheduled to work that they were responsible for covering the shift. If their replacement did not show up, then the originally scheduled employee would pay the consequences. This system made the host's job easy. The staff was motivated because they knew exactly when they had to work and knew that they could take a day off if some special event occurred. Of course, if employees knew far enough in advance before the schedule was to be made up that they needed a day off, they would inform the host and they would be accommodated.

Stations and Sidework

Regardless of how the stations are arranged in the restaurant (team or individual), they have to be posted. Sidework should be with the station. Figure 7-11 is an example of how stations and sidework can be planned. Notice that the sidework corresponds to the station assignment.

WEEKLY SCHEDULE, APRIL 1-10

Name	1	2	3	4	5	6	7	8	9	10
	Fri	Sat	Sun	Mon	Tue	Wed	Thu	Fri	Sat	Sun
Pam	7-3	7-3	7-3	OFF	OFF	7-3	7-3	7-3	7-3	7-3
John	7-3	7-3	7-3	7-3	7-3	OFF	OFF	7-3	7-3	7-3
Bill	7-3	7-3	7-3	7-3	7-3	7-3	7-3	OFF	OFF	7-3

Figure 7-9. A ten-day schedule for restaurant employees.

WEEKLY SCHEDULE, APRIL 8-17

Name	8	9	10	11	12	13	14	15	16	17
	Fri	Sat	Sun	Mon	Tue	Wed	Thu	Fri	Sat	Sun
Pam	7-3	7-3	7-3	7-3	7-3	7-3	7-3	7-3	OFF	OFF
John	7-3	7-3	7-3	7-3	7-3	OFF	OFF	7-3	7-3	7-3
Bill	OFF	OFF	7-3	7-3	7-3	7-3	7-3	7-3	7-3	7-3

Figure 7–10. A ten-day schedule for restaurant employees.

The host must be flexible, and on occasion must combine stations or service staff from different stations when it would benefit the guests. For example, a party of twelve went to a restaurant on New Year's Day. The host assigned two service people to take care of the table, even though it was on one station. The group was served more quickly than if one person had served them.

Menus and Checks

The host is usually responsible for making sure the menus are clean and ready to distribute to the guests. In some establishments, the host has to write (or type) and put the daily specials into the menu, and/or write them on the blackboard. When putting the specials into the menus, the host also checks the condition of the menus. Dirty, torn, or smudged menus should be discarded. If the restaurant serves three meals a day, the host checks that

STATIONS AND SIDEWORK, APRIL 1-10

Name	1	2	3	4	5	6	7	8	9	10
	Fri	Sat	Sun	Mon	Tue	Wed	Thu	Fri	Sat	Sun
Pam	1	3	2	OFF	OFF	1	2	1	2	1
John	2	1	3	1	2	OFF	OFF	2	1	2
Bill	3	2	1	2	1	2	1	OFF	OFF	3

1. Fold Fifty Napkins
2. Salt and Pepper shakers; perform sidework of station 3, when only two people are scheduled
3. Housekeeping of all coffee and beverage machines

Figure 7–11. A ten-day schedule of corresponding sidework for restaurant employees.

the menu is correct for that meal period. Have you ever received a menu that was for lunch when the other guests in your party had a dinner menu?

Guest checks are sometimes given out to the service staff by the host; at other times the job is assigned to a cashier. Regardless of who gives out the checks, all service staff should have to sign for the checks they receive. At the end of the meal period, the host verifies that all guests checks that were given out have been returned, either used or unused.

Check, Please!

One summer, the author was responsible for guest checks at one of the most prestigious Horse Racing Tracks during their racing season. Each morning the service staff would sign out for their checks. At the end of the day, all checks would have to be accounted for. During the first week of work, it was found that a few of the service staff had not turned in all of their checks. The checks averaged about $75. Word got out that management was looking for the individuals who had signed out for the checks. The next morning, another manager brought in one of the missing checks with the correct amount of money owed. He said that he was out at a night spot and one of the waiters (who had been working at the track for a few years) approached him and said, "I just found this check in my pocket. I hear you were looking for it." He gave the manager the check and the money and said, "Why are you guys keeping such tight controls on the checks; you never have before?" Why do you think this waiter was upset?

Staff Inspection and Daily Meeting

Before each meal period, the host has to conduct a staff inspection and hold a daily meeting.

It is at this time that the host inspects the employees regarding the grooming and cleanliness policies set by the restaurant. If a member of the staff does not meet the grooming standards that have been set, the host can not allow that individual to work. Allowing a service person to work who has not met the restaurant's standards will make it difficult to enforce the rules to the other staff members. Making exceptions will create problems with the other members of the staff. Once the service staff realizes that the grooming and cleanliness policies will be enforced, they will comply.

The daily meeting usually consists of a short information session that the host conducts before each meal period. Information is shared with the staff, such as the description and price of the day's chef's creations. Any new wines or beverages that the restaurant is featuring will be explained. The soup or vegetable of the day and items that the restaurant is temporarily out of are also communicated by the host. Any special requests from the reservations (birthday cake with the Smith reservation at 8 P.M.) and any items such as new promotions are also explained.

This informational session should not last a long time. There will be regularly scheduled meetings for the purpose of tasting food and wine, reviewing policies in depth, and soliciting new ideas from the staff. This meeting is only informational in nature, so that the dining room runs smoothly for that particular meal period.

Chapter Summary

1. The host must be attentive, courteous, dependable, honest, loyal to the establishment, tactful, knowledgeable, sensitive to guests' needs and moods, and persuasive.
2. The five P's of management are essential to any restaurant's efficiency. These are: *Prior Planning Prevents Poor Performance.*
3. The three most important factors in planning effectively are organization, forecasting, and scheduling.

Review Questions

1. You are the manager of the dining room. Your morning host is a bright, articulate, and personable individual. All the staff loves him. You have received many letters from guests complimenting him on the way he treats them at breakfast. However, he has an alcohol problem. About once a month he goes on a binge and does not show up for work. His wife does call in for him. What do you do with him?
2. The host has all the tables reserved and informs the guest of this. The guest produces a $50 bill and asks, "Are you sure?" The host and the guest both know that the patron is buying the table. What should the host do?
3. What does the phrase, "The taste of the roast is determined by the handshake of the host" mean?
4. Compare the jobs of the host of today with the four job titles of earlier times.
5. What qualities should a manager look for when hiring a host?
6. What behavioral traits should a person have in order to make a good host?
7. What are the five P's of management, and why is this phrase important in the restaurant industry?
8. What is forecasting, and how does it affect scheduling?

9. What is the purpose of having a ten-day schedule? Do you think it is a good idea? Explain your answer.
10. What factors have to be taken into consideration when scheduling?
11. What is a log book, and what is its purpose?

Reference

The Foodservice Editors of CBI, *The Professional Host* (Boston: CBI, 1981), 11–13.

Chapter 8
Planning Reservations and Blocking Tables

Chapter Objectives:

At the completion of this chapter, the reader will be able to:

1. take reservations;
2. state the advantages and disadvantages of a reservation policy;
3. state the advantages and disadvantages of a no reservation policy;
4. demonstrate how to block tables when reservations are accepted;
5. plan and organize a system to seat guests who come into the restaurant with a reservation;
6. explain the problems that occur when taking guest reservations, and propose solutions; and
7. recognize the problems with no-shows, and know how to reduce the number of no-shows.

The Decision on Whether to Accept Reservations

Each restaurant has to make a decision on whether it will accept reservations or rely on walk-ins to fill up its tables. A reservation is a promise for a table in a restaurant. Walk-ins are guests who patronize the restaurant without making a reservation; in effect, they walk in the door expecting to obtain a table.

Many restaurants will not take reservations. Instead, guests are seated on a first-come basis. However, before the decision is made not to take reservations, some facts have to be considered.

One of the most important considerations in not accepting reservations is the location of the restaurant. A restaurant that is located in an area where there is a large population, or in a busy tourist area, may prefer not to take

Figure 8–1. A restaurant located in a busy resort area like Flagler's Restaurant, at Walt Disney World's Grand Floridian Beach Resort, can take both reservations and walk-in guests. (© 1988 The Walt Disney Company)

reservations. A large population guarantees the restaurant the number of potential guests needed to fill up its tables. The same is true in a busy resort area that caters to tourists. If the establishment is located in an area where guests have to travel a long distance to reach it, this will be a negative factor.

A second negative factor would be the absence of choice, that is of other restaurants of the same quality in the general area. The guest will take both of these factors into consideration, and most likely will not attempt to patronize the restaurant. Why should a guest drive for a long period of time and not be assured of getting a table or even getting a decent meal? Would you?

The next factor is the size of the party. Because most restaurants have the majority of their tables as deuces and 4-tops, they are not equipped to accommodate groups larger than six people. It would be difficult, if not impossible, to accommodate a group of ten people at one table. Imagine a busy night at a restaurant. All the tables are occupied. A large group appears at the door and wants to sit together. The host would have to wait until three tables next to each other become vacant all at once. Then the host would have to move the tables so they could accommodate the party. To avoid this

Figure 8–2.   Victoria and Albert's Restaurant, which is a reservation-only restaurant in Walt Disney World's Grand Floridian Beach Resort. (© 1988 The Walt Disney Company)

problem, reservations should be accepted for large parties. The definition of large would depend upon the size of the tables in the individual restaurant. Usually, large is a party of six or more guests.

Reservations should always be accepted on a holiday. Easter and Mother's Day are special days for families. The families want to be assured that they can arrive at a restaurant, enjoy themselves, pay the bill, and leave in a definite period of time. For many people, it is the only time of the year that all members of the family can have a meal together. Because of the great difference in ages of most family groups, (young children, parents, and grandparents) having to wait for a table would not be tolerated or even considered.

Accepting Reservations

Once the decision is made to accept reservations, the restaurant will need to create a policy to deal with reserving tables for the guests. Some restaurants prefer not to take any reservations, relying exclusively on walk-in business. Other establishments will only reserve a certain percentage of tables. Many restaurants prefer the restaurant to be reserved completely. A gourmet restaurant like Victoria and Albert's Restaurant in Walt Disney World's Grand Floridian Beach Resort only takes reservations.

A reservation is a promise for a table in a restaurant. The promise works two ways. The restaurant promises to have a table available for the guest for a certain time period. The guest promises to show up for the reservation.

Reservations provide a mutual benefit to the guest and the restaurant. The guests know that they will have a table available to enjoy their meal. They will not have to wait for their table, or even worse, drive to the restaurant and find out they cannot be accommodated. Both the restaurant and guests have advantages and disadvantages with reservations.

The benefits for the guests include:

1. The table is available when requested.
2. The restaurant can be informed of special requests and have them available when guests arrive.
3. The host learns the guests' names.

The benefits for the restaurant are:

1. The restaurant will know how many guests to expect; forecasting and scheduling will be easier.
2. The menus and service staff can be planned exactly.
3. The host knows guests' names and can use them to create ego gratification.
4. A mailing list can be developed for future promotions.
5. If reservations are taken correctly, the restaurant will run smoothly, because the restaurant controls when the guests dine. The restaurant can prevent too many guests from showing up at the same time, thereby avoiding a strain on the kitchen and dining room.

However, reservations can also be a disadvantage. Among the disadvantages for the guests are:

1. If restaurants do not know how to take and plan correctly, reservations may not be honored at the stated time.
2. Some restaurants will reserve more parties than they have tables available. This practice is called overbooking. The restaurant does this to avoid losing revenue in case guests who have reservations do not show up. Others overbook because they do not know how to plan reservations.

The disadvantages for the restaurant may be:

1. When guests do not show up (called no-shows), revenue from that reserved table is lost.
2. When guests arrive late, the reservation plan may be put in disarray.
3. Restaurants that do not know how to block tables correctly will lose money because they are not getting maximum use from tables.

Taking reservations are a benefit to the guest and the restaurant only if both know their responsibilities concerning the reservations. Training the host in the proper way to take reservations is important. When guests make a reservation, it is an essential part of the host's job to explain to them their responsibilities.

Factors that Affect Taking Reservations

As was stated in the list of disadvantages for the guests, one of the main problems is overbooking by the restaurant. The first thing that will have to be established by management is a system that allows the people taking the reservations to know exactly how many tables can be reserved for the day. Also, if the restaurant takes more than one seating for the meal period, the *residence time* has to be established. The residence time is defined as the time it takes a party to eat their meal and pay their bill. For example, ninety minutes will be required for a complete meal with appetizers, drinks, main course, and dessert for a party of up to four people. Thus, leaving enough time to reset the table, reservations should be taken every two hours. Guests who have larger parties will take longer to eat, so the residence time must be adjusted. Other factors also influence the residence time of the guests. Items such as music, lighting, decor, mood, and ambience make the difference in how fast or slow the guests will eat. A menu that is easier to prepare will speed up the residence time.

Once the residence time and the system has been developed, the host can take reservations.

Taking the Reservation

Practically all reservations are taken via the telephone or in person. The people taking the reservation have to be trained properly so they will obtain all important information from the guests and explain to them the policies of the restaurant.

The person answering the phone must be competent in taking reservations, but also must have excellent telephone courtesy. This is the guest's first contact with the restaurant. To ensure this, management may check their reservation procedures by conducting mystery calls to determine the telephone courtesy and competency of the host. It is common telephone courtesy for the people answering the phone to identify the restaurant as well as themselves. A sentence such as this is appropriate: "Good day, thank you for calling the Speciality restaurant; this is Sue speaking, how may I help you?"

The reservations should be taken and placed on a preprinted form like the one shown in Figure 8-3, or directly into the reservation book. This depends entirely on the size of the restaurant. A small restaurant, would be able to put the reservations directly into a book. A large restaurant would have to use a form and then transfer them to the book afterwards. Some restaurants are using personal computers with software developed to manage the reservation process.

Regardless of what type of form the restaurant uses, the information required from the guest is generally the same.

Information to Obtain from the Guest

The Name of the Guest
Included in this step is the correct spelling of the guests' names.

The Date for Which the Reservation is Desired
Ask for the date that they request with the day of the week and date. For example when the guests state, April 2, reconfirm it by saying, "Saturday, April 2." If the date is open, proceed with other questions. If the date is booked, suggest a different day. If the guests are adamant and insist on that date, take the guests' names and phone numbers and tell them they will be placed on the waiting list. Depending upon the restaurant, there should be a

RESERVATION FORM

Day & Date of Reservation _____ Time _____

Guest's Name _____ Number of Guests _____

Phone Number, Home _____ Business _____

Special Instructions _____

Taken By _____ Date Taken _____

Figure 8-3. A typical reservation form. The host will fill in the information in the appropriate space.

maximum number of parties that can be on the waiting list. Inform them that they will be called if an opening occurs.

The Time of the Reservation

If the time is booked, again suggest other times. At this point, the host should explain the policy concerning holding reservations. For example, a restaurant may have the policy that when guests make a reservation they are told they must be at the restaurant fifteen minutes early. It is further explained to the guest that if their reservation is for 6 P.M., they must show up at 5:45. If the guest is not there at 5:45, the table is given to a walk-in.

Obtain the Number of Guests in the Party and any Special Requests

If they need a birthday cake, special seating, or anything else, this should be noted.

Ask for the Guest's Phone Number

Take both the home and business numbers, if possible. If there is a problem, the host can contact the guests. The host may want to contact them after the meal to find out how they liked their dining experience.

Other Items that Go On the Reservation Request

There are other items that the person taking the reservations should place on the reservation form. By placing these items on the form, they can be used in case any problems arise, as well as for planning future reservations.

The Name of the Person Who Took the Reservation

The people who booked the party must sign their names. This makes people responsible, and if a problem arises, the host will know who to ask. If the guest calls and changes the reservation in any way, the person who took the changes must also sign and date the reservation request form.

The Date the Reservation was Taken

Noting the date on which reservations have been taken allows the host to determine how far in advance reservations are demanded.

Explaining Policies of the Restaurant to the Guest

Before the person taking the reservation thanks the guest and hangs up the phone, the guest will appreciate being informed of any special policies of the restaurant. For example, if the restaurant requires jackets for men in the dining room, this is told to the guest. The guest can be told that a gratuity is automatically added to the check.

In order to avoid mistakes, the reservation information taken down by the person who answered the phone is repeated back to the guest. Finally, the guest is thanked for calling, and told something like, "We will be looking forward to seeing you on Saturday, April 2, Mr. Smith."

Advantages of Not Taking Reservations

When factors warrant not taking reservations, the advantages for the restaurant are much greater than for the guest. There are four main advantages for the restaurant.

1. Maximum use of tables is experienced.
2. No overbooking will occur.
3. Little preplanning of reservations is needed.
4. No-shows will not be a major problem.

Maximum Use of Tables Is Experienced

Many restaurants that accept reservations will lose the use of tables for a period of time. This is because the host will reserve the tables incorrectly. For example, if a party of ten has a reservation for 8:30 P.M., the host puts three tables together and sets the table up at 5 P.M. Those tables are lost for the first two and a half hours. Even when the host reserves tables correctly, some time will be lost. When tables are not occupied because the table is reserved, and other guests are waiting for a table, a reservation policy will lose money for the restaurant and service staff. With a no-reservation policy, the guests are seated on a first-come basis and the restaurant is not losing money from unoccupied tables.

No Overbooking Will Occur

With a no-reservation policy, there is no danger of reserving more tables than the restaurant has to accommodate the guests.

Little Preplanning of Reservations is Needed

The host only reserves tables for large parties. At all other times, the host will seat the guests at any table that is available.

No-Shows Will Not Be a Major Problem

Because reservations are not accepted (except for large parties), there is no danger of holding a table and not having the guest show up to use the table. Even if the large party fails to show up, the host can reset the tables and accommodate the guests waiting for a table.

Disadvantages for the Restaurant

There are a few disadvantages for the restaurant that has a no reservation policy.

1. Business may be lost because reservations will not be accepted.
2. Guests may refuse to patronize the restaurant because they believe they will have to wait for a table for a long period of time.

Both of these disadvantages have to do with the attitude, convenience, and beliefs of the guests. Many guests do not want to wait for a table. They want to be assured that they will have a table when they arrive at the restaurant. If reservations are not taken, the guest may decide to go to another restaurant where accommodations can be secured without waiting for a table.

The second disadvantage occurs after the restaurant has been in business for some time. The restaurant is a success and it attracts a large volume of business. The wait for a table becomes longer than an hour. The word of mouth network that the public uses so well informs other potential guests of this fact. This works negatively for the restaurant. Many people will not want to wait that long, so they do not try to get into the restaurant. Eventually, because so many people decide to go to other restaurants, the amount of business decreases. However, the belief that the restaurant still has a long time for a wait persists in the community, even though it might not be true.

Advantages and Disadvantages for the Guest

In a no-reservation system, the disadvantages far outweigh the advantages. There are no outstanding advantages for the guest. It might be argued that everyone has the same opportunity of obtaining a table; however, it is a common practice in many no-reservation establishments that "push" regular customers to the top of the waiting list.

The disadvantages for the guest are many. Most of them have been stated already. Two more are:

1. The guests have to wait for a table.
2. If the guests are planning some other event besides dinner (such as the theater), there is no guarantee that they will be seated in time to attend the show.

Regardless of whether the restaurant has a reservation or no reservation policy, knowing how to reserve tables is an integral part of the host's job.

This is because all restaurants are recommended to take reservations on holidays and for large parties (usually, six or more guests).

Reserving Tables, Blocking Reservations

The term blocking means to reserve a certain table at a certain time for a guest. Its purpose is to enable the host to avoid overbooking. As was previously stated, each restaurant must determine the residence time for each meal period. Once this is known, the dining room can be blocked correctly. The process of blocking begins with taking the reservation correctly. All reservations should be taken on some organized form like the one shown in Figure 8-4.

Successful blocking is dependent upon an organized system. There are a few common procedures involved in all systems. Regardless of the method that is used, all blocking is to be entered in one book or place, such as a three-ring binder. This is preferable to individual sheets of paper, which may become lost. The physical layout of the dining room (with tables and numbers) is designed and duplicated. Restaurants that have entered the computer age may block tables using a computer program. However, all methods use the same basic principle: A table can only have one party reserved to use the table at that time period.

Blocking in a Small Restaurant

The simplest way of blocking tables occurs when a restaurant has set meal periods and a limited number of tables. In addition to the preprinted

RESERVATION FORM

Day & Date .... Number 00100

Number in party............... Time of Reservation............................

Name ....

Phone .... Business ....

Special requests ....

....

Date taken............... By ....

Figure 8–4. A standard reservation form. All reservations are taken on a form like this one.

reservation pad, all that is needed is a chart. The chart should be designed as is in Figure 8-5.

Across the top of the chart is the day of the week and date. Obviously, the restaurant would have a different chart for each day of the week and for each meal period. The next line of headings show table number, number of seats at each table, and the times of the reservations. This restaurant is only accepting reservations at 5:30 P.M. and 8 P.M.

This is an easy chart for the host to use to avoid overbooking. Notice that Table 3 seats two people. It is booked for the evening. If a guest requested Table 3 for Sunday, April 3, the host would see that the table is booked. In this restaurant of six tables with twenty-two seats, there are only three unreserved tables. By using this form, the restaurant can avoid the problem of overbooking. All employees know exactly at all times how many tables can be reserved. When a guest desires a reservation, the host can turn to the date in the book to see if they can be accommodated. Then all the information needed for a reservation can be obtained from the guest.

Restaurants that Don't Have Set Meal Times for Reservations

Some small restaurants will take reservations on a first-come-first-seated basis. They will take reservations at any time during their meal period. Basically, the blocking is accomplished in the same manner as in Figure 8-5. But there are three differences. First, the restaurant must know the residence time of the guests. This residence time is then incorporated into the planning for reserving tables. Second, the times that the restaurant will take reservations are stated in time segments at the top of the chart. Third, the guests' names must be written on the chart and their residence time blocked out. Figure 8-6 illustrates how to block in this type of restaurant.

Notice that in Figure 8-6, table 5, the Zorn party, is booked from 6 P.M. to 8 P.M. The residence time for their party of three is two hours. The restaurant

SUNDAY, APRIL 3, 19____

Table Number	# seats	5:30	8:00
1	4	Smith (2)	Jones (4)
2	6	Strianese (6)	Larkin (5)
3	2	Phillips (2)	Woodcock (2)
4	4	Gepfert (4)	
5	2		Geleso (2)
6	4		Malary (4)

Figure 8–5.   A blocking form for a small restaurant.

MONDAY, APRIL 4, 19____

Table Number	# of guests	Time 5 5:30	Time 6 6:30	Time 7 7:30	Time 8 8:30
1	4	Smith -------	-----------		
2	2		Jones -----	------------	
3	2	Malary -----	-----------	------------	Strianese --
4	6				Glock (5)----
5	4				
6	2	Zorn (3) ---	-----------	-------	
7	2				

Figure 8–6. A blocking form for a restaurant that takes reservations with open seating.

can take another reservation at 8 P.M. What problems do you envision using this type of system? Will the restaurant obtain maximum use of the tables? This is another example of a system that will work well for a small restaurant. But how will a large restaurant avoid overbooking?

Blocking in a Large Restaurant

First, a decision must be made whether to accept reservations at any time the guest desires or only at specified times that the restaurant sets. The principle of blocking tables in a large restaurant is the same as for the small restaurant. But it is impossible to block out reservations using the same method because of the large number of tables involved. There would be too much paperwork at the host's desk. The system in a large restaurant relies on having a person responsible for the planning and blocking of all reservations. This person is also responsible for informing those who take reservations about the number of tables that are left for each meal period. A large restaurant may have a person whose sole job is to be the reservation manager.

Blocking with Set Meal Times

This method of blocking tables requires four steps. It is referred to as the checkoff method. The first thing that the manager determines is the amount of tables that are available to be reserved in the restaurant. For example, a restaurant has four tables that seat six or eight; twelve tables that seat two; and sixteen tables that seat up to four. A chart, shown in Figure 8-7, is made for the 2 P.M. seating and placed into the three-ring binder where the reservations are being accepted. Each seating has its own individual chart.

SUNDAY, MAY 9, 19___ (MOTHER'S DAY)

2 P.M. Seating

2	4	6-8
12	16	4
11	15	3
10	14	2
9	13	1
8	12	
7	11	
6	10	
5	9	
4	8	
3	7	
2	6	
1	5	
	4	
	3	
	2	
	1	

Figure 8–7. A checkoff sheet. The checkoff sheet is used to assist the reservation manager in blocking.

The person taking the reservations checks off the size of the table that has been reserved. When Mrs. Smith reserves a table for six at 2 P.M., the procedure for reserving and blocking would occur in the following manner. The person taking the reservation would look at the checkoff sheet for Mother's Day at the 2 P.M. seating. Seeing that there is a table available, all information would be obtained on the preprinted reservation form. The first table under the 6–8 column would be crossed out and the name Smith would be placed next to it. The first line of the chart would appear as it does in Figure 8-8.

The chart would continue to be crossed off and filled out until all the tables are used. If a guest desired a reservation larger than six or eight, the reservation manager would have to establish a policy for accepting or rejecting the request. As large parties require combining existing tables, the reservation manager must carefully plan for the large parties, or overbooking will occur. Each restaurant should decide the maximum number of large parties that can be accepted. A set formula has to be determined for checking off tables so the restaurant will not overbook. For example, a reservation for

SUNDAY, MAY 9, 19___ (MOTHER'S DAY)

2 P.M. Seating

2	4	6-8
12	16	⅄ (Smith) (6)

Figure 8–8. The checkoff sheet after a reservation for Smith has been taken.

twelve may include putting together four 4-tops and a deuce. When a reservation is made for a party of twelve, four 4-tops and a table for two must be crossed off. The reservation manager, to assist in the planning of reservations, will have a printed diagram of the dining room and will block the guests' names and time next to the table that they have been assigned, as shown in Figure 8-9. The Jones, Casola, and Phillips reservations have been

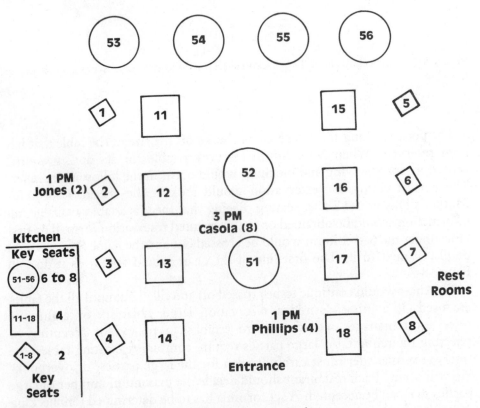

Figure 8–9. The dining room blocked with three reservations.

blocked off. As more reservations arrive, the remainder of the dining room can be blocked off. The key factor in making this system work is to have constant communication between the reservation manager and the people taking the reservations.

Accepting Reservations at Any Time

If the restaurant allows guests to reserve tables for any time (called open seating), then even more planning and organization must be done to avoid overbooking. The checkoff sheet would be used, except that the sheet would have the guest's name and the time of the reservation. Figure 8-10 shows how the sheet would look after the restaurant had accepted the first reservation for the Jones party of two guests.

The time is placed next to the Jones name. This informs all people taking reservations that the reservation is for 1 P.M. As the people taking reservations know that the residence time is two hours, they may accept another reservation at 3 P.M. for that table. However, this system could become very confusing when multiple reservations are made. Therefore, the reservation manager would be advised to block out tables daily on the master chart of the dining room, as you have seen in Figure 8-9. Each day, an updated sheet should be put in the three-ring binder showing the number of tables left to reserve. Understanding this system makes it easy to understand why a computer software program that reserves seats would be ideal for a large restaurant.

Blocking Effectively

The previous examples show how the blocking can be done in one step. For the small restaurant, blocking is a simple process. Large restaurants create more of a challenge. Blocking involves much planning and organization so that the guests will have their tables available when they arrive. In order to block effectively, the person doing the blocking (we will refer to

SUNDAY, MAY 9, 19____ (MOTHER'S DAY)

Open Seating

2	4	6-8
~~12~~ Jones (1 P.M.)	16	4

Figure 8–10.   The blocking sheet for open reservations after the Jones reservation had been accepted.

this person as the reservation manager) needs three items: a diagram of the dining room, the reservations, and the checkoff sheet.

The diagram of the dining room must have the table number and the number of people that can be seated at each table. The reservations are the preprinted forms that the person taking the reservations has completed. And the checkoff sheet is the control sheet that was located where the reservations have been taken.

Blocking is accomplished by way of an organized process. First, the reservation manager assigns the reservation to an appropriate-sized table. Then the guest's name and time is placed on the diagram at the table, as shown in Figure 8-9. Figure 8-10 shows the blocking sheet for open reservations. Finally, an alphabetized listing of the guests arriving is completed alongside their expected arrival time and their assigned table. An example of the list is shown in Figure 8-11. From the list, it is easy for the host to know what tables are blocked and what guests are to be seated at which table. Because the reservations are set up first by time and then alphabetized, the host's job becomes easier, as much planning has taken place before the guest has arrived.

This system will work well if planned and executed properly. The guests in Figure 8-12 had made reservations at the restaurant. When they arrived, their table was ready, and they are enjoying their dining experience. However, there are some problems that can be associated with this system. First, if the guests do not like the table they have been assigned, the host may have a problem with the guests. The host has a few options. For example,

RESERVATIONS FOR
SUNDAY, APRIL 30, 19____

Name	Number in Party	Table Assigned
	1 P.M.	
Feldman	4	12
Jones	6	51
Strianese	2	4
	1:30 P.M.	
Collins	4	16
Malary	6	55
Zorn	2	8

Figure 8–11. The alphabetized reservation list. After the reservation manager has blocked the tables, the guests' names are organized on a reservation form.

Figure 8–12. Guests enjoying a meal because their reservations were honored. (Photo courtesy of The Desmond Americana)

the guests' table could be switched to another comparable table (a 4-top for a 4-top). Or an apology could be offered and an explanation given why the guests cannot have the table they desire (e.g., all the other tables are reserved). If the host ever does switch a table for the guest, the master sheet also has to be updated.

Second, if the guests stay beyond the residence time, the next party will have to wait for their table.

Does the System Work?

I n a word, yes. However, the host must not deviate from the system. At the restaurant where the author was employed as the food and beverage manager, our policy was not to take reservations, except for holidays.

On Easter Sunday, we accepted reservations and served over eight hundred guests. A month later on Mother's day we served over twelve hundred. For both holidays, we used the open-seating policy on taking reservations. In addition to our regular dining room, we also used our three banquet rooms for parties of six or more. The dining rooms at Easter were running smoothly until 4 P.M. At that time, the staff began to get tired (both dining room and kitchen) and the residence time increased. Some guests had to wait for their assigned tables. As a solution, we deviated from the plan, putting guests at tables that they were not assigned. From 4 P.M. to 6 P.M., we had a mess on our hands. Guests were being brought to tables that should have been vacant and were not. The hosts could not keep up with the changes that were being made. Confusion reigned for those two hours. Fortunately, we learned from our mistakes.

A few weeks later, Mother's Day was almost perfect. Our planning took into account the fatigue factor of our staff. We increased the residence time of the guests for later in the day and did not deviate from the plan. The results of the planning was that just one party of guests were not seated at their assigned time. When the party arrived, an explanation was offered to them, admitting that it was our problem, not theirs. To show our concern, the restaurant invited them to go to the bar and to have either complimentary drinks or complimentary Champagne with their meal. In addition, the host kept checking back with the guests to advise them how long it would be before their table was available.

The result was phenomenal: over twelve hundred guests served with only one problem!

Taking reservations and blocking requires a lot of organization and preplanning, but it allows the restaurant to have a table ready for the guest and to avoid overbooking. Some of you reading this book will say it is too much work to do all that preplanning. Some of you will say, "I'll take some shortcuts and will not put the names next to the table." This can be done if the host is experienced and knows the room. But it comes only with time and experience. For a person using this system initially, follow the steps that were stated above, and the problems of overbooking will be eliminated. Once again, the reader can see the importance of the five P's of management: Prior Planning Prevents Poor Performance.

How to Alleviate No-Shows

A major problem that restaurants have in taking reservations is with guests who do not show up for their reservations. Restaurants have been trying to solve this problem of no-shows for many years. There are some proven methods that work in reducing the number of no-shows.

The first step in preventing no-shows is to properly train the person who takes reservations. Proper training means informing the guest of all policies of the restaurant pertaining to the reservation. Also, when the guest makes a reservation, information has to be obtained correctly.

Some restaurants request the guest to call them back on the day of the reservation to confirm their reservation. However, many people object to this, because the restaurant is making the guest do the work.

A better method is to inform the guests that on the day of the reservation, the staff will contact them within a certain time frame—for example, between 12 P.M. and 3 P.M.—to confirm the reservation. The guests are told that if they are unable to be reached, their reservation will not be honored unless the guests themselves confirm the reservation.

Other restaurants have begun to employ the same methods as hotels do for lodging rooms; to take a deposit for the reservations. In towns where there is a large demand for tables on weekends, restaurants have asked for a guest's credit card number or for cash to hold the table.

Leslie Reis, the owner of Cafe Provincial in Evanston, Illinois, has used a personal computer to keep track of guests who are no-shows. Once the guest becomes a no-show, the name is put on an alphabetized list for the reservation taker. When a guest calls and asks for a reservation, the name is checked against the list. If the name is on the list, the employee informs the guest that there was a reservation scheduled for a certain date for which the guest did not show up. The policy is further explained to the guest that if he or she do not show up for the reservation or does not cancel, then the restaurant will no longer take any reservations under his or her name.

By using one or a combination of these methods, the number of no-shows in the restaurant will be greatly decreased.

Chapter Summary

1. Each establishment must decide its own policy on accepting or not accepting reservations.
2. Both policies have advantages and disadvantages for guests and the establishment.
3. In taking reservations, it is important to follow established procedures to avoid the problem of overbooking.
4. Blocking tables in small restaurants differs from the method of blocking tables in large restaurants.

Review Questions

1. Your superior wants to have a no-reservation policy. The restaurant is located in a large metropolitan city. What reasons would you give to your superior to either have a no-reservation policy or to have the policy of accepting reservations?
2. Based on Figure 8-5, what type of cuisine would the restaurant that uses this type of blocking system have in order to make the system work? What will be

the cost of the average meal; high, average, or low? In other words, what factors must exist for a restaurant to use this system?

3. What are walk-ins? How are they different from guests who have a reservation?
4. What are the benefits and disadvantages for the guest at a restaurant that takes reservations?
5. What are the benefits and disadvantages for a restaurant that takes reservations?
6. What are the benefits and disadvantages for the guest at a restaurant that does not take reservations?
7. What are the benefits and disadvantages for the restaurant that does not take reservations?
8. What information should be obtained from a guest when taking a reservation? Why is this information important?
9. Guests arrives at the restaurant where you are the host. They have a reservation for 7 P.M. It is 6:45, but they are not dressed according to the restaurant's dress code. What will you do?
10. Should restaurants overbook when they take reservations? Explain your answer.
11. Explain how reservations can be structured to avoid overbooking. Include in your answer reservation taking, blocking, and drawing up seating charts.

Chapter 9
Managing the Dining Experience

Chapter Objectives:

At the completion of this chapter, the reader will be able to:

1. recite, recognize, and know how to correct or avoid the seven deadly sins of service, as stated in this chapter;
2. explain the method of handling complaints of guests who have a problem with reservations, the food, or any part of the dining experience;
3. use a turn sheet and knowing its purpose;
4. work the floor; and
5. seat guests (those with reservations, as well as walk-ins) using the tools available to the host.

The Operation of the Dining Room

A pleasurable dining experience will result in the guests returning to the restaurant for another meal. Return business is the key to making a restaurant profitable.

The restaurant business would do well to adopt the model concerning service that was created by the Swedish businessman Jan Carlzon. In the early 1980s, he sought to make the financially troubled Scandinavian Air System the best airline in Europe. He was able to change it from a losing business to a profitable one by using service as its main strategy. Carlzon keyed his system on "the moment of truth." A moment of truth occurs each time a customer (we should call them guests) comes into direct contact with the restaurant's people or system. The model states that the service image of your business (restaurant) is the sum of all your moments of truth.

The host is a key player in the restaurant's moment of truth. Many times, the first employee of the restaurant who comes in contact with the guests is the host. The host is also responsible for training and managing the service employees in the dining room. The service staff have many moments of truth with the guests. The author of the book *Service America,* Karl Albrecht, stated at a conference of chain restaurant executives in Orlando, Florida: "Your service image is not in the hands of your managers. Rather, it's won or lost by your service personnel."[1] It becomes the responsibility of the host to provide that the staff excels in giving the guests positive moments of truth!

The Seven Deadly Sins of Service

Karl Albrecht also states that there are seven deadly sins concerning service which are listed in Figure 9-1. Being aware of them and of how to prevent them is the obligation of both the host and the service staff. The seven deadly sins of service are: apathy, the brush-off, coldness, condescension, robotism, rule book excuses, and the runaround. Let's examine how each one of these sins relate to job of the host.

Apathy

Apathy can be described as a lack of emotion or interest. An example of an apathetic host is found in the following example. The guest enters the restaurant and sees the host standing at the host's desk (called the podium). The host does not acknowledge the guest's presence. Instead, the host appears to be interested in reading something that is much more important than greeting the guest. To avoid the sin of apathy, greet guests immediately when they enter the restaurant. Studies have shown that the impression made in the first thirty seconds of contact between the guest and the restaurant determines the feeling of the guest about the total dining experience. This is the first moment of truth for the restaurant. The host can create a positive one by greeting the guest within thirty seconds of arrival.

THE SEVEN DEADLY SINS OF SERVICE

Apathy
The Brush-off
Coldness
Condescension
Robotism
Rule Book Excuses
The Runaround

Figure 9–1.

The Brush-off

Brush-off is a slang term that means to rebuff, according to *The Random House Dictionary*.[2] Relating it to the host's job, an example of brushing off the guest occurs in the following case. The guest approaches the host and asks (most times, in a timid manner), "When will my table be ready? You told me it would be ready now and it isn't." The host replies, "In a few minutes," and walks away from the guest without any explanation or comment. The second moment of truth has been negative for the restaurant. To prevent committing the second sin, the host should strive to give the guest undivided attention. To avoid brushing off the guest, an apology could be offered to the guest by the host, and assurances could be made to the guest that the party would be seated as soon as possible. The host will then seat that party when the next table is available. If the problem persists and a table is not ready, it becomes the responsibility of the host to tell the guest about the status of the seating. It is recommended that eye contact be made with guests, so that they do not get the impression that the host is trying to brush them off.

Coldness

Have you ever been to a restaurant where the food was excellent and the prices reasonable, but you still felt something was missing? That something was a problem that you could not identify. Most of the time, it was that the restaurant left you with a cold feeling toward it. The host who responds to the guest's questions with one-phrase or one-word answers is guilty of committing the sin of coldness. For example, a guest might ask the host, "How long has the restaurant been in business?" The host answers, "Two years." The next question is also answered with a brisk reply. This is the opportunity for the host to make the guest the restaurant's ally; instead, the host has turned off the guest. Answers are best if they are complete and friendly. This will benefit the restaurant in two ways. First, the guest will have questions answered, and second, it will create a warm feeling toward the restaurant by the guest. Figure 9-2 portrays a group of regular guests at a restaurant bar. If you study the picture, you can feel the warmth of the regulars toward the person tending bar. This warmth results in a positive feeling by the guests toward the restaurant.

Condescension

Condescension can be described as a feeling of superiority that an individual has about another person. A host who is guilty of committing the sin of condescension would appear to be better than the guest. The host would give to the guest the impression that the guest does not belong in the

Figure 9–2. Owner Carol Philippi (standing) at the bar with a group of regular guests. Notice the warmth of the restaurant. (Photo courtesy of The Old Journey's End)

restaurant. Unfortunately, condescension is directed frequently at high school students. This most often occurs when they have a prom, and go to dinner before the dance. The host's attitude conveys the impression to the staff that the high school students are not very good customers. Notice, the word customers is used, not guests. That is an example of a condescending attitude. To correct this problem, the host should lead by setting an example, and should treat all the individuals who enter the restaurant as guests. All guests receiving positive treatment by all employees will increase repeat business for the establishment. The host or the staff should not be allowed to feel that they are better than any of the guests. By treating the high school students as guests, and by realizing that this is an important night for them, the host can make them feel important. Therefore, the host should greet them warmly and treat them like valued, respectable guests, which is what they are!

Robotism

Robots do not belong in the dining room of a restaurant. A robot can do many repetitive, boring tasks well. However, the job of the host is not repetitive or boring. An example of robotism is often seen when the host seats guests. The host picks up the menus; says, "Follow me"; and sprints to the table. The host then places the menus at the place settings and says, "Have a good meal." The next group of people are treated to the same robot-type antics. This method of dealing with guests is eventually transferred to the actions of the service staff. It becomes especially obvious when the service person is going through the "Hi, my name is . . ." canned speech. To alleviate the sin of robotism, the host should act natural, and should encourage the staff to act natural also. The host's movements should be energetic, and his or her speech should be cordial toward the guests. A robot would be great to do the dishes, but not to manage the dining room.

Rule Book Excuses

Rules are a necessary part of any business. However, when a host manages only by rules, and does not use common sense, the restaurant will suffer.

No Excuses, Please!

The two of us decided to try a new restaurant that had windows overlooking a beautiful view. The tables located directly in front of the windows were all booths for four people. When the hostess seated us at a deuce away from the windows, we asked for a window seat. The hostess said, "I'm sorry but I have to save those seats for parties of four." We tried to buy the table; that is, to give her a five dollar bill for the table. She still said that she could not give us the table. The time was 5 P.M., just when the restaurant opened and there were no other guests demanding to be seated. We could not understand why we could not have the table we desired. During our meal, we watched the table to see how many people she sat at the booths. When we left, an hour and a half later, there still was no guests seated at the table we wanted. Of course, we never returned to the restaurant—and apparently not too many others did either, because the restaurant has gone out of business. This was another example of a host failing at the moment of truth.

The host must not fall victim to the sin of rule book excuses, and may bend the rules when it benefits the guests.

The Runaround

The final sin of service has been experienced by everyone at one time or another in life—the runaround. An example of this as it relates to the host often occurs when the guest is waiting for a table at a no-reservation type of restaurant. When the guest approaches the host and asks how long it will be before the party is seated, the host replies, "Just a short time." The guest waits for a table to be vacant, and after twenty minutes returns to the host and asks the same question. Again the host says it will be just a short while. When the guest demands a specific time, the host pretends to check the dining room and gets sidetracked. The definition of the runaround is to give vague answers or to refuse to answer the question by ignoring or changing the meaning of the question. The way to avoid the runaround is for the host to give definite answers. A definite time will satisfy the question by the guest of "How long will it be before the table is ready?" An appropriate answer would be fifteen to twenty minutes, not "In a short while."

Knowing and training the staff to recognize and avoid the seven deadly sins of service is important for the host. The restaurant business is filled with many moments of truth. The restaurant can not afford to have sins committed at any moment of truth. The first moment of truth comes when the host greets guests into the restaurant. The last moment occurs when the guests leave the establishment. Throughout their meal, they will experience a series of moments of truth. All of these moments of truth add up to the total service in the restaurant. If the staff fails in one of these moments of truths, then service will suffer.

The Greeting

The host is exactly that: a host. The greeting should be warm and cordial, just as it would be in the host's home. The first thirty seconds are critical for the guest. In those few seconds, the guest forms an opinion about the restaurant; it wants or does not want the guest's business. This is all determined from the greeting offered by the host.

The size and the amount of volume of the restaurant determines the number of hosts on duty and their responsibilities. Smaller restaurants usually have one host who has to perform all the jobs. At larger establishments there may be as many as four hosts. Their job assignments are as follows: One remains at the podium to greet guests, take names, and assign tables. Another finds the guests in the waiting area or at the bar. The other two show the guests to their tables, each being responsible for one-half of the dining room.

Other establishments use three hosts. One always remains at the podium to greet guests, take names, and assigns tables. Another gets the guests when their table is ready. The third seats people and does table checks.

Figure 9–3. Steerman's Quarters on the Empress Lilly at Walt Disney World near Orlando, Florida. This restaurant employs three hosts to seat the guests. (© 1988 The Walt Disney World Company)

Regardless of the size of the establishment or the number of hosts employed, one host is always responsible for greeting the guests. This individual is always in a position to be able to see when a guest enters the restaurant.

Once the guest enters the restaurant, it becomes the host's responsibility to greet the guests immediately. If the host recognizes the guests, they will be greeted by addressing them by name. If the guests are new to the restaurant, the greeting is cordial. When at the podium receiving guests, the host should not be leaning over the desk, chewing gum, smoking, or drinking; instead, the guests receive the undivided attention of the host. If the restaurant takes reservations, the first question after the greeting will be, "Do you have a reservation?" If the guests do have a reservation, the host then takes them to their table.

If the restaurant does not take reservations, or the guests do not have a reservation, an inquiry will be made about the size of the party. The host should be aware of obvious facts and avoid saying to a single person, "Table for one." Instead say, "I have a nice table for you, sir; would you please follow me."

Assigning Tables

Like everything else in the restaurant business, there is a correct way to assign tables. And there are those hosts who take shortcuts and create problems for the guests, service staff, and the restaurant. Assigning tables correctly is another step to ensure that the restaurant will obtain maximum income and the guests will receive excellent service.

A good tactic used by many restaurants is to seat the guests who arrive when the restaurant opens at a table by the windows. Studies have shown that people would rather dine at a busy restaurant than one that is not busy. If the host seats the guests near a window, people walking or driving by will see the guests enjoying a meal, and it will create an impression in their minds that the restaurant is a good place to dine.

Rotation of the seating of the guests among the different stations is also advised. The wrong way to seat guests is for the host to seat the first twenty guests at one station, and then fill up the next section. Instead, the first party is seated at station one, the second at station two, and so on. Rotating the seating in this manner allows the service person to give the guests excellent service. If the service person's station was filled up all at once, the service person would have difficulty giving the guests good service because he or she would be overwhelmed (referred to as *swamped* or *in the weeds* in the business) with too many guests to serve at once. The rotation of assigning tables is also considered when stations are made and reservations are being blocked.

Occasionally a guest will request a special table or a different table from the one the host assigns. If the host can honor the request, it is good policy to do it. If there is a legitimate reason not to honor the request, it should be explained to the guest. For example, many times guests will request a 4-top for their party of two. If there is not too much business forecasted for the day, the host can give them the table they desire. If the host expects a heavy demand of business, or has a reservation for the table they desire, the guests should be told the reason why they cannot have the table. Of course, if they are regular guests, the host should break the rules and give them the table. Always seat parties of two at 4-tops if those tables are not in demand.

When a large group of people request a table together, the host should inquire whether they are on a time schedule (sometimes guests are attending a conference and have only a limited time to eat). If they are, it would be wise for the host to explain that it would be faster service if the party broke up into groups of four. The host could then sit the guests at different stations in the dining room. In this way, they will have more service staff to wait on them, instead of just one service person.

Forms Needed to Seat Guests

In addition to the ability to think quickly, the host needs a few forms that will assist in doing the job correctly and efficiently. The forms that are needed are: a diagram of the tables in the restaurant, the reservation list of reservations, the turnsheet, a table check form, and a waitlist.

Diagram of the Tables in the Restaurant

At the host's desk, there should be a diagram of the floor plan of the restaurant. Many restaurants place this diagram under a glass top. The hosts are given a grease pencil so they can write on the glass to indicate the vacant or occupied status of the table. By using the grease pencil and glass top, it makes it easier for the host to keep track of the status of the tables. Also, it makes it easier to erase and neater than trying to keep track on individual paper diagrams.

The List of Reservations

Along with the diagram of the restaurant, the host should also have an alphabetized list of the names of the guests who have reserved a table. Included on the list should be the names of the guests, the number of guests, and the table number they have been assigned. The list should be set up in chronological order. This will allow the host to check off the names as the guests come in to the restaurant, and will make for a smoother operation. Figure 9-4 shows the reader how the reservation list should be set up.

The listing would continue throughout the entire day. By setting this up in an organized fashion, the host can spend time attending to the guests' needs. If the host did not write this seating out in advance, he or she would have to spend an enormous amount of time and effort in correctly seating the guests with reservations.

The Turnsheet

The next form needed to seat guests effectively is called a turnsheet. Figure 9-5 illustrates how this form allows the host to keep track of how many guests have been seated at each station and what station should receive the next party.

**RESERVATIONS FOR
SUNDAY, APRIL 30, 19____**

Name	Number in Party	Table Assigned
	1 P.M.	
Feldman	4	12
Jones	6	51
Strianese	2	4
	1:30 P.M.	
Collins	4	16
Malary	6	55
Zorn	2	8

Figure 9–4. A reservation list set up for the host.

Our turnsheet shows that we have five service staff. After each person's name there are a series of numbers. Find the 6/6 fraction after Tom's name. The top number of the fraction represents the number of guests in the party. The bottom number is the cumulative total of all guests that have been seated on Tom's station during this meal period. From this example, Tom has only had 8 guests, while John and Jan have had 10 each, Jim 11, and Pam 13. The host will seat the next party at Tom's station. Most hosts use the turnsheet to seat the guests equitably among the service staff. However, when the restaurant becomes busy, often the host has no choice but to seat the guests at the next available table. However, in order to avoid controversy with the service staff, it is advisable for the host to keep track of the guests served by using the turnsheet.

TURNSHEET

Name			
Jan	3/3	3/6	4/10
Pam	2/2	4/6	7/13
Jim	1/1	2/3	8/11
John	4/4	4/8	2/10
Tom	6/6	2/8	

Figure 9–5. A turnsheet which keeps track of how many guests have been seated at each station and what station should receive the next party.

How Not to Seat Guests

Restaurants that do not take reservations, or only reserve a small percentage of tables, need a method to seat the guests. When there are tables available, there are no problems; guests are seated at an available table. Problems arise when all tables are occupied.

No guest wants to be treated in the following manner. In this no-reservations policy restaurant, when guests approached the host and asked for a table, the host would seat them. However, if the dining room was full, the host would tell the guest to go to the bar and check back in a few moments. The guest would say, "Aren't you going to put my name down?" The host would reply, "No." The guest wanted to know how he would know when his table would be ready. "Just come back, and if there is a table you get it," said the host. The guest suggested that a better method would be to take his name down. The host replied, "What do you think I am, a secretary?" The host is no longer employed at this establishment.

Table Check

The table check is a tool that allows the host to know the point of the meal that each table has reached. This form is continuously updated throughout the meal. For instance, some restaurants will have it done every twenty minutes. The table check is completed by one of the hosts whose job it is to walk around the dining room and observe each table's progress. The host writes down the course each table is on under the appropriate column. For instance, if table 71 is having coffee, a 71 goes under the coffee column, as you will observe in Figure 9-6.

From Figure 9-6, the reader can see that table 74 is available for a party of two, and table 61 is available for a party of four. *Up* means the table is

TABLE CHECK

# in party	JS	SS	Entree	Coff	Up
2	11	14	75	71	74
4	24	34	64	62	61
BT	17	18	19	20	

8:20

Figure 9–6. A table check form. This allows the host to know the point of the meal that each table is at in their dining experience.

available; *JS* refers to just seated; *SS* means soup or salad; *entree* means the guests are eating their main course; and *coff* means the guest is having coffee. Using this table check, which was completed at 8:20, the host greeting the guests at the podium knows the status of all tables at all times. When a party of two approaches the podium and requests a table for two, the host can seat them immediately at table 74. The next party of two will have to wait until table 71 finishes their coffee. The host will know that it generally takes fifteen to twenty minutes before that table will be vacant. When all the tables are filled, the table check gives the host a guideline of how long it will be before the guests can be seated. The approximate waiting times would be as follows:

If the guests are on:
Soup and salad   45–60 minutes;
Entree   30–45 minutes;
Coffee   15–20 minutes.

Some restaurants do table checks every twenty minutes, while other hosts do table checks informally. Once the host knows how long the wait will be, the proper method of informing the guest of the wait for the table can be used.

Informing the Guests about the Wait

When a guest arrives at a restaurant that does not take reservations and there is a long waiting time, the host has an obligation to tell the guests approximately how long they will have to wait for a table. Most guests do not mind waiting; however, some guests will object. The host should never state to a guest that it will just be a few minutes for a table. Instead, the host should give the guest an approximate time. This time has to be one which the host can honor. For example, if the host knows that a table will be vacant in fifteen minutes, the guest should be told that there is a wait of fifteen to twenty minutes. If the guest is seated before the fifteen minutes, that will be great for the guest. If the wait is more than twenty minutes, the restaurant has failed in this moment of truth.

By the host informing the guest of the length of the wait, the responsibility of staying or leaving rests upon the guest. Many restaurants have a friendly working relationship with their competitors. The host will phone the competitors and find out how long a wait there is at the competitor's restaurant, if any. The host can use this information in a variety of ways to assist the guests. First, if there is a long wait at the competitor's restaurant, this knowledge relayed to the guests may keep them at the host's restaurant.

This is especially true after the guests have to factor in driving time to the competitor's restaurant. However, if the competitor has space available or a much shorter waiting list, this can be relayed to the guests.

The host should keep the guests informed whenever possible about problems that arise that may keep the table from being available when promised. Again, the host performs some act (giving the guests some complimentary item) to let the guests know that their business is appreciated, if they cannot be seated when promised. One restaurant takes this a step further. Any guests that are told the waiting time and decide that it is too long for them to stay, receive a card that can be redeemed for a complimentary drink on their next visit to the restaurant.

The Waitlist

All restaurants that take walk-ins must have a waitlist. This form allows the host to seat guests in an organized manner. The waitlist is used when all the tables are occupied in the restaurant and guests are waiting for a table. The waitlist is shown in Figure 9-7.

The waitlist is set up with the names of the guests who are waiting for a table. The next column is for guests who want a table for four or more guests. The number in parenthesis, 51, represents the table that the host plans to use for that party. *Est wait time* refers to the amount of time the host has estimated that the guest will have to wait for a table. *Time in* refers to when the guest entered the restaurant. *Time seated* is when the guest has been seated at the table. The next column is for groups of two. Finally, the table number where the guest was actually seated is recorded. In our example in Figure 9-7, Mr. Smith entered the restaurant at 8:02 P.M. and wanted a table for two guests. From the host's table check chart, the host decides to seat Mr. Smith at table 51, because the guests at that table are on their entree. He informs the waiting guests that there will be a thirty to forty-five minute

THE WAITLIST

Name	4 or 6 guests	Est wait time	Time in	Time seated	2	Table Number
Smith	(51)	30/45	8:02	8:32	2	51
Jones	4 (62)	30/45	8:15			
Brown	6 (22)	30/45	8:17			

Figure 9–7.   The waitlist form. This allows the host to seat walk-in guests in an organized manner.

wait. Mr. Smith decides to stay and have dinner. The host gives Mr. Smith a card with his name on it, instructs him to give it to the host when his name is called, and keeps a duplicate copy for himself. This stops guests from trying to claim a table when it is not their reservation or name called.

Informing the Guests that Their Table is Available

Different establishments have different methods for informing their guests when their tables are ready. Many have loudspeakers that announce their names. Others have a system wherein they instruct their bartenders and cocktail waitresses to ask the guests if they are having dinner. If the guests say they are, they ask them for their card. When their table is ready, the host calls the bar and informs the bartender that there is a table available for the Smith party of two. At other times, a host walks throughout the waiting area and announces the names of the guests that they are seeking.

The Dishonest Table Snatcher

A t a twentieth-year high school reunion, a classmate boasted that he had never waited very long for a table at places that had a no–reservation policy. He and his date would go to restaurants that took the names of walk-in guests waiting for a table. Sometimes, they would go to the bar and have a drink; other times they would obtain their table immediately. This is how he did it. As soon as he heard the host calling the name and number of guests in the party, (for instance, the Smith party of two), he would go to the host and claim the table. Most of the time he was seated because the restaurant did not give out any cards to the guests.

Keeping the Waitlist Accurate

Each host must keep an accurate waitlist to avoid problems in seating guests, and to aid in planning future business. The time that Mr. Smith is seated is noted under the time seated column, along with the table that he has been assigned.

All restaurants have their own codes to assist them with the waitlist. At one restaurant, when a guest requests a table for six, the host places a big black mark around the guest's name. This is to signify that they have a large party waiting. As the number of tables that will accommodate six people are limited, the host does not want to make the guest's party wait longer than they are told. In addition, once the host sends for a party, they underline the name with the black pen. When the person has been located, they put a double mark under the name. If a person is not found, they put down the time they called them, give them fifteen minutes to appear, and if they are not there in that time, put in large letters *NS* (for No-Show) through their name.

The information gained from the waitlist can be valuable for the host. The host can see how many guests had to wait for a table, the time the first guest had to wait, the average waiting time, the longest waiting time, and other factors that will help the host staff and plan for the business. Above all, the waitlist will provide a fair and organized tool for the host to seat the guests.

Leading and Seating the Guests at Their Tables

Once the host has determined where to seat the guests and a table is available, they have to be shown to their assigned table. The host has to take into account the age and the physical condition of the guests. Once the host determines the condition of the guests, the host gages the walk leading the guest to the table at a comfortable pace. It is not a good idea to sprint to the table if the guest is elderly, because the guest may not be able to keep up with the pace.

Once the host reaches the table, it is proper to pull out chairs for the guests (women first) and assist them with seating. If the table is against the wall, it has become traditional to offer the seat that faces into the dining room to the female, while the male is seated facing the wall. The napkins are removed from the table by the host, opened, and handed to the guests.

Menus should be distributed next, both food and wine, if appropriate. Women are given their menus first. It is advisable to open up the menus to the entree page. This accomplishes two purposes. First, the host can see if the menu is the correct menu; second, it is another small detail that the guest will not have to do for themselves. Next, the host has to communicate important information to the guests.

Communicating Information

This is an area where most hosts fall short. Many hosts bring the guest to the table, drop off the menus, and are never seen again. Instead, after the guests have been seated and handed menus, the host's next duty is to recite any chef's creations (with the price) that are not offered on the regular menu. The restaurant should not have more than three chef's specials, because the guest may become confused. Many restaurants have a listing of daily specials which is placed on the guests' table. The host points out the list, which includes prices, to the guests as they are seated.

It is strongly suggested that the host use the guests' name as much as possible when they are known. Once the guests have been told the additions to the menu, the host may also ask them if they would like to order a beverage. This is a key moment of truth in the restaurant business. According to Professor Gary Brenensthul of Schenectady County Community College, this is transition time. It is the time when the host turns over the guests from his care to the care of the service person. When the guest must wait for the service person to approach the table and take the drink order, the wait can be an uncomfortable one. Professor Brenensthul says that "the guest should have the drink order taken immediately." By having the host take the drink order, the guest will have been serviced immediately. The restaurant is saying to the guest that we value your business and do not want you to wait for anything. In addition, there is the possibility of selling more drinks, whether they are alcoholic or nonalcoholic. This serving or taking of a drink order should be done with every meal period. At breakfast, the host would offer coffee to the guest immediately. The last thing the host should do as he leaves the table is to tell the guests the name of the service person. To be most effective, it is recommended that it be done in an informal manner, such as, "Jan will be your service person, she will be right over with your drink order." As the host leaves the table, the drink order is given to the service person so it can be delivered as soon as possible. The host can now concentrate on *working the floor*.

Working the Floor

Working the floor is a phrase used in the restaurant business to mean that the host is circulating around the dining room talking to guests and assisting service staff. When the guest has been seated by the host, the host should not go back and stand at the podium waiting for the next guest to come into the restaurant. Instead, the host has to walk around the dining room and make certain that the guests are being serviced properly. One of the key factors in working the floor is to communicate with the guests. If the host notices that the guests are sitting at the table with their menus for a long period of time, he should approach the table and ask, "Has Jan been here to take your order yet?" If she hasn't, the host should take the order or find Jan so that she can take the order. The host should not just walk around the dining room, but should stop at tables and talk to guests. Again the host is reminded to call the guests by name.

Working the floor also involves getting "your hands dirty." This means that the host may bus tables, serve food, serve drinks, and reset tables if a service person needs assistance. The host should not just be a pretty face but a vital working member of the staff.

The final responsibility of the host is to make sure that the guests are completely satisfied with their dining experience. As the guests complete their meals, the host inquires about their dining experience and shows appreciation to the guests for patronizing the restaurant. This appreciation can be shown in the form of a "Thank you," buying the guest a free dessert or after-dinner drink, or some other gesture that makes the guests feel special.

A Host Who Almost Got It Right

A couple were at a restaurant. They watched and listened as the host approached and spoke to a party of two after they had finished their meal. One guest had ordered swordfish that was served on a bed of pasta. The host inquired about the food, asking how they liked the food. The guest said that the swordfish was great, but the pasta was not cooked enough. The host replied that all the pasta is cooked the same way, *al dente*. He further added: "If you want, you can take the pasta home with you and microwave it. It will taste really good that way. The next time you come in, make sure you ask for it (the pasta) cooked more than al dente." If you were the guest would you be pleased with this response? What do you think the host did correctly and incorrectly? What improvements could you suggest to make the guest feel satisfied?

Seating Physically Disabled Guests

With more restaurants becoming accessible to physical disabled guests, the host has to be aware of the special considerations needed to make their dining experience enjoyable. The type of impairment the guest has should dictate the consideration that the host gives to that person. For instance, a visually impaired guest should be lead to the table and have the location of the utensils explained by the host by imagining the table as the face of a clock (e.g., the coffee cup is at five o'clock). If the guest has a seeing-eye dog, the host leads the guest to a table where the dog can lie down without being in the traffic flow.

The same is true of a guest in a wheelchair. Seat that guest out of the flow of traffic, but where the guest is comfortable. The host may assist the guest in whatever way possible to make the person feel welcome. It may be necessary to move the table so the guest can position his or her wheelchair comfortably at the place setting. In some instances, it might be necessary to raise the table to a height which will accommodate wheelchairs.

Regardless of the physical condition of the guest, the host has to remember, and impress upon the staff, that these individuals are as valuable to the restaurant as guests who are not physically disabled. The staff has to be taught to treat all guests with courtesy, and to put forth extra effort so that all can enjoy themselves and have a pleasant dining experience.

The Problem Guest

Unfortunately, there will be times when a guest has a complaint about the wait for the table, the food, the service, or prices. The host must know how to handle complaints and be able resolve the situation so the guest feels that the problem has been solved satisfactorily.

Regardless of the complaint, it is recommended that the host take the following steps to solve the problem. First, the host should **listen carefully** to the complaint. If the guest is loud or creating a scene, move off to a side area. Clarify the complaint by repeating it back to the guest. This will calm the guest down and make the person realize that you understand the complaint. Next, agree on some point about the complaint. Finally, solve the problem or offer the guest some solution to the problem. Throughout the meal, return to the guest's table and check to ensure that the problem has been solved. Using this approach, the host can turn a bad situation into a good situation. Throughout this chapter, you have read about guests that have had problems, and you have been asked to solve the problems. This skill in handling complaints is another area that the host must excel in to create a positive moment of truth for the restaurant.

Reservation Not Honored

Unfortunately, one of the major problems that occur in restaurants are that reservations are not honored. The reasons for this happening are

STEPS TO HANDLE COMPLAINTS

1. Listen carefully to the guest's complaint.
2. Clarify the complaint by repeating it back to the guest.
3. Agree with the guest on some point about the complaint.
4. Solve the guest's problem or explain why the complaint can not be solved.
5. Check back throughout the meal to be certain the problem was solved.

Figure 9–8.

numerous. Occasionally there will be a problem because reservations have been taken incorrectly. Other times, guests will stay longer than their residence time. Regardless of the problem or the reason why the restaurant does not have a table for the guests, it is the fault of the restaurant, not the guests.

To solve the problem, the host must seat the guests as soon as a table becomes available. However, the host first should explain the problem to the guests and offer an apology for their inconvenience. It is recommended that the host make some positive gesture to the guests to soothe their feelings for the inconvenience. If it is legal in your state, buy them a bottle of wine with the meal; or have them go to the bar and buy them a drink. If they don't drink, offer them a free dessert.

In the meantime, the host also has to deal with guests who are staying past their residence time. The host should find out the reason for the delay. If it is a problem that can be solved quickly (the service person has not given the guests their check), the host can rectify it immediately. The table can now be set (called turning tables) for the next guest. If the guests are sitting with an extra cup of coffee, the host may not be able to do anything. Or an offer may be made to move the guests to another area (such as the bar or a sitting room), where they can continue their conversation. However, this is a very tricky situation, and the host may do more harm than good by asking the guests to move. This is a decision that the host would make after considering whether asking the guests to move would result in negative feelings by the guests.

After the problems have been solved, the host must identify the reason why the reservations were not honored. Then, adjustments to the reservation policy must be made so the problem will not occur again. The host needs to have the ability to solve the problem of not honoring reservations, so the guest will want to return to the restaurant for another meal.

Final Jobs of the Host

The host's job is not complete until long after the guests leave the restaurant.

After the guests have received their entrees, the host works the floor and talks to the guests, inquiring about a variety of items, such as the food and their personal interests. Before the guests leave the restaurant, the host should inquire about the dining experience and offer the guests a **free** something. This offer of something could be an after-dinner drink or a food or complimentary coffee. The key is to let the guests know that their business is appreciated.

When the guests leave the restaurant, it is imperative that the host thank them for their business and invite them to return to the restaurant.

Some restaurants employ a person to call up on the following day those guests that have had reservations to inquire about their dining experience. This gives the guest an opportunity to give the restaurant feedback without having to do it face to face. It gives the restaurant an opportunity to find out

Figure 9–9. Fisherman's Deck on the Empress Lilly at Walt Disney World in Orlando, Florida. A restaurant that uses both the table check and waitlist forms to seat their walk-in guests. (© 1988 The Walt Disney World Company)

about its performance and if there were any problems. If the person calling is told of a problem, the restaurant can take steps to correct it.

The Logbook

Each restaurant should have a book that includes a record of what went on for that day that management feels is important. Items such as the number of meals that were served, the waiting time of reservations, the time first seated, and other items that will assist in the forecasting of the business may be included. In addition, there usually is an area where messages are left for the next shift. By having this special area in the logbook, no messages are lost and there is proof that information was passed to the next shift. This logbook will help the restaurant run smoothly and efficiently.

The information in this chapter gives the reader the knowledge to be the perfect host. Does one exist? Have you ever found one?

The Perfect Host

In a little community ten minutes from Schenectady, New York, is a restaurant called The Bears. The owners of the restaurant, Bob and Pat Payne, or Papa and Mama Bear, along with their three cubs, operate an excellent restaurant. This restaurant has been in business for over twenty years.

This is one of the few, if not the only, restaurant known that employs no advertising and does not have a business phone. In fact, The Bears restaurant is not listed in the white or the yellow pages of the phone book. The restaurant takes reservations only for specified times; it will not take walk-ins. The only way to obtain its unlisted phone number is from a regular patron of the restaurant. Because the restaurant seats only sixty and is so popular, it is almost impossible for a new guest to get a reservation. But once you become a regular guest, it is an experience that you will never forget.

Everything works! The food, the service, the cleanliness, and the price value. When guests arrive at The Bears, they are greeted by name by the owners. The owners act as if they are greeting long-lost friends. The new guests are introduced to the owners by the regulars. Once that is completed, the owners return to the kitchen to prepare the meal.

Next, the service person explains the menu thoroughly and knowledgeably. However, for most guests, it is not necessary. This is because The Bears is noted for its beef. When the guests make their reservations, the meals have been ordered in advance. Usually, it will be Chateaubriand or prime ribs.

Next comes the food. And the food is great. Their speciality, Chateaubriand, is so tender that it can be cut with a fork. All the other items are just as good, and all are presented attractively. The service is proper and the service staff makes certain that they take care of the needs of all their guests.

When the meal is completed, Papa Bear makes it a point to visit each table and ask all the guests if they liked their meal. He then offers them more food if they are still hungry; which almost everyone refuses because there is enough food left over for another complete meal. That left-over food is quickly placed in a container by the service staff to be taken home by the guest.

The guests leave The Bears completely satisfied, and their word of mouth promotion fills the restaurant completely, week after week.

Chapter Summary

1. The seven deadly sins of service are apathy, the brush-off, coldness, condescension, robotism, rule book excuses, and the runaround.
2. The first thirty seconds after a guest enters the restaurant are critical to the guest's opinion of the establishment. In this regard, the host's greeting is all-important.
3. The essential tools for seating guests are the reservations list, the turnsheet, the table check, and the waitlist.
4. Among the host's chief responsibilities during the dining experience are working the floor, accommodating physically disabled guests, dealing with problem guests, and showing the establishment's appreciation for the guest's patronage at the end of the dining experience.
5. The restaurant's logbook is important as a record of the day's business, a tool for forecasting future business, and a vehicle for leaving messages for the following shift.

Review Questions

1. Why should a restaurant owner or host send business to the competition?
2. List the seven deadly sins of service. Explain what they are and how they relate to the host's job.
3. Explain how you would handle the following problem. A party of four comes into your restaurant. The host tells them it will be a short wait for their table. They are asked if they want to go to the bar, which they do. The service person ignores them in the bar. When they finally are seated after their short wait (thirty minutes), the service person takes and serves their appetizers almost immediately. One half hour goes by and then the service person returns to the table and says: "I made a terrible mistake, I forgot to put your order into the kitchen. I just did it

now." The food comes out twenty minutes later. One of the steaks was ordered medium well and comes out rare. The guest is upset. She asks to see the manager. You come to the table and she shoves her plate at you, complaining about your restaurant. What do you do?

4. What is a turnsheet? What is its purpose and how is it set up?
5. How is a table check form set up? What is its purpose?
6. What should a host do when seating a guest? What are the steps needed to seat the guests properly?
7. What is a wait list, and what is its purpose?
8. What does the phrase "working the floor" mean?
9. What considerations should be given to physically disabled guests?

References

1. Jack Hayes, "Albrecht Stresses Need to Service America," *Nation's Restaurant News,*14 March 1988, 4.
2. Jess Stein, ed. in chief, *The Random House Dictionary* (New York: Ballantine Books, 1978), 116.

Part 3:

BANQUET MANAGEMENT

Chapter 10

The Banquet Business and the Banquet Manager

Chapter Objectives:

At the completion of this chapter, the reader will be able to:

1. define the term banquet;
2. verbally explain the importance of banquets as they relate to the profitability of any hospitality establishment;
3. list and explain the advantages that the banquet business has over restaurants that serve a la carte meals;
4. define the difference between a caterer and a banquet manager;
5. list the advantages and disadvantages of having a career as a banquet manager;
6. name the types and styles of service available for banquets;
7. explain the qualifications for being a banquet manager;
8. list the job knowledge that a banquet manager must possess in order to do the job effectively;
9. explain the banquet manager's main responsibility as it relates to the host of the banquet; and
10. explain the key to being a successful banquet manager.

What is a Banquet?

A banquet is a meal that has a menu that is preselected by the hosts for all of the guests attending the event. The number of guests at a banquet usually ranges from ten to ten thousand or higher. The only reason there will be a maximum number is because the banquet facility has a limited amount of space to accommodate the guests. However, if the space is available—as it is with a domed stadium like the Houston Astrodome—a banquet can accommodate up to two thousand guests.

Figure 10–1. The Houston Astrodome, in Houston Texas, which accommodates up to two thousand guests for a banquet. (Photo courtesy of Hall Puckett)

Any restaurant that can successfully serve a banquet of ten people can serve any size banquet. This is because the principle of serving a banquet to a large group is the same as serving it to a small group.

Guests Reasons for Having a Banquet

There are many reasons why guests hold banquets. Some hold them for the purpose of personal entertaining, while others must conduct them for business; still others hold banquets for fraternal reasons. Regardless of the reason, the banquet serves one main purpose: it allows the guest to be host to a large group of people, without doing the planning, buying, cooking, and serving of food. Nor does the guest have to clean up after the party is finished. Having a banquet allows the guest to be a host rather than a cook or a service person.

REASONS FOR HAVING BANQUETS

Personal Entertaining	Business	Fraternal Organizations
Religious Ceremonies	Meetings	Weekly Meetings
Celebrations	Conferences	Sports Banquets
Social	Celebrations	Award Banquets

Figure 10–2. Guests' reasons for holding a banquet.

Personal Entertainment

The first thought most people have about the reasons why banquets are held concern personal entertaining. These type of banquets are conducted because the host wants to entertain his or her friends. Personal entertainment banquets are usually a result of religious ceremonies, celebrations, or social affairs.

One of the largest markets in the personal entertaining banquet business comes from wedding receptions. However, there are many other religious ceremonies that will add to the list. For example, baptisms, first communions, confirmations, and even funerals. In communities where there is a large Jewish religious population, bar and bat mitzvahs may make up a large portion of a banquet establishment's business.

Each one of these requires the banquet manager to understand and know the religious customs of each group. For instance, a banquet celebrating a Catholic confirmation would require a different set of rules from a Jewish bar/bat mitzvah ceremony. The banquet manager must know the protocol regarding who is to give the blessing and when and how it will be given. The host of the event will often ask the banquet manager for guidance to perform it correctly.

The twenty-fifth and fiftieth wedding anniversaries are the ones that are most celebrated with banquets. However, birthday and graduation parties also contribute greatly to the social business.

Finally, there are parties for social entertaining. Guests are invited to a banquet facility or to a party catered at the host's house for the purpose of having a party. Many of them occur during the winter holiday season; but they are a viable business all year long.

The personal entertaining business is an excellent market for a banquet facility or a caterer. There will always be a demand for banquets from this type of clientele.

Business Entertaining

Entertaining for the purpose of doing business is another large source of income for the caterer or banquet facility. The individual responsible for planning business entertaining is employed by that particular business. This type of entertaining differs from personal entertaining because the business, not the individual, pays for the banquet. One of the main purposes for business entertaining is to conduct conferences or meetings. Other reasons are for celebrating a special business occurrence (anniversary, grand opening) and having parties to honor employees.

Conferences and meetings are often held off premises of the business, at a hotel or restaurant. Some large companies employ a meeting planner to

Figure 10–3. A business banquet set up at the Astrohall in Houston, Texas. An example of business entertaining. (Photo courtesy of Hall Puckett).

select the facility to hold these conferences. However, the vast majority of companies assign an employee to head the event who has little or no experience in planning and conducting a conference. This person utilizes the experience and organization of the banquet manager to have a successful conference. These conferences can last from as short a time as one meal or as long as a week. They usually involve the renting of meeting rooms and provisions for food and liquor service.

Another great source of income for the banquet manager or caterer are business anniversary parties. Along with these anniversary parties, businesses often have special parties for their employees. These consist of retirement, Christmas, and special recognition banquets. Also, many schools have a "welcome party" for their new employees at the beginning of the school year.

The business market is a valuable addition to the caterer's market, as the vast majority of functions are held Monday through Friday; but a certain percentage also are held on weekends.

Fraternal Organizations

A fraternal organization can be defined as a group of people who belong to an organized club. Some examples would be service clubs, like the Rotary and Lions. Youth sport groups such as soccer, baseball, football, and basketball would also be considered fraternal organizations. Bowling leagues are another fraternal group which can be a large source of revenue for a banquet house. These fraternal organizations can bring an enormous amount of business to a banquet house or a caterer.

The Key to Successful Banquet Management

The reasons explained above are only a partial list of why people have banquets. The reader can add to the list many more groups of people who would need the services of a banquet manager. However, regardless of the reasons for holding banquets, there is one key to being a successful banquet manager. It is the statement highlighted in Figure 10-4.

Why Banquets?

More and more restaurants are getting into the banquet business for a very simple reason: A restaurant can make more money, with a lot less chance of failure, by holding banquets at their restaurant. Put simply, the profit potential is much greater for selling banquets than for a restaurant that has an a la carte business only.

The reason that the above statement is true becomes evident when a comparison is made between the a la carte restaurant and a banquet house. Let us look at how an a la carte restaurant must conduct business as compared to a banquet establishment.

At a banquet, the establishment knows in advance many more facts about the food it has to prepare than does an a la carte restaurant. First, the banquet manager knows what all the guests are going to eat at the banquet. Because the banquet has been prearranged, the banquet manager knows how many guests are going to attend the banquet and how much food has been ordered.

THE KEY TO SUCCESSFUL BANQUET MANAGEMENT

The banquet manager must take the
RESPONSIBILITY
for the party off the guest's shoulders
and put it on his or her shoulders.

Figure 10–4.

At the a la carte restaurant, the manager never knows what or when the guests will eat. Therefore, the a la carte restaurant has to have more inventory to satisfy the guest's requests, while the banquet house only has to buy the food that has been ordered for the banquet.

The banquet manager knows in advance exactly how many guests will attend the banquet; as a matter of fact, the host of the party must guarantee the number of guests that will attend. If that number does not show up, the host must pay for the guaranteed number. On the other hand, the restaurant has to forecast the amount of guests that will patronize the establishment. If there is bad weather or some other event is scheduled that the guests would rather attend, then the guests do not show up at the restaurant. In addition, the banquet manager may obtain an advance payment; most banquet houses obtain a deposit large enough to cover all their expenses. The restaurant has to wait until the guests consume their meals before getting any money.

Staffing is another advantage the banquet house has over the a la carte restaurant. Because the banquet manager knows the number of people attending, the menu, and the time the food will be served, the banquet manager can staff for the event without any wasted labor cost. On the other hand, the restaurant has to be prepared for a large group of guests, when in fact no one may show up. The a la carte restaurant may have many people scheduled to work, with little work to do. As the restaurant has to pay these employees, their labor cost rises and their profits decrease.

There is virtually no leftover food at a banquet. Everything is purchased in advance and cooked correctly; therefore, waste is kept to a minimum. At a restaurant, there may be an enormous amount of waste, since the restaurant manager does not know what the patrons will order. Thus, the restaurant may have too much of one item and not enough of another. In an a la carte restaurant, specific items are often sold out; at a banquet, this never happens.

Advertising and selling of banquets is easier than for an a la carte restaurant. For an a la carte restaurant to get two hundred guests to have dinner at the establishment, it has to convince a large group of guests to patronize it by using a variety of advertising methods—often at a cost of between 3% to 7% of its gross sales. On the other hand, a banquet facility in order to get two hundred guests has to convince one or two people (just the host or hosts) to have the banquet at its establishment. In addition, because everything is known about the banquet before the guests arrive, the quality of food and service will most likely be higher than at the a la carte restaurant. The end result is that when the banquet house does a superb job on the party, the banquet manager has two hundred more potential guests to book a banquet.

Monaco's Palace: the Banquet Specialists

There was a restaurant in Columbus, Ohio, called Monaco's Palace. The owner of the restaurant, Baldino Monaco, chose to change the business from a la carte and banquets to strictly banquets. The restaurant had a banquet room that seated four hundred. The room was booked a year in advance for banquets. Baldino had a very good a la carte weekend business; his restaurant would have an hour and a half wait on Saturday night and a short wait on Friday. But during the week, there was never a wait for a table. In fact, business was very slow. He found he was getting more requests for his banquet room and had to turn business away. So he did the logical thing: he eliminated the a la carte business and changed the name of the restaurant from Monaco's Palace to Monaco's Palace: the Banquet Specialists. As a result of the change he was able to reduce his full time staff to five from about twenty-eight. He also appreciates the banquet business because it is guaranteed, and it has been a lot less strain on him.

The main reason a restaurant would seek out the banquet business is because it is a profit maker. A restaurant which serves banquets knows a vast amount of information about the party before the guest arrives. The restaurant knows how many people will be attending, how much food to order, the time of the event, its food cost, and its labor cost for the banquet. Everything about the banquet is known before the guests arrive, so costs can be kept to a minimum while profits are maximized.

Catering vs. Banquets

Many people do not understand the difference between a caterer and a banquet manager. In reality, there is very little difference. In some areas of the country there is no distinction whatsoever. Both serve the guests by providing them with food, service staff, and cleanup. There is only one difference.

In some geographical areas a caterer performs the service away from his own establishment. In other words, the caterer brings the food and the service to the guests. This can occur at many different locations. On the other hand, the banquet manager usually works at the establishment that has space to hold a banquet and has the guests come to the establishment to partake of the food and service.

DIFFERENCE BETWEEN CATERING AND BANQUETS

Catering	Banquets
Takes place AWAY FROM the establishment	Takes place AT the establishment

Figure 10–5. The difference between a caterer and a banquet manager. In some geographical areas, the terms are interchangeable, while other areas use this distinction.

Both the caterer and banquet manager basically conduct their business in the same manner. However, the caterer must utilize a tremendous amount of pre-planning and organization in order to have a successful banquet. This is because all the equipment and food must be brought to the job. The banquet manager has the luxury of working in a familiar facility. If the banquet manager forgets or runs out of some item like salt, it is much easier for him to replace it than for the caterer. The banquet manager will go to the storeroom and get more salt; the caterer will have to find a store that sells salt, which will involve wasted time and money on the caterer's part. The caterer will have to charge for travel time and for transportation costs; obviously, the banquet manager does not have these costs. Because the jobs of caterer and banquet manager are so similar, many people use the terms interchangeably. However, as has been explained, there is a difference between them.

Staffing a Banquet Facility

The person responsible for the success of the banquet is the banquet manager or caterer. In larger operations, the banquet facility may have a sales manager, a head banquet waiter, and banquet captains, as well as the banquet manager. But in a smaller operation, the banquet manager or caterer performs all of the duties.

The job of the sales manager is to book the banquets. Booking of banquets can be done by conducting outside sales or inside sales. The outside salesperson travels to the client's home or business to convince the guest to have the banquet at the salesperson's facility. The inside salesperson works at the banquet facility. Guests come to the restaurant and book the party.

A head banquet waiter is generally employed at an establishment where there are many function rooms. In these large banquet establishments, many banquets will be occurring simultaneously. The head banquet waiter is responsible for the success of the party in the room in which he is supervising.

Banquet captains are responsible for the service in a section of the banquet room. They would be used when the banquet is large, perhaps over two hundred guests. Both the head banquet waiter and the banquet captains are working supervisors.

The banquet manager is the person who has the final responsibility for the success of the banquet. The banquet manager must make sure that all the details of the party are completed. He or she must make certain that whatever the guest requested and was promised is delivered. If there are any problems with the banquet, it is the banquet manager's duty to solve the problem. The key in being an excellent banquet manager is to concentrate on **details.**

The banquet manager has one main purpose in doing his or her job. It is not to cook the food. It is not to serve the food. *It is to take the responsibility off the guest's shoulders and put it on to his or her own shoulders.* The main responsibility of the banquet manager or caterer is to allow the host to have fun with the guests while the banquet manager or caterer takes care of all the details of the party.

Banquet Manager Qualifications

A banquet manager or a caterer has to be a truly unique individual. The job requires a person who can be referred to as a generalist, rather than a specialist. The banquet manager will have to have the ability to deal with all types of guests. These guests are on many different socioeconomic and psychological levels.

The qualifications for becoming a banquet manager include having a cheerful personality; being attentive to details; having a neat appearance; using tact and diplomacy; having the ability to react quickly to change; having the ability not to become flustered when problems occur; and having the ability to work with many different groups of individuals at the same time. In addition, the banquet manager has to be able to competently express himself or herself orally and in writing. Above all, the banquet manager must be organized.

Personality

The banquet manager will have to deal with a never-ending group of guests that will test his or her limits of patience and endurance. Their

BANQUET MANAGER QUALIFICATIONS

To become a banquet manager you
MUST

1. Have a cheerful personality
2. Be attentive to details
3. Have a neat appearance
4. Have tact and diplomacy
5. Be able to react quickly to change
6. Not become flustered
7. Have excellent oral communication skills
8. Have excellent written communication skills
9. Have the ability to work with many different types of people at once

Figure 10–6.

personality must be cheerful, because the banquet manager is almost always dealing with guests who are in a stress situation. They (the guests) want their party to be perfect. Even though the banquet manager may have conducted a thousand wedding receptions, the mother of the bride feels that this is the only one that the banquet manager has ever done. One fact that the reader must realize is that all guests, regardless of how rich or poor, no matter the type of education they possess, no matter their ethnic background, share the same trait when they are the host of a banquet. They are all placed in a stressful situation. Because of this stress, they exhibit behavior that will test the limits of the banquet manager's patience. Almost always, their personality changes; they change from a nice, friendly, relaxed individual to a stressed out person, which demands that the banquet manager handle them in a firm, yet friendly manner. In short, they could be referred to as temporarily insane or crazy.

The Bride's Parents

A t a very extravagant wedding, both the wedding and reception took place in the same location. The wedding took place in a garden under a tent. When the ceremony was over, the guests were to proceed into one room for cocktails and hors d'oeuvres. After an hour and a half, they were to go into the dining room for the meal.

The parents of the bride had planned everything in a calm atmosphere. They, their daughter, and their future son-in-law were well educated and articulate. The numerous meetings conducted with them were cordial and relaxed. The caterer had explained all that would happen on the day of the wedding.

After the ceremony, the bride's mother came into the dining room and began to panic because none of the tables had been set. The caterer had to calmly escort her out of the room while explaining that the room would be set up in time for the meal. In the meantime, the father of the bride came into the room and his wife asked him to put some gifts into their car. He checked his tuxedo for the keys and discovered that he had locked them in the car. They started an argument, not because the room was not set up, nor because he had locked the keys in the car, but because they were both so stressed out over the wedding. It was the caterer's job to calm them both down and decrease their level of stress by assuring them that everything would be all right with the wedding reception. When the room was set up, the bride was brought into the room to see it. She immediately broke down in tears because the florist had put the wrong type of flowers at the place setting. Because the florist did not have the type of flowers she requested (and had never told her), it was up to the caterer to solve the problem. All that could be done at this point (five minutes before the guests were to enter the room) was to give her a reassuring hug and again calmly tell her everything would be all right. She calmed down and enjoyed her wedding reception.

A banquet manager will incur this type of behavior at every wedding and almost all parties that he or she conducts. The banquet manager must have the personality to deal with these stressed out guests.

Attention to Details

This trait is considered the most important for the banquet manager to have. Being attentive to details makes the difference between a good and great banquet manager.

Raspberries

While working for a caterer, the author was sent to a fiftieth birthday party given by a woman for her husband. The staff arrived at her house and set up for the party. Everything was progressing smoothly; the food was being unloaded and cooked; the dining room was being set up; the hostess was acting normal—crazy and stressed out. Then she asked the fatal question that sent her over the edge: "Where are the raspberries?" The response was that the caterer had not given us any raspberries; instead, she gave us other fruits as a substitute (mangos and papayas). The hostess broke down and started to cry. She said that the party was ruined because raspberries were her husband's favorite dessert and she was promised them by the caterer. The caterer was immediately called and the hostess talked to her about the problem. The hostess was not at all pleased about the lack of raspberries. The caterer claimed that she had told the woman only that she might be able to get the fruit for the party. The woman heard what she wanted to hear—that the caterer would have raspberries for the party. By the way, all the guests at the party loved the birthday celebration. But the hostess was convinced that the party was ruined.

It is worth repeating: Attention to details makes the difference between being good and being great.

Neat Appearance

A banquet manager should look neat and clean. His or her appearance has to be professional at all times.

Tact and Diplomacy

The banquet manager must be able to react with tact and diplomacy at all times.

 # No Sugar, Thank You!

At one party, two of the honored guests were seated at the head table. Another guest wanted to buy them an alcoholic beverage. However, because other guests would have been offended if they had seen the two drinking alcohol, the drinks had to be served without calling attention to the fact. An experienced waiter said, "Leave it to me, I'll solve the problem." He went to the honored guests, obtained their order, and served them their drinks. No one knew that they were drinking an alcoholic beverage. This waiter was a master in the art of tact and diplomacy. He had exercised tact by not turning down or insulting the guest who wanted to buy the honored guests a drink, and he did not offend any of the other guests by blatantly serving the alcoholic drinks in a glass. He showed his diplomacy in this situation by serving the drinks in coffee cups!

The banquet manager has to use these traits often in dealing with different groups of guests. Tact is the ability to say or do the correct thing without offending the guest. Diplomacy is the ability to act tactfully with the guest.

Reacts Quickly to Changes

Another qualification needed by the banquet manager is the ability to think and react quickly when a change has to be made. For instance, there are many times when more guests show up for a party than has been planned. The banquet manager has to be able to accommodate the extra guests without the other guests realizing there is a problem.

Doesn't Become Flustered

In the same vein, when a problem occurs, the banquet manager must remain calm and solve the problem without becoming visually annoyed with the guests. The banquet manager should give the impression that everything is OK, even if there is a catastrophe in the kitchen.

Ability to Work with Many Different Personalities at Once

The banquet manager is a boss. He or she has to manage his or her staff, as well as interact with the guests. In the banquet room, there may be a guest who holds an important position in the country or community. In the kitchen there are dishwashers and potwashers. The banquet manager generally is responsible for the performance of the dishwashers and service people, as well as for the success of the banquet. This means that at one moment the banquet manager may be talking to the dishwasher, while a second later he or she has to return to the banquet room and discuss an item with the host of the party, who may be the Vice President of the United States. Most likely these two individuals come from different social and intellectual classes, but the banquet manager has to be able to converse and act appropriately with both people. The banquet manager has to know and understand psychology and how to use it to make the banquet a success.

Oral Communication

The banquet manager needs to possess excellent oral communication skills. In addition to the obvious responsibilities of communicating with the guests, at times the banquet manager may have to act as a master of ceremonies for a party. This may involve speaking before a group of five hundred guests. The banquet manager will also be conducting meetings with staff, as well as having to present proposals to committees of guests wishing to hold a banquet at the banquet facility.

Written Communication

The ability to express communication clearly and concisely through the use of memos and forms to the staff is another qualification needed by the banquet manager. In addition, the banquet manager must be able to communicate effectively through the use of letters and contracts to the guests.

Organizational Skills

Along with taking care of details, this is the critical skill that a banquet manager must have. He or she must be organized to do the vast amount of planning that goes into a banquet. Food has to be ordered, cooking time and service have to be coordinated. Often, the banquet manager arranges for music, flowers, wedding cakes, audio equipment, photographers, and even entertainment for a banquet. This person has to know where to find all of these services and have an organized system to obtain them.

At times, most likely on weekends, a second banquet is scheduled within one hour of the first banquet in the same room. The banquet manager must be organized and have a plan so that the room can be reset and ready for the next party at its scheduled time. Regardless of the time factor, without organization, any banquet becomes a disaster.

The above list of qualifications is not an all encompassing list. But it is a list of the most crucial skills that the banquet manager must have in order to perform the job of banquet manager or caterer successfully.

Banquet Manager Benefits

There are many benefits for choosing a career in banquet management. Prestige, salary, gratuities, and perquisites (perks) are among the benefits a person can attain as a banquet manager.

Prestige

Prestige comes naturally to the banquet manager. This is because the job puts the banquet manager in direct contact with the most important and influential people in the social and business community. A banquet manager who excels at the job soon receives the accolades of the community. In addition, the manager makes valuable contacts that may be used to further his or her career. Because the banquet manager is the most visible employee and the one that comes in contact most often with the guests, the manager **is** the establishment in the eyes of the guests.

Psychic Income

Another important benefit in the prestige category is the factor called *psychic income*. This is not money that the banquet manager receives; rather, it is the positive feeling that the manager obtains from doing a job well, or from serving important guests and sometimes becoming the confidant of those guests.

Pay

The banquet manager is generally paid an excellent salary. Since the banquet manager represents the establishment to the guests, they identify with the banquet manager rather than the establishment. If the banquet manager leaves the establishment and goes to work for a competitor, the guests generally follow the banquet manager. Therefore, the banquet facility does not want to lose good banquet managers. They will pay them handsomely for their services and contacts. In addition, the managers may receive a percentage of the gratuity as an extra incentive to remain at the banquet house.

The banquet manager deals closely with the hosts of the parties, and in doing so usually creates an excellent rapport. If the banquet manager is competent in performing the job, it appears to be done effortlessly. The host often asks the banquet manager to do jobs that are not normally associated with the position. At the end of the party, it is not unusual for a satisfied guest to give a monetary gratuity to the banquet manager for a job well done.

Perquisites

Perquisites or "perks" are additional benefits that are given to the banquet manager in addition to the regular salary. There is usually an allowance for clothing, and the expense of cleaning the clothes is generally paid for. The banquet manager generally has an expense account for the purpose of entertaining potential or repeat guests. Sometimes lodging may be included as a benefit. The value of the banquet manager to the business will determine the amount of perquisites he or she is offered.

Disadvantages of Becoming a Banquet Manager

As in any good job, there are also detriments to the banquet manager's position. Long hours, stressful parties, and the availability of food and liquor are all negative factors in the banquet manager's job.

Long Hours

The job of banquet manager requires the banquet manager to work when everyone else is playing. Social events occur on weekends, evenings, and holidays. The banquet manager may have had twelve parties during the week, but to the guests, their party is the only one that matters. The banquet manager is responsible for all the parties being conducted at the establishment. Many times, this means supervising all the parties. Larger banquet houses will have assistant banquet managers, but the vast majority of operations can not afford an assistant. Therefore, the banquet manager has to be in attendance at all parties.

Stress

The banquet manager is under a tremendous amount of stress to do an excellent job. Even though guests do not expect the same high quality as they do when they go to an a la carte dining establishment, the hosts of the party want a gourmet meal. They also want everything done one way—perfectly. The hosts have chosen the banquet facility with the expectation that the party will be perfect. They want to enjoy themselves. At times this creates an unbearable amount of stress on the banquet manager.

Availability of Food and Liquor

Often the banquet manager, as a response to the stress in the job, turns to "the bottle" to solve problems. Because of the perquisite and the stature in the establishment, the banquet manager can "drink" as part of his job. By the same token, many people in this profession have poor diets. They have so many different foods available, they reward themselves with a poor nutritional diet that is detrimental to their health.

Illegal Activities

In addition to the above problems, there usually is the opportunity for the manager to engage in illegal activities, such as drug use and gambling. Because of the high-prestige position of the banquet manager, he or she is often exposed to this type of activity.

Job Knowledge Needed

The banquet manager must know how to sell, plan, organize, and conduct banquets so they are a success for the guests. There are many detailed items that make the difference between a successful or unsuccessful banquet. The following chapters will go into more depth on these nuances; however, to begin with, the banquet manager must know the following to conduct business successfully:

1. the size of each room and how to diagram rooms;
2. how to book banquets;
3. the difference between tentative and firm reservations;
4. how many main entrees the guests can choose;
5. the importance of communication with the guest and the kitchen;
6. how to construct a menu that will be eye appealing, nutritionally sound and one that the kitchen will be able to serve;
7. the timing of the party so that the food arrives when the guest desires it; and
8. should know the manner in which banquets can be served to the guests.

Styles of Banquets

There are two general styles of banquets. The first is a sit-down meal, the second is a buffet. Both refer to the type of service the service staff gives to the guests. The sit-down banquet refers to the fact that the guests are served their complete meal by the service staff. At a buffet, the guests either obtain a portion or all their food by serving themselves from buffet tables.

Type of Service for Banquets

There are two types of service for sit-down banquets. Restaurants either use American or Russian banquet service. For buffets, there are three types of buffet services: buffet, modified buffet, and deluxe buffet.

American banquet is the type of service that most restaurants use because it is simple. It is referred to as "On the plate, no wait." It is easy to learn and use.

Russian service requires more skill by the service staff. The staff must transfer food from platters to guest plates by using a fork and spoon. This

TYPES OF SERVICES AT BANQUETS

Sit Down Meals	Buffets
American	Simple Buffet
Russian	Modified Deluxe
	Deluxe

Figure 10–7.

type of service most often occurs at expensive banquets, usually in large metropolitan hotels or at a catered event.

The service that does not deserve to be called service is the first type of buffet service. In this service, the guests obtain all their own food, utensils, and beverages. The only thing the service staff does is clean up the dirty tables.

A modified buffet service requires the service staff to serve beverages and, perhaps, the dessert courses, while the guests obtain their appetizers, salad, and main entree items from the buffet table.

The deluxe buffet provides the guests with the most service. All the courses except the main course are served to the guest.

Chapter Summary

1. The three main types of banquets are: personal entertaining, business meetings, and fraternal organizations.
2. The main difference between a banquet manager and a caterer is that the banquet manager hosts the guests in his own establishment, whereas the caterer brings the food and service to the guests.
3. The key to banquet management is for the banquet manager to take the responsibility for the banquet's success off the guest's shoulders and on to his or her own.
4. The qualities that a successful banquet manager must possess are many; among the most important are: attention to details, tact, a neat appearance, the ability to react quickly to change, the ability to work with many different types of personalities, the ability to communicate well both orally and in writing, and a high degree of organizational skills.
5. The advantages to the banquet manager's position are good pay, prestige, "psychic income," and perquisites.
6. The disadvantages to the banquet manager's position are long hours, stress, the availability of food and liquor, and the opportunity to engage in illegal activities.
7. The two types of banquet are sit-down and buffet.
8. Sit-down banquets may be of American service or Russian service.
9. Buffets may be: buffet service, modified buffet service, or deluxe buffet service.

Review Questions

1. A party of 150 is served their meal. You, as the banquet manager, observe that the noise level in the room is very high. No one is eating their main beef course! It is obvious that there is a problem with the meal. How do you solve this problem?

2. Referring to the story about raspberries: What should the caterer have done to avoid this problem? Explain why the caterer did not exhibit the trait of attending to details.
3. Define the term banquet.
4. Explain the importance of banquets as they relate to the profitability of a hospitality establishment.
5. List and explain the advantages that the banquet business has over restaurants that serve a la carte meals.
6. Define the difference between a caterer and a banquet manager.
7. What are the advantages and disadvantages of the banquet manager's job?
8. What are the types and styles of service available for banquets?
9. What are the qualifications needed to become a banquet manager?
10. What job knowledge should the banquet manager possess in order to do the job effectively?
11. What is the banquet manager's main responsibility as it relates to the host of the banquet?

Chapter 11
How to Book Functions

Chapter Objectives:

At the completion of this chapter, the reader will be able to:

1. define the term *function;*
2. name the sizes of the standard banquet tables and their uses;
3. describe the different types of room setups available for functions;
4. draw a diagram of a function room in a simple and concise manner;
5. define the difference between tentative and firm bookings;
6. explain the importance of a function book, or computer program, and how to book functions at the establishment;
7. explain the word *qualified* as it relates to booking business;
8. explain the meaning of the word *guarantee* and its importance in the banquet business;
9. describe the difference in policies on room rentals; and
10. explain the importance of setting up policies as they relate to payment of functions.

What is a Function?

A function is any use of banquet facilities. The room may be rented by the guest, or the establishment may allow the guest to use the room at no charge. Examples of functions are meetings, dinners, conferences, and cocktail parties. Guests deal directly with the banquet office for the purpose of conducting these functions. Depending upon the size of the banquet facility, the banquet manager may be the only management person that comes in contact with the guest from the initial booking until the function is complete. In larger establishments, there may be a catering and sales manager, as well as a group sales office that has the responsibility of booking the function. Once the event is booked, the responsibility for the success of the event depends upon the performance of the banquet manager. One of the keys in conducting successful functions begins with proper booking of the event.

What Must be Known about Function Room Setups

Regardless of the type of function that will be booked, the person booking the function must know specific facts about the individual banquet facility. First, the booking person has to know the number of rooms available and each room's capacity for either meal or meeting functions. Second, the type of physical setups that will accommodate guests comfortably and efficiently in each room should be known. Third, the banquet manager has to know the equipment available to be used in the establishment, as well as how and where to obtain extra equipment if needed. Finally, the manager will have to be able to diagram a room simply and concisely so the person physically setting up the room will be able to perform the job without having to ask any questions about the room layout.

Room Availability and Capacity

Architects and banquet managers never see a room the same way. It has been well documented that most restaurant facilities (especially kitchens) are designed by people who do not or have never worked in a kitchen. The same is true of function rooms. Many times, the square footage available is calculated upon the general formula of eight to twelve square feet of space for each person at a sit-down meal function. Often, even though the formula is mathematically correct, the projected number of guests will not fit into the room. This is because each function is an individual party which may require different table configurations, resulting in a different capacity for the room. The location of exits, the shape of the head table, the traffic flow, the dance floor, the audio-visual equipment, and the type of function must be taken into consideration before the capacity of a room can be determined. For instance, more people will be accommodated into a room that is being used for a stand-up cocktail party as opposed to a meeting scheduled for that room. Therefore, the banquet manager should get the "feel of the room" by setting up tables and conducting a few sample functions in it. By doing this, the banquet manager will know the capacity of each room for each type of function.

Another "moment of truth" occurs when guests sit down to have their meal. If there is enough room at the table, they are pleased. If the room is too crowded, the banquet facility has failed this "moment of truth." Therefore, each person booking functions has to be aware of the realistic capacity and use of every room for every type of function, not relying on the proposed capacity determined by the architect.

Types of Room Setups for Functions

Guests do not want to be too crowded into a room; nor do they want a room where there is so much extra space that it looks as if the party is a failure. It is the banquet manager's responsibility to know the different ways a room can be set up to create a successful social or business event. Banquet managers must know how to use room space effectively to maximize revenue. In addition, anyone booking parties has to know the definition of the standard types of functions. The following descriptions are of those functions most widely used, but the list is not all-inclusive.

Tables

All guests are seated at tables and are waited on by a service person. For social events, such as weddings or dinners, round tables are ideal because they encourage conversation. For business meetings, a block table, a T-shaped table, or an E-shaped table is better because it eliminates unnecessary conversation. Figures 11-1 through 11-3 illustrate the different shaped tables.

The block table is made up of four rectangular tables put together to form a block. This is an ideal setup for a maximum of twenty guests at a small business meeting where all guests can communicate freely.

The T-shaped table is ideal to use in a long, narrow room. The illustration shows three rectangular tables; however, in actual practice, four or five tables would make up the base of the T.

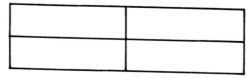

Figure 11–1. An illustration of a block table. Made up of four rectangular tables put together to form a block.

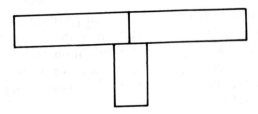

Figure 11–2. A T-shaped table. Made up of three or more rectangular tables.

The third, the E-shaped table is ideal where there is a large delegation of guests who must be seated at the head table.

Meeting Setups

Usually there are two general types of setups for meetings. The easiest one to set up is referred to as theater style. The guests are provided only chairs, all facing in the same direction. This type of physical setup would be used when the guests are listening to a presentation.

The second type of meeting where all the guests have to face the front of the room is set up in a style called schoolroom or classroom. Figure 11-4 illustrates how all the guests are facing the front of the room while seated at a table for the purpose of writing notes. This setup would be used for a teaching seminar. Schoolroom style takes up the most amount of space, which results in a lessening of the amount of guests that may be accommo-

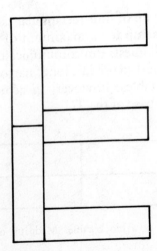

Figure 11–3. An E-shaped table. Made up of five or more rectangular tables.

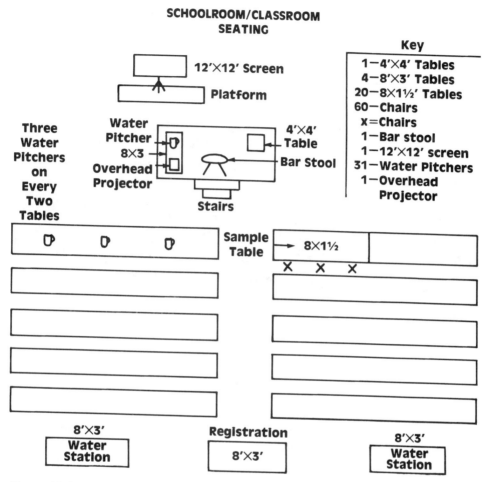

Figure 11–4.   A classroom or schoolroom style setup for a function. All seats are facing the front of the room.

dated in a room. Figure 11-5 shows a room set up for a classroom or schoolroom style meeting.

Head Tables

These tables are placed in front of the room, with the guests seated only on the side of the table from which they are facing the other members of the party. A new trend, at social events, is to have a round head table placed in the middle of the party. This eliminates the formality of the event and allows the guests at the head table to enjoy themselves more.

Figure 11–5.   A schoolroom style set up for a function. (Photo courtesy of The Desmond Americana)

Cocktail Parties

The flow of guests is important for this type of function. The banquet manager can become creative and use all types of space for these parties. It can be the lobbies or pools of hotels, or it can be a function room. The position of both the bars and food stations become important for guest comfort and ease of service. Setting up a cocktail party is relatively easy because the banquet manager only has to use a few tables.

At a cocktail party, there should be fewer chairs than the number of guests that are expected. This forces the guests to socialize. Figure 11-6 shows guests enjoying themselves at a cocktail party. Care must be used in locating food and drink stations away from one another to minimize traffic jams. A popular cocktail party concept that has caught on in the 1980s is to have stations where food is cooked and small portions are served to the guests. For instance, there may be a fettuccine station, a chicken cordon bleu station, and a veal marsalla station. More room must be allowed for this type of cocktail party than the traditional one in which food is precooked and put out for the guests in chafing dishes and on trays. However, at all cocktail parties, many more guests can be accommodated into the room than at a sit-down dinner.

Figure 11–6.   Guests enjoying themselves at a cocktail party. They have plenty of room to move around. There is a lack of seating at cocktail parties. (Photo courtesy of The Desmond Americana)

Once the banquet manager has determined the type of setup the guest wants for the function, and how many people can be accommodated comfortably and efficiently in a function room, a diagram has to be drawn in order for the room to be set up correctly. But before this can be done, the banquet manager needs to know what equipment is available for setting up rooms.

Available Equipment

The manager knows the capacity of all the rooms and the types of functions that may be booked into a room. The next thing the banquet manager needs to know are the types and sizes of tables available, so the function can be planned with comfort for the guests and efficiency for the banquet establishment. Figure 11-7 illustrates the types of tables that are available for the banquet manager to use in setting up functions.

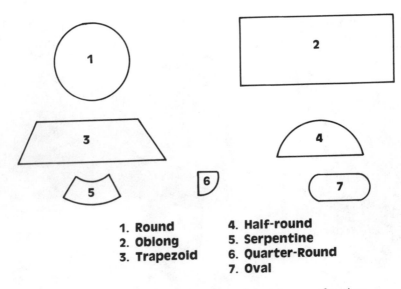

1. Round   4. Half-round
2. Oblong   5. Serpentine
3. Trapezoid 6. Quarter-Round
                  7. Oval

Figure 11–7. Shapes of tables available to use in setting up banquet functions.

Round Tables

Round tables are used to create a jovial atmosphere. They always should be used when the guest wants a function where fun and enjoyment are part of the key ingredients for the success of the party. Round tables are a must for wedding receptions. Most banquet houses use one of two sizes of round tables. The standard round table is sixty inches in diameter. This will seat eight people comfortably at a meal. The other size is seventy-two inches, which seats ten. The main disadvantage of a banquet facility using round tables is that round tables take up more space than rectangular tables. Therefore, the banquet facility cannot seat as many people at a function using round tables as it could using rectangular tables. However, the banquet facility that uses round tables has an advantage over a competitor that only uses rectangular tables because the round tables encourage socialization.

Oblong or Rectangular Tables

Figure 11-8 shows the three basic sizes of oblong or rectangular tables. They are 30″ wide × 96″ long (called an 8-foot table); 18″ × 96″ (8-foot × 1½-foot, or skinny); and 30″ × 72″ (6-foot). Each guest needs twenty-four inches of linear space to be comfortable. Therefore, an 8-footer will seat eight people (four on each side of the table). The 6-footer will accommodate six people, and the 8-×-1½-footer will only accommodate three people. The skinny table is used when guests have to sit on one side of the table (at a head

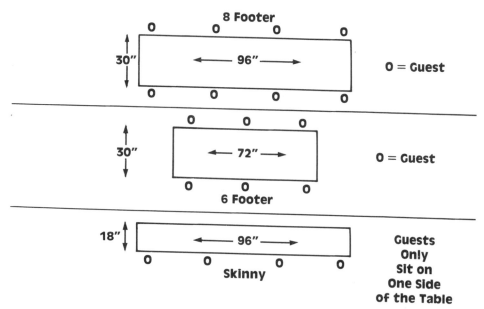

Figure 11–8.

table or for a schoolroom style setup). Eight foot by one and a half foot tables can also be used for a block table.

Space Between Tables

When guests are seated back to back, which is the case when rectangular tables are used, it is recommended that sixty inches are allowed between tables. Using round tables, fifty-four inches of space is allowed. Both of the above guidelines take into account that chairs are placed in the sixty inches and fifty-four inches of space. However, this is another area in which the banquet manager should experiment by actually setting up the rooms to determine if there is enough space between tables for the guests to be comfortable and to allow enough space for the service personnel to do their job efficiently. When doing this experiment, the banquet manager should instruct the person setting up the chairs to not push them under the tables but to keep them pulled out as a if a guest were sitting at the table. The banquet manager will soon discover the capacity of the function rooms in the establishment.

Special-Shaped Tables

The serpentine, quarter-, and half-round tables are best used for setting up food or bar stations rather than for the guests' dining. A banquet manager and chef can create an interesting food setup using the different shaped tables.

Lecterns

Lecterns are placed in the center of the head table and take up twenty-four inches (the same amount of space that a guest requires). On the lectern there is a place for the notes of the guest speaker, a light, and a microphone.

Podium

A podium serves the same purpose as a lectern. The difference between the two is that a podium is freestanding, while the lectern sits on the table. It also takes up twenty-four inches of space.

Microphones

Every banquet manager has to be aware of the types of microphones available for use in the function room. The banquet manager should know where the power source is for the microphone outlet, how to turn the system on, adjust the volume, and eliminate annoying feedback. One common mistake most people make when testing a microphone is not setting the volume loud enough. The microphone system should be tested before the guests arrive in the function room. Often, the person testing the system does not take into account that there will be many more people in the room when the system is in use. A room with four hundred guests will produce a higher decibel volume of miscellaneous sounds than one with no guests; so the microphone must sound loud when it is being tested.

Audiovisual Equipment

Most banquet facilities have movie screens, and some may have slide projectors. Other facilities have state-of-the-art rear projection systems. Regardless of the type of equipment the establishment owns, the banquet manager needs to know how to operate it. If a guest makes a request for equipment that the facility does not own, the banquet manager can rent it. Therefore, a knowledge of where to obtain the rental audio-visual equipment is needed, as must the amount of money to charge the guest for the rental.

Things to Keep in Mind

Every banquet manager must realize that planning the correct setup of a function room can be an integral part of the success or failure of a business meeting or party. There are a couple of facts that have to be stressed for the reader about equipment and use of function rooms.

Especially important is the fact that all equipment must be in the room and thoroughly tested before the guests arrive. For example, if the slide projector is rented, the banquet manager should have extra bulbs available, and know how to change bulbs if one burns out during a slide presentation. If the equipment is owned by the establishment, a regular maintenance schedule should be set up for changing bulbs so there will be no problem during the presentation. All equipment must be in working condition and ready to operate when the guests walk in.

The second fact that the banquet manager must consider has to do with the placement of different types of functions in the rooms. Many modern facilities have large function rooms that can be made into smaller rooms by the use of moveable walls. Many times these walls are not as soundproof as the manufacturer claims. A banquet manager would be wise not to place a business meeting in the same space as a wedding reception, with only the wall separating them.

The banquet manager can play an integral part in the success or failure of a party by the planning and use of tables, setup, and equipment that is available to the guests. Practice, common sense, and the banquet manager's experience all will benefit the guests. Satisfied guests mean more repeat business for the establishment. However, sometimes the banquet manager will get some unusual requests for equipment.

A Quick Fix

A few days before a function was to take place, Governor Rockefeller's advance man made an appointment with the banquet manager to inspect the facilities for the Governor's speech. They entered the function room, the advance man checked where the windows were (to make sure the Governor would not be susceptible to a sniper's shot), told the banquet manager exactly what side the television cameras could be set up on (to present the best side of the Governor), and then asked to test out the lectern. The lectern was positioned on the head table as it would be for the Governor's speech. The advance man took out a tape measure and discovered that from the floor to the place where "The Man's" (as he referred to him) notes would be placed were forty-three inches from the floor. "This will never do," he said. "The notes must sit on a lectern or podium that is forty-four inches from the floor." The question was asked, "Why?" "Because that is the perfect distance that allows the Man to read his notes without putting on his glasses," he replied. With that information, the problem was solved by getting the carpenter to cut a one-inch piece of wood that would fit under the lectern. On the day of the speech, the wood was under the lectern, which elevated it to forty-four inches from the floor, and the event was a success. From that day on, the wood was kept in the banquet manager's office and used every time the Governor was the guest speaker at functions at the hotel.

A Final Point about Room Setups

In scheduling functions for rooms, the banquet manager should see to it that there is enough room to accommodate all the guests comfortably in the room. There is one exception to this rule. Often guests who plan this type of function want to schedule a room that is much too small for the number of people that is expected at the event. What type of event is it?

It is a press conference. This is done to make the event look like an overwhelming success. Think of a room that seats 100. If 110 people show up, the room is filled to capacity. Put the same press conference in a room that seats 500. Even if 200 people attend the event, it still appears that the event was a flop, because there are 300 empty seats.

Physically Setting up the Function Rooms

Once the banquet manager knows the proper manner of setting up and the use of the function rooms, the next step is to physically set up the rooms for the function. The banquet manager should not set up the rooms. However, he or she should know how to diagram the function so the setup people will be able to accomplish the task without asking any questions.

Most of the time, the people who have the responsibility of setting up the rooms are entry level workers. If they are trained properly (generally the banquet manager's job), they become excellent employees and are a valuable asset for the banquet manager. Regardless of their training, it is the banquet manager's responsibility to diagram all parties as the guests request them. After this diagram is prepared, it is then given to the setup people so they can physically set up the room. Figure 11-9 shows the setup for a wedding reception for 198 guests. Figure 11-10 is the same party for 198 guests. Compare the two diagrams and decide which one is easier to understand.

Figure 11-10 should be easier to understand. There is a key on the bottom of the diagram. All tables are clearly marked with their sizes, and there is a sample table for the setup person to follow. The head table has the exact specification of how many guests should be seated and where they should be seated. The key tells exactly how many tables, their sizes, and the number of chairs the setup people need to do their job. This diagram makes the setup of this party easy.

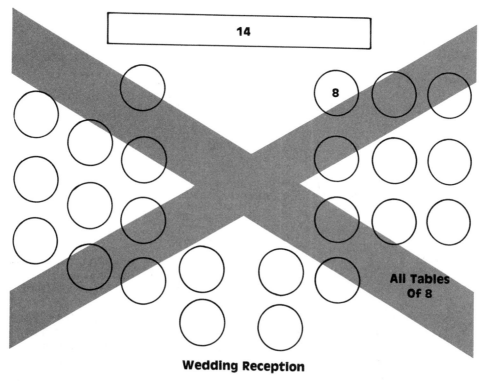

Figure 11–9. A setup for a wedding reception for 198 guests. It is a general setup with no landmarks and little details. There are many items wrong with this setup, which are corrected in Figure 11-10.

Every function should have a diagram such as that in Figure 11-10. Because most setups are done during the night when the banquet manager is not working, the diagrams should be as complete as possible. In the morning, the first thing the banquet manager will do is check the rooms to make sure they are set up correctly. If there is a problem, it can be corrected, and it can be determined whether the mistake was the setup person's or the banquet manager's. The banquet manager must know how to diagram function rooms simply and concisely.

Two Final Tips

All illustrations should be done on paper that is 8½″ by 11″ (so the setup people can carry them around in their pockets). The diagrams do not have to be done to scale.

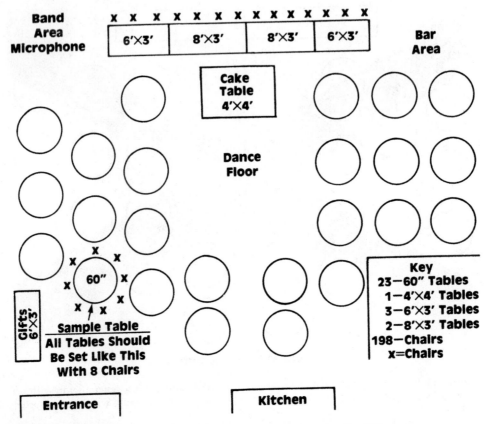

Figure 11–10.   The correct way to diagram a wedding reception for 198 guests.

Finally, the banquet manager should try, whenever feasible, to suggest the same physical setup to the next guest as was used for the previous function. This will cut down on the banquet facilities labor cost, as well as increase the morale of the setup crew.

Booking Functions

Once the banquet manager knows the capacity and use of the function rooms, the next task is to book functions. The booking of functions is done by either a sales, catering, or banquet manager or secretary. For the purpose of this chapter, the title banquet manager will encompass all of these job titles.

The banquet manager has to know exactly what types of meals, accommodations for meetings, and charges for these services the establishment can offer to the guest. Usually this information is provided by the owners or the general manager of the establishment after the food has been costed out and the profit margin is added into the meal. Most banquet managers work from a set-price menu; caterers usually do not. Caterers set their prices based upon a variety of factors, such as what the guest desires, the location of the party, day of the week, and how much demand there is for the caterer's services. Knowing all of this information, the booking process can begin.

How Would You Like to be in this Situation?

One Saturday morning a banquet establishment was setting up for their wedding of two hundred. As they were just about completed with the setup, the waiter looked out and saw the wedding party arrive. He thought this was odd, as they were half an hour early. The banquet manager went out to greet the bride and groom; but to his surprise it was a different bride and groom who showed up. Another manager had booked another wedding on the same day, at the same time, with the same menu. In thirty minutes the other wedding party of two hundred showed up. And no, this is not made up. It really happened!

Function Book

To avoid the above situation, every facility must have an organized system to keep their bookings straight. In the past, the tool to use was a function book. Today, the function book is being replaced with the use of computer software. However, whether a banquet establishment uses a function book or a computer, the basic principles are the same.

A function book is an organized piece of equipment that lists the rooms that the establishment has to rent on a daily basis. A typical page from a function book looks like the one in Figure 11-11.

Looking at Figure 11-11, each meal period and each day of the year are in the book. In addition, every room would be listed in the book. The person doing the booking would open the page to the date and see if anything was booked into the room. If there was nothing entered, then the booking person could sell the space to the guest. In Figure 11-11, the booking person can see that the SeVille room is booked for Mr. Zorn. Furthermore, AJS

MONDAY, SEPTEMBER 12, 19____
LUNCH

Room	Group	Estimated Number	Time
SeVille	Society of Wine Educators Ted Zorn 28 Oakbarrel Drive Hammensport, NY 617-555-WINE (B) 315-555-6589 (H)	250 Firm 3/21/19____ $300.00 Deposit	11-1:30 AJS

Figure 11–11. A typical page from a function book. Its purpose is to avoid overbooking.

booked the party and accepted the deposit on 3/21 and made the notation that the party was firm.

If another guest wanted the SeVille room for lunch on September 12, the guest would be told that the room had been previously booked. The banquet manager should then attempt to sell the guest a date, a different room, or a time that is open. If there are no open dates or if the guest cannot change the requested date, the banquet manager may make suggestions or even assist the guest in finding another banquet facility that is comparable in service and price. This practice is beneficial to the banquet manager in a couple of ways. First, the guest will be impressed that the banquet manager is taking the time to assist in finding an alternative banquet establishment. Second, the competition will reciprocate when they are booked up.

The function book does not provide any information about the menu or the party; only who reserved the room, whether it is a firm or tentative booking, and the approximate time and number of guests that will attend the function. The main purpose of the system is to avoid overbooking, which is defined as having two parties in the same room at the same time.

Care and Storage of the Book

Because the function book is such an integral part of the banquet business, the book should be kept in a permanent place. It should not be brought into another office or to a person's home when booking a party. When no one is in the office it should be kept in a locked area.

The banquet facility must make certain that only authorized people are allowed to make entries into the book. All entries must be made in pencil, and the people who books the parties must identify themselves by putting their initials in the entry.

One advantage computer software has over the traditional function book is that backup copies of all bookings can be saved and/or printed. There has always been a fear that if the book was stolen, lost, or damaged by fire, it would be difficult to reconfirm the bookings, and, thus, overbooking would occur. Figure 11-12 is an advertisement that appeared in a newspaper. From the ad, it appears that the function book has been lost. In fact it was stolen.

By taking the above steps, the establishment should almost eliminate the possibility of overbooking.

Qualifying Business

Each banquet establishment has to set up a policy to determine the amount of money that must be made when a room is booked. Once that determination and policy has been set, the banquet manager should attempt to book parties that will bring in the most revenue for the establishment. Some banquet establishments will accept any and all business, while others attempt to specialize in certain market areas, such as the social business.

Qualifying a client means to determine how much money the client will be spending at the establishment. At some establishments there will be more demand for function space in particular months. "September is a peak season for us as far as functions go," states Kim Spiak, Sales and Catering Manager at the Desmond Americana in Albany, New York. "It is primarily our large conference and convention season. There is minimal space available. If a

Figure 11–12.   An advertisement for a lost function book.

room is available for fifty guests, we are going to try to find a client that has an open-bar, extensive hors d'oeuvres, high revenue dinner, and possibly wine sales, in comparison to a cash bar and a chicken dinner."

Qualifying should also mean to determine if the guest can pay for the party. Some guests have booked parties with no intention of paying for them. Unfortunately, this is usually people running for political office. It is best to make candidates pay for their functions in advance. There are many documented stories about candidates who have both won and lost elections, and still owe for their parties. The accepted method of payment should be explained to the guest when the party is booked. The establishment has to decide if it will accept personal checks and/or credit cards, and how much of a deposit to charge the guest.

Once the business is qualified, the date can be entered into the function book as either a tentative or firm booking.

How Far in Advance may Banquets be Booked

Each banquet facility has to determine, based upon the demand for space, a policy concerning how far in advance banquets may be booked. The goal of the facility is to obtain the most revenue. For example, a new banquet business would probably book any business, while one that is established and more in demand may set a limit on advance bookings.

Guidelines are clearly outlined at the Desmond Americana, says Ms. Spiak. "We have specific booking policies. For instance, the group sales office can take bookings far in advance, as long as the business is qualified. On the other hand, the catering office can take social events only nine months in advance of the event. The exception is on holiday weekends. We can book as far in advance as requested on a weekend such as Labor Day. So if I were to have a request for a wedding, it cannot be booked a year in advance unless it was on a holiday weekend. Small business meetings of between fifteen or twenty-five people may only be booked three months in advance of the date. This is done in order to maximize the space."

Once the guidelines and policies are set, the banquet manager should "qualify the business" before booking the party.

The Difference between Tentative and Firm

Bookings can be either called *tentative* or *firm*. Firm bookings are the easiest to understand. A guest gives the banquet manager a deposit for a party. Once the establishment receives the guest's money for the party, the amount and date of the deposit, as well as the word "firm," is entered into the function book.

Tentative means that the banquet manager will put the guests name into the function book, and the guest will have first refusal if another person calls and wants the same room at the same time. Again, a policy is established by the banquet facility about tentative bookings. At many banquet establishments, the space is held tentatively without a deposit for one week. After the week, the person who booked the party will call the guest and ask if he or she is still interested in the date. If the guest is still interested, a deposit must be brought in. The person who books the function writes in the book the term "*FIRM,*" with the date and the amount of the deposit received. If the guest does not bring the deposit within one week, he or she is called and informed that the deposit must be brought in before the close of business that day or the function will be canceled.

Problems with Tentative Bookings

Banquet managers find that some dates are more popular than others. Often, the manager will have a tentative booking and then a guest will come in a day later with a deposit for a firm booking. The banquet establishment needs a policy to determine which party to take and which party to refuse.

Deposits

A deposit is required for almost all banquet events. The deposit protects both parties. The banquet house will not sell the date that the guest has reserved to another client; while the client will not cancel the event without losing the money that has been put down for the event.

Each banquet house should determine the amount of deposit that it will charge. It should be expensive enough to deter the guest from canceling the party, while moderate enough not to deter the guest from booking the party with the banquet house. As an example, one banquet facility requires a $200 deposit for social events that occur in any month except December. Deposits on Christmas parties vary from $500 to $1,000. Other establishments have a different policy. However, excellent repeat customers often are not charged a deposit.

Different operations have different policies on refunding the deposits. Some will never refund a deposit; other places will refund the deposit if the party is canceled four months prior to the event; still other banquet houses will not give back the deposit unless another group rebooks the date. Of course, there are always circumstances in which the manager will have to determine if giving back or keeping the deposit would be in the best interests of the business.

Guarantees

When booking functions, guests should be informed of the policy on guarantees of the establishment. A guarantee is a promise made by the host of the party that a certain number of guests will show up for the party and that the host will pay for that number unless more guests attend.

When a guest originally books an event, he or she gives an estimate of how many people will attend the party. Most banquet establishments require that the guarantee must be given three or four days prior to the event. Most establishments will take that number and set up 5% above that guaranteed number (100 guaranteed, 105 seats). The guest pays for a minimum of 100 people unless more guests show up.

Room Rentals

Guests will be using the function rooms for food and beverage functions or meetings. There are different ways to charge for room rentals.

If a guest has a food and beverage function in a room, usually there is no charge for the room. If the guest has to use two rooms, one for a meeting and one for a food and beverage function, the guest may be charged the full price for the meeting room. Naturally, if a guest uses just a meeting room, the full price for the meeting room is charged.

At times, meeting room charges can be waived if the guest spends additional money at the facility. For instance, if a guest has booked two hundred rooms at a hotel, the meeting room charge is waived.

Chapter Summary

1. Knowledge of room availability and capacity are necessary when booking functions.
2. There are four types of setups for functions: meal functions, meetings, head-table functions, and cocktail parties.
3. Equipment available for the various functions include: round tables, oblong or rectangular tables, serpentine tables, quarter-round tables,

half-round tables, lecterns, podiums, microphones, and audio-visual equipment.
4. A diagram should be drawn to guide the setup crew for each function.
5. A function book must be kept to avoid overbooking.
6. All business should be qualified as to the amount of revenue that a function will bring in, the guest's ability to pay for the function, how far in advance a booking may be taken, whether a booking is firm or tentative, and whether a deposit is required.
7. A guarantee is a guest's promise to pay for a minimum number of guests at a booked function.

Review Questions

1. You are the banquet manager of a brand new hotel. You plan to open in December of this year. It is November and there is a lot of demand for June weddings. You have been very successful in booking parties. The one and only room you have is in demand for weddings. In the afternoon, a bride and her mother come into the establishment. You show them around, and by the time they leave they have a tentative booking on the room for June 21. That evening you go out on a sales call with your food and beverage manager to book a wedding. He has tentatively reserved June 28 in the logbook. You do a great job of selling your services. The parents of the bride say, "Yes, we would like to firm up the date." You say, "Great, that will be June 28." They reply, "No, it is the 21st and we want that date!" What do you do?
2. Referring to Figure 11-9, what problems would the setup people have with this diagram?
3. Referring to Figures 11-9 and 11-10, what positive details does Figure 11-10 have that Figure 11-9 does not have?
4. Referring to the problem of the two simultaneous wedding receptions that were cited earlier in this chapter, how would you handle the situation?
5. A guest has booked a tentative party. Unfortunately, you did not qualify the business. It is the stereotype chicken dinner for fifty guests with a cash bar. One of your best customers comes into your office and says that his boss is retiring and he wants the same date as that booked for the tentative party. In addition to being a great customer, he informs you that they want a filet mignon party for two hundred guests with an open bar, wine, and a cocktail party. What party should you take, and how will you explain the rejection to the guest to whom you deny the date?

6. Would you give back a deposit if a couple broke up two weeks before their planned wedding? What if the prospective bride got killed in an accident?
7. What does the term "function" mean?
8. What are the sizes of the standard banquet tables, and what type of parties use them?
9. Explain the difference between a tentative and a firm booking.

Chapter 12

The Banquet Function Sheet

Chapter Objectives:

At the completion of this chapter, the reader will be able to:

1. define a banquet function sheet and know its purpose;
2. obtain information from the host concerning the event;
3. suggest items to make the event a success;
4. complete the information needed on the banquet function sheet;
5. explain the different meal options a host can have for a banquet;
6. define "details" as it pertains to the banquet business;
7. explain the importance of details in organizing and planning a banquet;
8. illustrate how to serve more than one main course item to guests at a banquet;
9. understand the importance of cooperation with all the staff, especially the chef;
10. plan, staff, and organize a banquet to result in a perfect event;
11. explain the different alcoholic beverage choices to a host at a banquet; and
12. set up seating arrangements for a party.

Organization: a Key to a Successful Banquet

Having completed Chapter 11, the reader now knows how to book function rooms. The next step in the banquet management process is to obtain all information concerning the event. Once the banquet manager has the information, it has to be transmitted to the staff in a clear, concise manner.

Different banquet managers use different techniques for accomplishing this task. However, they all have one thing in common; every successful banquet manager has an organized system. Kim Sibson Williams, the banquet manager at the Astro Hall in Houston, Texas, uses informal lists to

keep herself organized. "I'm a great list maker," she says. Kim is responsible
for parties from ten to one thousand in the Astro Hall. In addition, her
responsibilities also include serving all banquets that are booked in the
building next to the Astro Hall, the Houston Astrodome. She has had parties
as large as two thousand guests that must be served in the same area in which
baseball and football games are played. In such cases, she becomes the caterer
to the Astrodome.

Both facilities have a limited kitchen area and equipment to accommodate
the large number of guests. She must plan and organize the banquets,
keeping in mind the limitations of both facilities. She also has the responsibility for obtaining all utensils and plates to feed the many guests. In addition,
she must obtain all the service staff to serve the guests.

Once a party is booked, she begins her practice of making lists. By
compiling these lists, she makes certain nothing is forgotten for the event.
Finally, she must have everything the host has ordered and make sure it is
served the way the host desires it. Her success rate is evident, based upon the
large amount of repeat business she receives. Another banquet facility, The
Desmond Americana, in Albany, New York, uses a more sophisticated
process in the planning and operation of functions. Each day, the sales and
banquet staff receive a computerized print out which consists of five parts.
These five parts are: deposits due, banquet event order (beo) due, guarantee
due, personal thank you, and signed beo received.

All tasks are assigned to the staff in the sales and catering office. They are
to complete these tasks daily. Figure 12-1 illustrates page two of the
Morning Report for Kimberly A. Spiak. This page is concerned with
personal thank you notes and the signed beo. Once the task has been
completed, Kim will check off the task.

Organization is one of the keys for a banquet manager to be successful in
this business. Both of the above women have a system to help them do their
job. Without organization, their jobs would be impossible to accomplish.

Obtaining Information about the Function

Once the host has reserved a date, the banquet manager must schedule an
appointment to discuss all the particulars concerning the event. At this
meeting the banquet manager will listen, then suggest and guide the host to
make correct choices about the function. Included in the discussion will be
the physical setup of the room, planning the program and time schedule, and
selecting the food and beverage menu.

The banquet manager usually will offer suggestions to the host to make

```
DELPHI -- Morning Report for Kimberly A. Spiak - KS
2

PERSONAL THANK YOU............

Group Name                     (Account ID)   Arrival Date Trace Date Action
- - - - - - - - -              - - - - -      - - - - -    - - - -    - - - - - - - - - - - -
Quench Beverage                (Quench Bev)    7/ 5/88      7/ 9/88   __ Complete/New Trace: __/__/__
Scarlett County Farmers Assoc. (Scarlett Farm) 7/ 6/88     7/10/88   __ Complete/New Trace: __/__/__
APEX Savings and Loan          (APEX S & L)    7/ 7/88      7/11/88   __ Complete/New Trace: __/__/__
Red Rupert Insurance           (Rupert Ins)    7/ 7/88      7/11/88   __ Complete/New Trace: __/__/__
Professional Paints            (Prof Paint)    7/ 7/88      7/11/88   __ Complete/New Trace: __/__/__

SIGNED BEO RECEIVED?..........

Group Name                     (Account ID)   Arrival Date Trace Date Action
- - - - - - - - -              - - - - -      - - - - -    - - - -    - - - - - - - - - - - -
Glucose Associates             (Glucose)       7/ 5/88      7/ 9/88   __ Complete/New Trace: __/__/__
Wildnut Spring Corp.           (Wild Spring)   7/ 6/88      7/10/88   __ Complete/New Trace: __/__/__
Ardor, Beetle and Beason, Inc. (Ardor, Bee)    7/ 7/88      7/11/88   __ Complete/New Trace: __/__/__
Wearever Tires and Shocks      (Wearev Tires)  7/ 7/88      7/11/88   __ Complete/New Trace: __/__/__
People's Bank                  (People Bank)   7/ 7/88      7/11/88   __ Complete/New Trace: __/__/__
```

Figure 12–1. A morning report form for a banquet manager. This comes from a computer printout that she obtains daily. It assigns her tasks to complete concerning past and future functions.

the party a success. Often, a host has a general idea of what he or she desires for the function. But, most of the time, the host relies on the banquet manager to assist him or her in planning the function. It is the job and the responsibility of the banquet manager to help plan the event so it will be precisely what the host desires.

In order to do the job effectively, the banquet manager has to rely on the sense of hearing more than any of the other senses. The banquet manager must listen carefully to the host. The banquet manager's mind cannot be thinking of next week's party; all attention must be given to the host. By listening to the host, the banquet manager can offer suggestions to make the party a success.

The Policy Sheet

Each banquet facility must have a printed sheet that lists specific policies concerning banquets. This policy sheet must be given to the host at the initial planning meeting. Items on the sheet should include: the length of time a room would be reserved; the cost of extra service staff and bartenders; how long in advance a function room will be set up; and the policy on deposits, guarantees, and contracts. The list can be as short as one page or, for conferences, can be several pages. With a printed policy statement, most questions are answered. This alleviates misunderstanding between the host and the banquet manager. Figure 12-2 illustrates the first two policies of our banquet establishment.

The Function Sheet

When the banquet manager and host decide what is desired for the function, it must be placed on an organized written document. The purpose of this document is to have the banquet house give the host exactly what has been requested, when it is requested. Everything that the host and the banquet manager have agreed upon appears on this document.

This document has many different names, depending on the banquet establishment. For the purpose of this book, it is called the **function sheet.** It is sometimes named the banquet event order or banquet stencil. Regardless of the name, the purpose is to list in detailed form everything that the host desires for the event. Every banquet establishment must have a function sheet in order to successfully serve banquets. Figure 12-3 illustrates a standard function sheet.

Function sheets are generally broken down into three main areas. The top third is information that is obtained at the time of the booking. Only the banquet and sales office employees need this information. Part One begins at the top of the sheet and includes the information through the estimated number of guests.

Part Three, from price to the date, is also information primarily needed by

BANQUET & MEETING POLICY INFORMATION

Thank you for your interest in our facilities.
The following is an outline of our standard policies:

1. Rooms will be set one hour before an event is to begin. If the host desires to have the room set up earlier, they must pay the standard room rental fee for the time period.
2. One bartender is provided for every 50 guests. Additional bartenders may be requested at the current rate of pay.
3. The rest of the policies will be continued.

Figure 12–2. The policy sheet. All banquet facilities need a sheet that will list all the policies of the banquet establishment.

FUNCTION SHEET

Event Date _____ Payment Arrangement _____

_____

Organization _____ Business Phone _____

Address _____ Home Phone _____

_____

Person in Charge _____

Estimated Number _____ Guarantee _____ Set _____

Room _____ Time _____

Food   Program

Liquor

Price _____ Booked By _____

Guest Signature & Date _____

Figure 12–3. All banquet establishments need a form to transmit information from the person who booked the party to the rest of the staff. This is accomplished through the use of a standard function sheet.

the banquet office. This part can only be completed after the host and banquet manager have agreed upon all items desired for the event. The banquet manager completes this area by filling in the price, signing, and dating it. Then it is sent to the host to be signed.

The Part Two of the function sheet is the key to the success of the event; this is where all of the information about the event is recorded. In effect, this part of the function sheet becomes a work order for the event.

Read on as Mr. Lockwood books his daughter's wedding, and we fill in the function sheet.

Part One of the Function Sheet

Figure 12–4 illustrates Part One of the function sheet.

Notice that the date includes the day of the week. This will avoid any mix up by the staff. Many times, people get confused about what day of the week

FUNCTION SHEET

Event Date <u>Saturday, August 1</u>   Payment Arrangement <u>Cash</u>

Organization <u>Lockwood-Jones Wedding</u>   Business Phone <u>555-0978</u>

Address <u>7 Lark Ave</u>   Home Phone <u>555-0878</u>

<u>Cranston, RI</u>

Person in Charge <u>Jim Lockwood</u>

Estimated Number <u>200</u>

Figure 12–4. Part One of the function sheet. This part is concerned with information that is obtained at the time of the booking.

a date such as August 1 falls on. The banquet manager needs to put the day of the week on the function sheet to avoid any confusion.

Usually, there are so many departments involved with a large event such as the Lockwood wedding that everyone knows what day of the week August 1 falls on. However, mistakes are more likely to occur for small functions (groups of ten to twenty), because fewer employees are scheduled to work. A party of twenty may be served by the staff on duty rather than having a separate banquet staff.

Sorry, Chief!

W e once had a party that was scheduled for twenty guests. The function sheet was completed and distributed. At noon, the guests arrived for the luncheon; no food was prepared, nor was the room set up. Both the waiter and the cook misread the date on the function sheet, which said only July 1. Fortunately, it was the New York State Chiefs of Police Organization, regular guests of the hotel, who were most understanding of the problem. They conducted their meeting while we set up the room and prepared the food. But from that day on, the day of the week always went on function sheets.

The rest of Part One of the function sheet is straightforward information. The banquet manager should always obtain both the host's business and home phone in case a question occurs concerning the event. By having both phone numbers, the banquet manager can contact the host of the event with relative ease. Information in Part One should be filled in completely, and be verified to be correct.

Right a Wrong

A t one party, the host guaranteed one hundred people for breakfast for an organization whose goal was to legalize marijuana. Only twenty-five of the invited state legislators attended. At the end of the event, the head waiter gave the host the check for one hundred breakfasts. The guest signed it and was billed directly for the event. A few days later, the bill was returned with the words, "addressee unknown." A call was made to the one phone number listed in the function book and on the function sheet. It was the number of a pool hall in a large city. They had never heard of the guest. The phone number and the address were never checked. No money was ever received for the party. It ended up in the bad debt category.

The estimated number is the amount of guests that the host expects to attend the event. It is usually the number of people that will be invited. This number is almost always larger than the guaranteed number. For instance, at wedding receptions, the banquet manager can calculate that 20% of the invited guests (which is usually the estimated number) will refuse the invitation because of traveling distance or other commitments. Of course, sometimes the guarantee will exceed the estimate. But this number is always a general figure; the host is never responsible for paying for the estimated amount of guests.

Part Three of the Function Sheet

Figure 12-5 illustrates the last area of the function sheet. This area is completed after all the information about the event has been received from the host.

Notice that the price includes the gratuity and the sales tax. The price area should specify all the charges. Some banquet houses eliminate this section on the copy that goes to the staff.

The only thing left to be completed on the function sheet is for the host to read, sign, and date it. The function sheet is often used as a contract between the host and the banquet establishment.

FUNCTION SHEET

Price $35.00 + 20% grat and Sales tax Booked By AJS _____

Guest Signature & Date _____

Figure 12–5.   Part Three of the function sheet. This part is filled in after all the plans have been made for the party.

Part Two of the Function Sheet

This is the area of the function sheet that is of utmost importance to the employees. In reality, it is their work order. For example, it specifies exactly the time that all events are scheduled. The service staff can obtain the information needed to lay the place setting and cover from the function sheet; the chef knows how much food to order; the kitchen staff has an exact description of the food that must be cooked and served; and the bar knows what liquor the host has ordered and when to serve it. In short, everything about the function should be written on this sheet.

However, before Part Two can be completed, the banquet manager has to discuss and suggest different ideas to the host. Figure 12-6 is a blank Part Two of the function sheet. The following sections will illustrate the step-by-step process that the banquet manager will go through with the host in order to obtain all the information needed to fill in the sheet.

Purpose of the Function

The first thing that the banquet manager must determine about the function is the purpose. It will either be for a social or a business event. Once

PART TWO OF THE FUNCTION SHEET

Estimated Number 200 _____   Guarantee_____   Set _____

_____

Food   Program   Liquor

Figure 12–6.   Part Two of the function sheet. This part becomes the work order for the employees after the banquet manager determines the guests' needs.

the purpose is determined, the event can be planned. Keep in mind that most of the time the main purpose of an event is not to consume a gourmet meal. The food, even though it is an important part of the success of the event, becomes secondary to the purpose of the event. The banquet manager has to plan the meal to serve the guests quickly and efficiently so the host can begin the program.

When the host is having a social event, the purpose of the party is to honor someone or something. It could be celebrating a wedding or an anniversary. It may be a retirement party, or a company may have a banquet as a reward to honor its top sales producers.

Business meetings have many purposes. Some are held to introduce a new product. Others are held for the staff as a reward for a job well done. Other meetings serve as a sales meeting for the staff; while still others are actually used to sell a product to a potential customer.

Once the banquet manager determines the purpose of the event, the room and meal can be chosen.

Menu Planning

Choosing a meal is important for both the host and the banquet manager. A meal has to be chosen that can be served efficiently by the banquet establishment, taste good, and meet the needs of the guest.

For instance, one guest wanted his party served quickly. He stated that his guests had been up since 6 A.M. and they did not want to spend a lot of time over a meal. The banquet house suggested having the appetizer placed on the table before the guests arrived. It is standard practice to preset the appetizer. However, the guest wanted not only the appetizer but the salad and dessert on the table before the guests arrived. The only item that was served was the main course.

The banquet manager and host have to agree upon a meal that will meet the nutritional needs of the guests, as well as the financial needs of the host.

The meal should look appealing on the plate. A boneless breast of chicken, with a white sauce served on a bed of rice with mashed potatoes looks bland. It has no color, and having two starches (potatoes and rice) is not nutritionally sound.

Menu planning also takes into account whether the host desires a heavy or light meal for the guests. This is determined by the purpose of the event. A lunch, followed by a meeting, should be light, with a chicken or fish item. A dinner celebration may include hearty meats, wines, and even a decadent chocolate dessert buffet bar.

Other factors that determine the menu selection are the makeup of the guests who will be attending the event. For instance, at Italian weddings it is customary to serve a pasta course before the main course.

Once the menu has been set, the banquet manager and host can plan for the event.

Planning the Details of the Event

The main part of the function sheet is an open-ended area in which the banquet manager writes exactly what the host desires. All facets of the event must be included in this area: serving times for food and liquor; color of linen; complete detailed menu specifying everything that was promised to the host; liquor service; and special instructions. All this information must be included on Part Two of the function sheet. This is where the word **details** takes on utmost importance for the success of the event.

Details

Details are defined in *The Random House Dictionary* as "attention to a subject's individual or minute parts."[1] That is how the banquet manager should approach running every event. The guest wants the banquet manager to take care of all the little things (called details) that will make the party a success. Again, the premise of this section on banquet management is stated: the main job of the banquet manager is to **take the responsibility of the party off of the host's shoulders and put it on his or her own shoulders.** Doing this will make the event a success and result in repeat business for the banquet establishment.

Discussing the Details of the Party

The banquet manager needs to discuss every aspect regarding the event with the host. This is a must for obtaining all the information necessary for running the function. The banquet manager should always listen to what the host desires and then offer proper suggestions based upon the discussion. Once the host makes the decisions about the event, the function sheet can be completed.

Because no two functions are alike, the following text will include discussions concerning different options that the host can have at banquets.

Types of Meals

Banquet houses offer three types of meals. They are: the cocktail reception, serving drinks and finger foods; the sit-down served meal; and the buffet meal.

The cocktail reception is beneficial for the host who wants the guests to mingle with each other. There usually are a variety of food and drinks for the guests, located at set places (called stations) in the room or passed by the service staff (called butler service).

Many times a cocktail reception precedes a sit-down dinner. As a general rule, guests should have approximately five hors d'oeuvres to eat per person if the cocktail reception precedes a sit-down meal. If the cocktail reception is the only meal, the amount of food must be doubled. However, one fear almost all hosts have is that they will not have enough food to serve all of their guests. Therefore, the banquet manager should find out from the host the makeup of the group of people who will be attending the event. The banquet manager can then suggest the correct amount of food based upon the information provided by the host. For example, younger guests will eat more food than senior citizens.

The sit-down meal is the most popular type to be served at a banquet. At this type of banquet, all guests receive the same meal, chosen by the host of the party. Many times a host will ask if the banquet establishment can offer the guests a choice of more than one main course meal. This will depend strictly on the capability of the kitchen and the serving staff.

Because the purpose of a banquet is to serve the meal quickly, limiting the

Figure 12–7. Guests having a sit-down banquet meal at the Houston, Texas, Astrohall. This is the most common type of banquet function. (Photo courtesy of Hall Puckett)

number of choices is a wise idea for the banquet establishment. If the host insists that the guests have a choice of food, offer a choice only for the main course and limit it to two selections. The number of guests ordering each choice has to be given when the guarantee is called into the establishment. The host will be responsible for identifying which guest gets which entree choice. The easiest way to do this is by having different colored tickets (red for beef, yellow for chicken) for the host to distribute.

Also, it is a poor idea to have the service staff take guest orders on how food (such as steaks) is to be cooked at a banquet. Taking individual orders takes too much time for the service person and too much time for the cook. Imagine serving steak for two hundred guests!

If the host wants the guests to have many food choices, then the best meal selection is the buffet. Buffets offer guests an enormous choice of foods and a variety of serving options. The kitchen staff enjoys preparing buffets because they have an opportunity to present foods artistically.

Hosts have three service styles of buffets from which to choose. The first is referred to as the simple buffet style, where guests serve themselves. Service staff is only needed to clear dirty dishes. The guest obtains all food, drinks, and utensils.

The second, called the modified deluxe buffet, has waitstaff set up tables with utensils, clear each course, and serve guests beverages. The guests obtain all additional food.

The third, the deluxe buffet, combines excellent service with the opportunity for the guest to have a wide variety of foods. The guests are served their appetizer, salad, beverage, and dessert. They obtain their main course meal from the buffet.

A banquet manager can tailor a buffet type service to meet the needs of the host. The above three types of buffets are only a guideline to the style of services for buffets. The banquet manager can be creative and mix up the styles of service to create a new style to meet the needs of the host.

Once the host decides on the type of meal service desired for the guests, a menu may be chosen. Most banquet houses have preprinted menu selection choices. Figure 12-8 illustrates the dinner selection, while Figure 12-9 illustrates the buffet menu that the host may choose from. All banquet houses should have this type of menu to distribute for each meal period. Banquet houses usually have separate menus for each meal period, as well as a separate price list that includes the cost of all meals. Using a separate price list, the hotel only has to reprint one sheet of paper, rather than printing up an entire set of menus.

Once the host has decided on what type of meal to have, the next item to discuss is alcoholic beverage service.

Dinners

Special Preludes

Scrimshaw Salad

Chilled Romaine Lettuce Topped with
Sliced Mushrooms, Mandarin Oranges,
Sliced Almonds, Cheddar Cheese and
Our Creamy Scrimshaw Dressing

Tortellini 'N' Dill

Chilled Tortellini in a Dill
Cream and Laced with
Imported Prosciutto Ham

Shrimp Cocktail

Large Shrimp Served with Traditional
Cocktail Sauce

Baked Brie Almondine

Ripe French Brie Served En Croute
with Raspberry Glaze and Fruit Garnish

Shrimp Scampi

Gulf Shrimp Sauteed with Garlic Butter and White
Wine and Served on a Puff Paste Crouton

Fruit Sorbet

Choose from a Variety of Fruit Ices
as an Intermezzo Addition

Figure 12–8.   A preprinted dinner menu that is given to the host of the party for selection of food for a sit-down dinner banquet.

Dinner Appetizers

Fresh Fruit Cup

A Delightful Assortment of Fresh Seasonal
Fruits Topped with a Frosty Sherbet

Crab Bisque

A Delicate Creamy Soup Laced with Sherry

Scrimshaw Salad

Chilled Romaine Lettuce Topped with
Sliced Mushrooms, Mandarin Oranges,
Sliced Almonds, Cheddar Cheese and
Our Creamy Scrimshaw Dressing

Caesar Salad

Chilled Romaine Lettuce Tossed with
a Zesty Caesar Dressing

Consomme Celestine

Fine Beef Consomme Accompanied by
Julienne Slices of Crepes
and Laced with Sherry

Dinner Entrees

Your Entree will be Accompanied by a Fresh
Vegetable Selected by Our Chef. All Selections
Include Fresh Rolls, Brewed Coffees or
Tea. Please Choose One Appetizer and One
Dessert to Complement Your Entree Selection.

Breast of Chicken Normande

A Roasted Boneless Breast of Chicken with an
Herbed Apple Stuffing and Sauce Bercy.
Served with Roasted New Potatoes

California Pistachio Leg of Lamb

Roasted Leg of Lamb Stuffed with a
Pistachio Herb Dressing and
Served with Roasted New Potatoes

The Desmond
Albany, New York

Figure 12-8.   *(Continued)*

Prime Rib of Beef

The Finest Aged Rib of Beef, Slowly Roasted
with Crushed Herbs. Served with Creamed
Horseradish and a Baked Potato

Broiled Sirloin Steak

A Tender New York Sirloin, Topped with
Mushrooms Sauteed in Herb Butter. Served
with a Baked Potato

Roasted Sirloin of Beef

Sliced Loin, Served with Bordelaise Sauce and
a Golden Browned Potato Croquette

Filet Mignon

A Filet Broiled and Topped with a Mushroom
Cap and Sauce Perigourdine. Accompanied by
a Baked Potato

Stuffed Shrimp

Baked Jumbo Gulf Shrimp with a Seafood Dressing.
Accompanied by Saffron Rice

Roast Veal A la Creme

Roasted Medallions of Veal Served on a
Bed of Imported Pasta
with a Sauce of Tarragon, Cream and
Sweet Basil

Salmon On The Green

Poached Fresh Salmon on a Dill Sauce
Garnished with Julienne of Leek, Carrots and
Zucchini. Accompanied by Golden Browned
Potato Croquette

Chicken Pomeray

Breast of Chicken Sauteed with Mushrooms,
Heavy Cream and Pomery
Mustard. Served with Saffron Rice

Roasted Breast of Duck

Boneless Breast of Duckling
Slowly Roasted with Seasonings and
Served with a Raspberry-Orange Sauce.
Accompanied by Long Grain Wild Rice

Surf & Turf

The Traditional Combination of Broiled
Lobster Tail and Filet Mignon. Served with a Baked
Potato and Drawn Butter

Beef 'N' Shrimp

Sliced New York Sirloin Accompanied by Stuffed
Jumbo Shrimp. Served with a Golden Browned
Potato Croquette

Filet Of Sole Mediterranean

Baked Paupiette of Sole Filled with Mouseline
of Seafood and Served on
a Bed of Pasta Mediterranean

The Desmond
Albany, New York

Figure 12-8.   *(Continued)*

Dinner Desserts

Chocolate Mousse

Fluffy Chocolate Mousse Served in a
Chocolate Shell with Raspberry Sauce
and Fresh Whipped Cream

Praline Pecan Crepe

A Thin French Pancake Stuffed with
Pecan Ice Cream and
Served with Chocolate Sauce

Our Sinfully Rich Cheesecake

Topped with a Seasonal Fruit Selection

Mississippi Mud Pie—A
Desmond Specialty

Rich Mocha Ice Cream in a Chocolate Crumb
Shell Afloat in a Pool of Hot Fudge

Midnight Layer Cake

A Rich Creamy Chocolate-Covered
Chocolate Layer Cake

May We Offer the Following Desserts Flambéed
In Your Dining Room at an Additional Charge

Cherries Jubilee

Marinated Bing Cherries Simmered in Kirsch Wasser
Flambéed with Cognac and Served over Ice Cream

Strawberries Chambord Flambé

Fresh Berries Simmered in Chambord and Flambéed with
Cognac and Served over Ice Cream

The Desmond
Albany, New York

Figure 12-8.   *(Continued)*

Dinner Buffets

The Courtyard
(Minimum of 100 Guests)

Chef's Salad Bar

A Selection of Fresh Salad Greens
Accompanied by Julienne of Ham, Turkey,
Salami and Cheese,
Bacon Bits, Crumbled Bleu Cheese,
Chopped Egg
Croutons and Assorted Dressings

Almond Chicken Salad

Chilled Gulf Shrimp Salad

Chicken Stir-Fry

Seafood Pasta

Sauteed Shrimp, Scallops and Crabmeat
Served with a Lobster Sauce

Roast New York Sirloin Of Beef

Served with Bordelaise Sauce,
And Carved Buffetside

Roasted New Potatoes
Garden Vegetables
Fresh Rolls
Brewed Coffees and Tea

A Selection Of Pastries

The Patroon
(Minimum of 100 Guests)

Selection of Imported and Domestic Cheeses
An Array of Chilled Fresh Vegetables and
Assorted Dips

Salad Fare

Spinach Salad
Caesar Salad
Seafood Tortillini Salad

Chicken Tarragon

Served with a Mushroom Cream Sauce

Seafood Saint Jacques

Prime Rib of Beef

Carved Buffetside. Served with Creamed
Horseradish Sauce

Roasted New Potatoes
Selected Stir-Fried Vegetables
Rice Pilaf
Fresh Rolls and Butter
Brewed Coffees or Tea

Pastry Table

A Selection of Assorted Pastries and Sweets

Menu Builder

To Enhance Your Dinner Buffet, May We Suggest the Following at an Additional Charge

- *Ice Cream Sundae Buffet*

Vanilla and Chocolate Ice Cream with a Let-Yourself-Go Selection of Banana Nirvana, Hot Fudge,
Butterscotch, Marshmallow, Nuts, Cherries and Chocolate Sprinkles

- *Flambé*

Cherries Jubilee or Strawberries Chambord
Flambéed in your Dining Room

The Desmond
Albany, New York

Figure 12–9.   A preprinted dinner menu that is given to the host of the party for selection of
food for a sit-down dinner buffet.

Alcoholic Beverage Service

There are two basic styles of alcoholic beverage service that are used for functions. Guests can obtain their drinks from a host (often called open) bar, because the host pays for all drinks consumed. The other option is for the host to have the banquet establishment set up a cash bar. At the cash bar, the guests have to pay individually for each drink that they consume. Of course, there are some functions where it will not be appropriate or practical to have a bar in the function room; so none is set up. At those functions, guests who desire an alcoholic beverage will purchase one from the bar open to the general public if one is available.

Alcoholic Service Choices

The open or host bar have many different options for serving alcoholic beverages. Like the meal service, the banquet manager has to suggest the correct type of alcoholic service based upon the desires of the host. The banquet manager should be able to estimate how much liquor the guests will consume. This should be based upon previous experience with parties of similar groups. For instance, the average consumption at an event used to be two-and-a-half drinks per person per hour. However, this number goes down significantly after food has been consumed, because the guests are full. Another reason for lower alcohol consumption after a meal is the public's awareness concerning drinking and driving.

Because alcohol laws differ state by state, the banquet manager must check the liquor laws in the state where the banquet establishment is located. The choices of service listed below should only be used as a guideline. Each establishment must decide on its own policy of alcoholic beverage service based upon the laws of its state.

Alcohol Placed on the Guests Table

In this type of service, each table is provided with some type of alcoholic beverage. It may be pitchers of beer or bottles of wine. It could be two bottles of liquor with the appropriate mixers (called set-ups). The host is charged for the number of bottles that are placed on the tables. The guests serve themselves.

Open Bar

In this service, guests order a beverage at the bar and are served by a bartender. They may have whatever type of liquor the host has ordered. Generally, one bartender is needed for fifty guests at a cocktail party, and one for one hundred guests after the meal has been served.

With this type of service, the host may be charged in a variety of methods. The first is that the host pays for all bottles of liquor that are opened. Another way is that the host is charged for only the amount of liquor that is used. Another method is to use the public bar and charge the host for the number of drinks that have been consumed. The method that most hosts prefer is a per person charge. This way they know exactly how much money they will spend for the event. Another method involves the guests being provided with tickets which are good for a drink.

A La Carte Drinks

At some events, the host wants the service staff to take individual drink orders and serve them to the guests. This may be done at an additional cost to the host if the banquet manager has to employ more staff to take and serve drink orders. The main job of the banquet staff should be to serve the food for the banquet, not to serve drink orders.

Cash Bars

This arrangement may cost the host nothing. The guests purchase their own drinks. Cash bars bring in less revenue than open bars. Therefore, most banquet houses have a minimum amount of liquor sales that must be attained. If the guests do not meet this minimum, the cost of the bartender has to be paid by the host.

The banquet manager should attempt to convince the host to have an open bar, if at all possible. First, the open bar increases the profits of the establishment. But more importantly, an open bar contributes to making the event a success. An open bar does not mean that all guests get drunk; but it does mean that the host is hospitable. Guests attending a wedding reception or any banquet are more likely to be in a positive state of mind when they are provided with drinks than when they have to purchase their own. This goes back to Maslow's theory, the love and belonging stage. The host has invited the guest to the banquet. Guests should be treated as if they were guests at the host's home.

Once the bar service has been decided, all the other details concerning the event must be determined. Look at Figure 12-10, as the guarantee and set are filled in on the function sheet.

Guarantee and Set

The guarantee and set pertain to the number of guests that will attend the event. Both of these numbers are written onto the function sheet only after the guarantee from the host has been given to the banquet establishment.

PART TWO OF THE FUNCTION SHEET

Estimated Number 200 _____ Guarantee 198 _____ Set 198 _____

Food   **Program**   **Liquor**

Figure 12–10.   Part Two of the function sheet. This part is concerned with the set and guarantee for the banquet.

Guarantee

The guarantee is the minimum number of guests that the host must pay for, even if fewer guests attend the event. Most banquet establishments demand the guaranteed number of guests seventy-two business hours in advance of the event.

Most often this system works well. However, some establishments have found that hosts play a dangerous game by underestimating their guarantee. If they have 200 affirmative replies for the event, the host knows that the banquet facility will set up approximately 10% additional seats, so he or she only guarantees 180. This way, the host saves money if some guests do not attend. This creates a problem with seating arrangements (which is explained in the set information), because many times all 200 guests show up. Some establishments, to solve this problem, have allowed the guarantee to go 10% in either direction. Therefore, if the host guarantees 200, a minimum of 180 will be charged; but the room is set for 220. What do you think of this technique?

Set

Once the guarantee has been given, the banquet manager decides on how many extra seats to set in the banquet room. Oversetting generally ranges from 5% to 10% above the guarantee. As the party becomes larger, the percentage of extra seats must diminish; otherwise, a banquet manager such as Kim Sibson Williams would be setting up two hundred extra seats for her banquets at the Astrodome. Therefore, many establishments state on their policy sheet the maximum number of seats that will be overset.

The reason for oversetting is that more guests may attend the banquet than had been guaranteed. Another, more common, reason is that often guests are in groups of two or more, and they do not want to break up their group. Therefore, the banquet manager sets extra seats because it is easier to set them before the guests arrive. Banquets are staffed economically with service people. If a service person has to stop what he or she is doing and set up extra tables, chairs, and covers it detracts from the event and almost always makes the staff play a game of "catch up."

The only time the banquet room is not overset is when the host has seating arrangements. With seating arrangements every guest is assigned a seat.

Setting up the Time Schedule

Most hosts want their guests to eat promptly and their program to start immediately. The banquet manager must be firm in allowing the service staff enough time to serve and clean up the meal. For American banquet service, it usually takes between one-and-a-half to two hours from the time that the guests are seated until the dessert and extra items are removed. For instance, if the party starts at 7 P.M., speeches should be scheduled for 9 P.M.

One of the most challenging events to plan for is the wedding reception. There may be a receiving line, pictures, blessing, toast, first dance, cake cutting, and bouquet and garter ceremonies. A wedding reception meal generally takes three hours from the time the guests sit down. Time must be planned for extra alcoholic beverage service if there are cocktails before the meal.

Once the host has decided on all the details of the event, this information must be placed onto the function sheet. The information should appear on the function sheet exactly as has been discussed with the host. There should be no surprises. Look at the completed Part Two of the function sheet in Figure 12-11. This is a completed work order for the wedding that will take place in the SeVille Room from 7 P.M. to 11 P.M.

As you notice, the banquet manager has specified everything that the host desires on this function sheet. The reader can see exactly what time the cake is to be cut and what time each course is to be served. This function sheet is set up thoroughly. Even to the pink fan-folded napkins. Each function should have this type of function sheet. By doing this, mistakes will be kept to a minimum.

Confirming the Arrangements

Once the function sheet is completed, the banquet manager must send a copy of the function sheet to the host of the party. Along with the sheet, a

PART TWO OF THE FUNCTION SHEET

Room SeVille   Time 7 P.M. - 1 A.M.

Toast   7:00 P.M.
   NV Moet Chandon

Food   7:10 P.M.
   1/2 Pineapple filled with fresh fruit in season (preset on
     table)

   Tossed Garden Fresh Salad, Italian Dressing   7:25 P.M.

   Prime Ribs of Beef, au jus   7:40 P.M.
   Baked Stuffed Potatoes
   Fresh Green Beans with Fresh Onions
   1961 Chateau Lafite Rothschild served with the meal
   Homemade Rolls and Butter served as soon as the guests
     are seated
   Coffee, Tea and Decaffeinated Coffee served immediately
     after the Prime Ribs have been served
   Wedding Cake served with SuperFudge Ice Cream   8:45 P.M.

Liquor Service
   Open Bar from 8 P.M. to 1 A.M.
   Three bars, 4 bartenders. Bars will open at 8 P.M.
   Seagrams VO; Dewers White Label; Smirnoff Vodka; Peach Schnapps;
   Molson Golden; 1961 Chateau Yqueem available for after dinner wine.
   Fetzer Chardonnay & Chenin Blanc
   Iron Horse Cabernet Sauvignon (at least 10 years of age)

Program
   White tablecloths with pink napkins fan folded
   Head table skirted with candelabras and fern
   Seating arrangements
   Cocktails from 5:45 to 6:45 at Pool (see attached function sheet)
   7:00 P.M.—Announcement of Bride & Groom
   7:05 P.M.—Blessing by Father Fitzpatrick
   7:06 P.M.—Toast by best man
   7:10 P.M.—First Dance
   8:40 P.M.—Wedding Cake Ceremony
   Midnight—Bouquet & Garter

Band—Rhythm & Rain 877-3245 (obtained by the bride)
Cake—Chocolate with white frosting (we supply)

Figure 12–11.   The completed Part Two of the function sheet. This provides everyone with complete information of what will be occurring at the wedding.

cover letter must be included. Figure 12-12 is a sample cover letter that the banquet manager will send out to the host.

Scheduling Parties

Many banquet operations have more than one banquet room. Therefore, they may have more than one party occurring during a meal period. The banquet manager should not schedule two events to take place at the same time. Instead, try to stagger the times at fifteen minute intervals.

It would be great for the banquet manager to sell the hosts the same meal items. If it is impossible to sell them the same main course item, at least give them the same accompaniments. This is another way to improve relations with the kitchen, and also it will make the parties run smoother. Remember that the reasons American banquet style service is used are speed and profitability.

Distribution of the Function Sheet

The banquet establishment should set up a policy of when to distribute the function sheet to the department heads. This should be determined based on

Dear Mr. & Mrs. Lockwood,

We are pleased to enclose the function sheet for Jill's wedding that will be held in the SeVille Room on Saturday, August 1 of this year.

Please examine the function sheet carefully. If you are satisfied with the arrangements specified on the function sheet, please sign, date it, and return it in the enclosed stamped self-addressed envelope. If you desire to change any item, please call me at 555-6211.

Our staff is proud of the job we do for our wedding receptions. We are excited to be able to share in your family's special day. A few weeks before the wedding, I will call you to set up a meeting with Chef Brown, Head Waiter Larkin, and Bar Manager Verrigni to review all the details of the wedding.

August 1 will be an exciting day for Jill. I am looking forward to sharing in the happiness of the day!

Sincerely yours,

Mr. Toby
Banquet Manager

Figure 12–12.   A sample cover letter that is sent to the host with the function sheet.

the amount of time needed to order the food and schedule the staff. Many establishments find that two weeks in advance of a party is a good time to distribute the sheet. Each department should receive its own copy of the function sheet.

Meeting with the Staff

In order for functions to run smoothly, there should be weekly staff meetings for the purpose of discussing all events. All specifics about functions can be discussed. The banquet manager will be able to explain any special requests that hosts want for their event. Discussions can take place on any problems that occurred at previous functions.

Many establishments use this meeting to have a dress rehearsal of the meal for the upcoming event. After the food is prepared and eaten, the staff discusses any potential problems that may occur with the meal.

By conducting these weekly meetings, problems and misunderstandings are alleviated between the members of the staff.

Working with the Kitchen

The banquet manager must learn how to work effectively with the kitchen staff, and especially the chef. The secret is to treat them with respect and make them your allies.

In order to make the chef your ally, always ask the chef if it is possible to comply with a host's special request about a meal item before you promise it to the host. Include the chef in the planning for special menus for parties. Ask for and use the chef's knowledge in planning events. Most importantly, introduce the chef to the host of the party.

The kitchen staff should always be told when the food is excellent, as well as when there is a problem. One of the most effective methods of encouraging the cooks to prepare excellent food is to bring the host of the party into the kitchen immediately after the meal. The cooks will look forward to this positive feedback. As a result, meals will always be prepared superbly.

Communication and respect will make it easy to work with the kitchen. If the banquet manager does not have an excellent working relationship with the kitchen, major problems will occur with functions.

Checking Details

The banquet manager should check with the guest three or four days before the event. At this time, the guarantee must be obtained from the host. This is also the time that the banquet manager **must** verbally recheck every item step by step to make sure there will be no misunderstanding with the host. The banquet manager must do this even though the host has signed the function sheet; the host may not have read what he or she has signed.

If the host gives the banquet manager any changes, it must be communicated on all the function sheets. Whenever any written changes are made on the function sheet, they must be initialed, and the department head must be verbally told of the change.

Seating Arrangements

Many times the banquet manager is asked to help plan seating arrangements for the party. The following is a step by step procedure for planning seating arrangements.

1. The estimated number is received from the host. Give the host a tentative floor plan. The circled number is the number of guests to be seated at the table; the other number is the table number.
2. As the host receives positive responses, guests are placed in groups that correspond to the circled numbers.
3. The host assigns groups to tables.
4. After all guests have been assigned a table number, the host makes an alphabetized listing of the guests' names and table numbers.
5. The host makes out cards that read "Mr. Mars Jones you are seated at table 7." The host does all the planning and writing of the names.
6. The host brings the alphabetized cards and list to the banquet establishment on the day of the party.
7. On the day of the party, the staff puts table numbers on each table that correspond to the floor plan that the banquet manager has given the host.
8. On a table at the entrance to the banquet room, the cards are placed in alphabetical order. The guests find their names, read the cards, and proceed to the tables with the numbers that correspond to their cards.
9. The banquet manager should have the alphabetized list as a double check in case there is a problem with the cards.

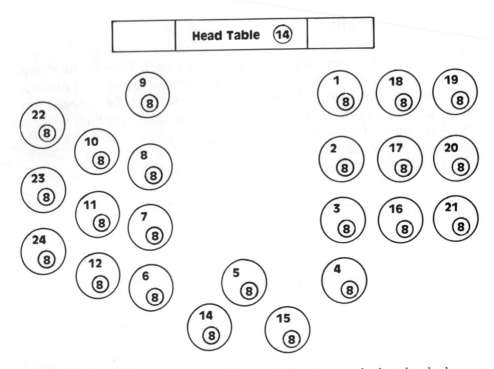

Figure 12–13. A tentative floor plan that would be given to the host by the banquet manager to set up seating arrangements for a party. The number in the circle represents the guests that can be accommodated at that table. The other number is the number of the table.

The banquet manager now has all the information necessary to run the event completed on the function sheet. In order to let all the staff in the establishment know what events are happening, the banquet office uses two other forms.

Weekly and Daily Function Sheet

Each week, a listing of all the events for that week should be distributed to all departments. In addition, an updated daily function sheet should be distributed. See Figure 12-14 for an example of a daily function sheet.

The weekly function sheet should be distributed on the same day every week. This lets all departments know what is going on at the banquet establishment.

DAILY FUNCTION SHEET

Saturday, July 9

KILROY MANNERS SKILLS WORKSHOP

POD/Joan Starker/KS/525

7AM	Regent Room	*ACCESS*, 3 6' registration tables, 3 chairs, 2 wastepaper basket, water/glasses, have 10-13 of their boxes under this table by 7AM
7AM	5, 7, 9 Madison Room	*ACCESS*, Classroom f/300

No ashtrays/no smoking signs
8×12 stage 10' away from wall
6' table on left side of stage
4' table on right side of stage
Steps center of stage
Barstool center stage
Water station in back of room in addition to water on each table
Light colored linen (if available)
Flipchart w/markers (at registration table)
8×8 screen (on stage)
Lavalier mic w/45 ft. cord

8:30AM	Regent Room	Registration begins
8:30AM-5PM	5, 7, 9 Madison Room	Meeting

BILOXI/KING RECEPTION

POD/Kevin Biloxi/KS/

12 Noon-1PM	Lancaster Gallery	Open bar f/75
		Hors d'oeuvres
1-5PM	24, 25 High Cafe	Dinner: set 75, GTD 71 (*SEE DIAGRAM*)

Headtable f/10 on risers
Predesignated seating
Placecard Table
Gift Table
Cake Table

Figure 12–14. A daily function sheet. Each day, a sheet is distributed to all departments informing them of what events are taking place in the banquet establishment.

JOHNSON/PEABODY RECEPTION
POD/Julea Johnson/KS/

1:30-2:30PM	Lancaster Gallery	Open bar f/58
		Hors d'oeuvres
2:30-6PM	6, 8 Lancaster	Dinner set 58, GTD 55 (*SEE DIAGRAM*)
		Headtable f/6 on risers
		Predesignated seating
		Placecard Table
		Gift Table
		Cake Table
		No ashtrays not even on request, send people into courtyard

Figure 12-14.   (*Continued*)

The daily function sheet is simply an update of the weekly function sheet. The guarantee is on this sheet.

Once all this information has been gathered, the banquet manager can proceed to run the party.

Chapter Summary

1. Organization is the key to a successful banquet.
2. The purpose of the function determines the planning of the menu.
3. There are three types of banquet function meals: cocktail reception, sit-down meal, and buffet meal.
4. Buffets can be simple buffet, modified deluxe buffet, or deluxe buffet.
5. Alcoholic beverage services are: alcohol placed on guests' tables, open bar, a la carte drinks, or cash bar.

Review Questions

1. Three days before the function, you contact the host for the guarantee. When checking the details of the event, you discover that the host has told the guests that they are going to receive sirloin steak for their main course. The signed function sheet clearly states that the meal will be top sirloin of beef. Because this is a retirement party of 150, and the guests have purchased their own tickets, you know a problem will develop. What would you do? Take into consideration the potential for repeat business in your answer.

2. Should Part Three of the function sheet be distributed to all employees? Or do you believe that Part Three would be better left off the function sheet? Explain your answer.
3. What problems would occur by having the service staff take individual cooking orders for guests at a banquet? For instance, the staff is told to ask the guests how they would want their filet mignons cooked: rare, medium, or well.
4. What is a banquet function sheet, and what is its purpose?
5. What important information should the banquet manager obtain from the host of the party? Why is that information important?
6. What does the term *details* mean as it pertains to the banquet business? Why is it an important term?
7. How would a banquet manager serve more than one main course entree to the guests at a banquet? Explain the steps that a banquet manager would have to take to achieve this goal.
8. What is the difference between a cash bar and an open bar?
9. Explain the different options of open bars that a host can choose for the guests at a banquet.
10. Explain how seating arrangements are set up. Give a step by step explanation.

Reference

Jess Stein, ed. in chief, *The Random House Dictionary* (New York: Ballantine Books, 1978), 248.

Chapter 13

Managing the Function

Chapter Objectives:

At the completion of this chapter, the reader will be able to:

1. diagram the setup of a place setting from information provided on the function sheet;
2. plan all equipment needed for the banquet service based upon information contained on the function sheet;
3. list the three styles of service for serving a sit-down banquet;
4. illustrate the quickest way to serve food from the kitchen to the banquet room;
5. explain the methods for keeping food hot when serving banquets which are a distance from the kitchen;
6. describe the proper sequence for setting up and serving a banquet room;
7. explain the methods for staffing and ending bar service correctly at a banquet;
8. explain the methods for controlling the amount of canapes and hors d'oeuvres at a party;
9. illustrate the proper method for setting up a buffet and controlling traffic flow; and
10. describe how to clean up a meeting room and how to provide the guests with water, paper, and pencils.

Preparing for the Function

As was stated in the preceding chapter, three days before the event is to be held the banquet manager obtains the guaranteed number of guests from the host. Now the banquet manager's most critical part of the job begins.

The banquet manager must plan and organize the minute details of the function to make it a success. The host has chosen the banquet establishment for the event. It is up to the banquet manager to *take the responsibility for the event off of the host's shoulders and put it on his or her own shoulders.* This is the banquet manager's opportunity to provide the host quality service. Quality service will be made up of many moments of truth that the banquet manager will control. If the banquet manager attends to the details of planning, organizing, and managing the function, the event will result in success.

In order to illustrate the importance of details that the banquet manager's job encompasses, we will use the function sheet from the Lockwood wedding, Figure 13-1.

The Function Sheet

The banquet manager must use the information on the function sheet to organize, plan, and manage the wedding. The function sheet has been distributed to the department heads. They have scheduled employees and obtained the food and beverage needed for the event. The banquet manager will make any last minute changes on the function sheet. These were obtained when the guarantee was obtained from the host.

Staffing the Wedding

The first job the banquet manager has to perform after the guarantee is received is to make certain there are the proper number of employees to serve the party. Not only should the banquet manager be concerned with the amount of service staff that is needed, but also with the bar and kitchen staff. The banquet manager is the one ultimately responsible for the service of the banquet. Having too few bartenders or kitchen staff results in slow service for the guests. Once again a reminder: American banquet service must be a fast service.

Service Staff Needed

The amount of staff that is scheduled by banquet establishments varies depending upon the number of guests at a table, the competency of the staff, and whether the staff is covered by union representation (in the case of union representation, the amount of staff required is clearly stated in the contract). Figure 13-2 can be used as a guideline for staffing service personnel and bartenders. Generally, one service person can serve between sixteen and twenty-four guests efficiently. Using this figure, one service person should be scheduled to serve two or three tables, depending on how many guests are seated at each table. For a buffet or cocktail party with butler service, one service person is needed for thirty-five guests. At a cocktail party, without butler service, one server is needed for every fifty guests.

FUNCTION SHEET

Event Date Saturday, August 1   Payment Arrangement Cash

Organization Lockwood-Jones Wedding   Business Phone 555-0978

Address 7 Lark Ave   Home Phone 555-0878

Cranston, RI

Person in Charge Jim Lockwood

Estimated Number 200   Guarantee 198   Set 198

Room Seville   Time 7 P.M.–1 A.M.

Toast
  NV Moet Chandon   7:00 P.M.

Food
  1/2 Pineapple filled with Fresh Fruit in season   Preset on Table
  Tossed Garden Fresh Salad, Italian Dressing   7:25 P.M.
  Prime Ribs of Beef, Au Jus   7:40 P.M.
  Baked Stuffed Potatoes
  Fresh Green Beans with Fresh Onions
  1961 Chateau Lafite Rothschild served with the meal
  Homemade Rolls and Butter served as soon as the guests are
    seated
  Coffee, Tea, and Decaffeinated Coffee served immediately
    after the Prime Ribs have been served
  Wedding Cake served with SuperFudge Ice Cream   8:45 P.M.

Liquor Service
  Open Bar from 8 P.M. to 1 A.M.
  Three bars, 4 bartenders   Bars will open at: 8 P.M.
  Fetzer Chardonnay & Chenin Blanc
  Iron Horse Cabernet Sauvigon (at least 10 years old)

Program
  White tablecloths with pink napkins fan-folded
  Head table skirted, candelabras and fern
  Seating arrangements
  Cocktails from 5:45 to 6:45 at Pool (on attached function
    sheet)
  7:00 P.M.—Introduction of Wedding Party
  7:05 P.M.—Blessing by Father Fitzpatrick
  7:06 P.M.—Toast by best man
  7:15 P.M.—First Dance after first course has been eaten
  8:40 P.M.—Wedding Cake Ceremony
  Midnight—Bouquet & Garter
Band—Misty Rain 555-3425 (obtained by the bride)
Cake—Chocolate with white frosting (from L & G Goodies, we
  obtain)
Price $50.00 +20% grat and Sales tax   Booked By AJS
Guest Signature & Date

Figure 13–1.   The function sheet for the Lockwood-Jones wedding reception. The banquet manager will use the information stated on the function sheet to make the wedding a success.

STAFFING TABLE

Position	Meal	Number of Employees
Service person	Lunch or Dinner	1 for 16-24 guests
Service person	Breakfast	1 for 24 guests
Service person	Buffet	1 for 35 guests
Service person	Butler Service	1 for 35 guests
Service person	Cocktail Reception	1 for 50 guests
Bartender	Cocktail Reception	1 for 50 guests
Bartender	Bar after Meal	1 for 100 guests

Figure 13–2. A staffing table to be used as a guideline for staffing banquets using American banquet service.

At the Lockwood wedding, ten service personnel should be scheduled. Each person will serve approximately twenty guests. Because the cocktail party is before the main meal, some of the same staff can be used to pass the food butler-style during the cocktail reception.

Bar Staff Needed

Normally, at a cocktail reception, either before dinner or by itself, one bartender is needed for every 50 guests; after dinner, one is needed for 100. This applies to both cash and open bars.

Often extra bartenders are needed only for the cocktail reception. As they are only needed for a short period, it becomes expensive to employ them for the entire night or for the minimum required by some state laws. One way to alleviate this problem is to have service people act as bartenders. Another method is to schedule bartenders from a previous party to work one or two hours overtime. For instance, if a bartender is scheduled to work from 10 A.M. to 6 P.M., have the bartender stay for two hours of overtime. During that period from 6 P.M. to 8 P.M., the bartender can set up the bar and serve the guests at the cocktail party. When the cocktail party is finished, the bartender is done working.

At the Lockwood wedding we have a special request to have four bartenders throughout the evening. Because most guests remain at their table when the meal is being served, we will use three bartenders for opening and serving wine during the meal. The other one will get the bar prepared for service after dinner.

Kitchen Staff

This is an area of the banquet that most banquet managers do not give proper consideration. At a banquet it becomes extremely important to serve the food as quickly as possible from the kitchen to the guests. In order to do this, the kitchen must be organized and the service planned.

There are two methods for serving that work well. Both methods need teamwork to serve the meal quickly, but only one skilled person is required to be at each serving station. The other employees put the food on the plate and have to be able to work quickly. Both systems work fastest when the meat has been sauced before being placed on the plate.

The first method, which was used at The DeWitt Clinton Hotel, is shown in Figure 13-3. This requires four people at each station to serve the food. Each person has a specific item to put on the plate. There are two piles of plates. Employee 2, the skilled employee, puts on the main course, while employees 3 and 4 put on the potato and vegetable. Very quickly, they develop a rhythm to avoid crashes. The plate never moves until employee 1 removes it and puts the sauce on the meat, if needed. The service person garnishes the plate, covers it, and takes it out of the kitchen.

The other method, just as effective, is shown in Figure 13-4. This method, used at the Hall of Springs in Saratoga, New York, is similar to the DeWitt

SERVING FOOD FROM THE KITCHEN AT A BANQUET

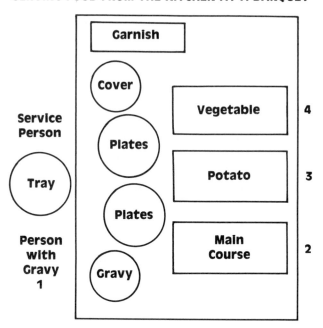

Figure 13–3.   The DeWitt Clinton method of serving a banquet. This requires four people at each station to serve the food. Each person has a specific item to put on the plate. There are two piles of plates. Employee 2, the skilled employee, puts on the main course, while employees 3 and 4 put on the potato and vegetable.

SERVING FOOD FROM THE KITCHEN

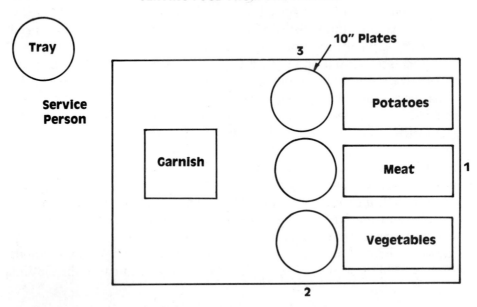

Figure 13–4. The Hall of Springs method of serving a banquet. Three piles of plates are set up on a rectangular table. Employee 1 puts the main course item on any one of the three piles of plates. Employees 2 and 3 put on the potato and vegetable. Both employees (2 with the left hand, 3 with the right hand) pull the plates from the pile when the dish is complete. They place them on the table, and a service person garnishes the plates, covers them, and brings them out into the dining room.

Clinton method. Three piles of plates are set up on a rectangular table. Employee 1 puts the main course item on plates from any one of the three piles. Employees 2 and 3 put on the potato and vegetable. Both employees (2 with the left hand, 3 with the right hand) pull the plates from the pile when the dish is complete. They place them on the table, and a service person garnishes the plates, covers them, and brings them out into the dining room.

For the Lockwood wedding, there must be two serving stations for the 198 guests. A few days before the wedding, the banquet manager confers with the chef to develop a plan to serve the function. This plan has the names of the employees who will be serving the food; for example, Anne puts on the potatoes; John the prime ribs, and so on. In a non-union establishment, the extra bartenders, service people, or even dishwashers may help with the plating of the meal.

Both systems described above are workable. The key is to plate the food quickly. Plates should only be handled by one person when the food is being plated. Never allow the plates to be passed in an assembly line fashion. That slows up the service. Using either system, it should take between eight and twelve minutes to serve the main course to the guests. The time should always be the same, regardless of the size of the party, as the number of serving stations are increased proportionately.

Once the staffing has been organized, the banquet manager can plan and obtain the equipment that is needed for the event.

Planning for the Equipment

Information required for the planning of equipment that is needed for the function is obtained directly from the function sheet. The banquet manager determines exactly what plates and utensils are needed to consume the meal. Using the Lockwood wedding function sheet, the banquet manager can plan the equipment that will be needed.

It is best to list the menu item along with the equipment that will be needed to eat the item.

ITEM	EQUIPMENT NEEDED
Toast	
NV Moet Chandon	Champagne Glass
Food	
1/2 Pineapple filled with Fresh Fruit in season (preset on table)	Spoon, 7″ Plate
Tossed Garden Fresh Salad, Italian Dressing	Fork, Salad Plate
Prime Ribs of Beef, au jus	Fork, Steak Knife, Dinner Plate
Baked Stuffed Potatoes	Served on Dinner Plate
Fresh Green Beans with Fresh Onions	Served on Dinner Plate
1961 Chateau Lafite Rothschild, served with the meal	Red Wine Glass
Homemade Rolls and Butter, served as soon as the guests are seated	Butter Knife, Bread and Butter Plate
Coffee, Tea, and Decaffinated Coffee, served immediately after the Prime Ribs have been served	Coffee Cup, Saucer, Coffee Spoon
Wedding Cake, served with SuperFudge Ice Cream	Spoon, Fork, 7″ Plate

From the above information, the banquet manager can now plan how much equipment is needed by multiplying the amount of each item by the set number (198) on the function sheet. For instance, 198 coffee cups and saucers are needed, while each guest requires 3 forks for a total of 594.

It is helpful to have a document such as the banquet checklist shown in Figure 13-5.

Using the banquet checklist, complete the planning of equipment for the Lockwood wedding.

Planning for the Needed Extra Equipment

In addition to figuring out how much equipment is needed for the guests, there are other items the banquet manager must make sure are available for the event. These are items such as salt and pepper shakers, butter dishes, sugars, roll baskets, and cream containers. Figure 13-6 represents a guideline for equipment that should be placed on the guest tables.

Having the correct amount of this equipment adds to the success of the event. The next time you attend a banquet notice how many sets of salt and pepper shakers are on the table. Most banquet houses provide one for a table of eight guests. Doesn't it make more sense to have one set for every two people? When the main course is served, the guests do not have to wait for the salt and pepper to be used by the other seven people at the table. While they are waiting to use the shakers, their food gets cold. Many will probably question the amount of shakers, but remember it is the job of the banquet house to make the guest have a pleasurable experience. Catering to that experience is having everything run so well that the guests never have to ask for any item. The guests should leave feeling great about the event, but without noticing how the banquet establishment accomplished it.

The same provisions should be made for the other items. All the items should be placed within easy reach of the guests. Try it yourself. Sit at a table like the one your guest will sit at and try to reach the items. This little experiment will give you a good idea of what your guests have to go through to obtain these items.

There should be one sugar and creamer for each four people. The rolls should be served hot, in a bread basket. The banquet manager should plan on having one and a half rolls for each guest.

In addition, the banquet manager has to order extra napkins for use as sidetowels and for use in the center of the banquet table. These napkins are usually a contrasting color from the tablecloth, but the same color as the

BANQUET CHECKLIST FORM

Tables

_____ 6 Foot

_____ 8 Foot

_____ 72" Round

_____ 60" Round

_____ 8 Foot by 1½ feet

Linen

_____ 72 × 72

_____ Napkins

_____ 81 × 81

_____ 120 × 48

_____ 84 × 48

Flatware

_____ Teaspoons

_____ Soupspoons

_____ Cocktail Forks

_____ Dinner Forks

_____ Bread & Butter Knives

_____ Dinner Forks

_____ Steak Knives

_____ Ice Tea

Plates

_____ Bread & Butter

_____ Dinner

_____ Saucers

_____ Soup Cups

_____ Monkey Dish

_____ Coffee Cups

_____ Roll Baskets

_____ Bread Board

_____ Ashtrays

_____ Sets of Salt and Pepper

_____ Sugar

_____ Cream Pitchers

_____ Salad Bowls

_____ Parfait

_____ Water

_____ Punch

_____ Water Pitchers

_____ Coffee Pots

_____ Tea Pots

_____ Ice Tea Glasses

_____ Table Number

_____ Candles

_____ Bud Vases

Figure 13–5.   A banquet checklist helps the banquet manager organize the amount of supplies needed for the banquet.

EQUIPMENT NEEDED FOR TABLE SERVICE

Item	Head	Round or Oblong
Whipped Butter	1 for 2	1 for 4 people
Butter Pats	2 pats on each Bread and Butter Dish	
Salt and Pepper Sets	1 set for every 2 people	
Sugar, Ashtrays	1 for 2	1 for 4
Cream	1 for 2	1 for 4
Amount of Cream	3 oz.	5 oz.
Roll Baskets	1 for 3	1 for 4

Figure 1/½ rolls per person. Rolls go on table with salad course. All sugar, cream, and butter are placed on underliners.

Linen

SIZE	FOR WHAT TABLE?
45 × 45	Deuces
54 × 54	4-tops
72 × 72	60 inch Rounds, Head, and Buffet
54 × 90	6 Foot By 3 Foot
54 × 108	8 Foot By 3 Foot

NOTE: Place a napkin in the center of the table, to place sugar, cream, etc. on. Only do this if the napkin is a different color from the tablecloth.

Figure 13–6.   A guideline for equipment to be placed on guests tables.

guest napkins. On the napkin will be placed the ashtrays, rolls, salt and pepper shakers, and other items that the guest needs to enjoy the meal. Another item that has to be ordered are extra bread and butter plates to be used as coffee shields.

Once all this equipment has been calculated, the banquet checklist will be completed. The equipment can be obtained before the service staff arrives by a dishwasher or banquet steward. It should be ready for the service staff to set up the tables when they arrive. Obviously, if some equipment is not available, the banquet manager will know before the party is ready to be set up and can make adjustments.

A Little Tip for Planning for Equipment

Many times it becomes impractical to have all the plates and utensils that are needed to serve the party. The banquet establishment simply may not have a sufficient inventory to have three forks for each guest. If a caterer is renting the equipment, the cost may be prohibitive to rent an additional two hundred forks.

The banquet manager has a couple of choices. First, the guests can use the same fork for the salad and main course. The service staff are instructed to leave the fork at the place setting when picking up the salad course. This is not proper service, but it is done.

The best method is to determine what items can be washed and used for another course. For example, at the Lockwood wedding, the plate that is used for the pineapple can be washed, dried, and used for the cake course. The guests would have no idea that they are eating off of the same plates that contained the pineapple. Can you discover any other multiple uses of equipment?

Organizing the Jobs for the Service Staff

When the service staff report to work, there should be a detailed work schedule for them. The banquet manager must plan these jobs **before** the employees report to work.

The banquet manager makes a job duty roster. It should be posted in the same location for each banquet. The service staff are usually scheduled to report to work two hours in advance of the function, or at a time determined by the banquet manager. Once the banquet manager masters this system, the amount of time needed to set up the function room is reduced. This is valuable if the establishment is paying the service staff by the hour. For instance, if a service person gets paid $5 per hour, eliminating one hour's work for ten staff members is a savings of $50. Over the course of a year, it would be a great savings.

When the service staff arrive to work, the roster will be posted on the wall. Figure 13-7 is the job duty roster for the Lockwood wedding. Notice that there are three columns. The first is the time by which the job must be completed; the second is who is responsible for doing the job; and the third is the specific job to be done. This duty roster should be completed for all banquets.

By having this duty roster, the banquet manager has an organized plan of

LOCKWOOD DUTY ROSTER

Time Completed By	Staff	Job
7 P.M.	All	Room completely set up
	All	Champagne poured (head table poured last)
6:50	All	Assignments given out
6:40	Pam, Jane Beth, Sue	Water poured at tables
	Jim, John Tom, Gerri	Pineapples preset at tables
6:20	Pam, Jane	Head Table skirted
	Beth, Sue Tom, Gerri	Tables checked, Fan Fold napkins, set up
	Jim, John	30 Butters on tables, 30 creamers in walk-in
6:00	Pam & Jane	Water glasses
	Beth, Sue	Wine glasses
	Tom, Gerri	Champagne glasses
	Jim, John	Salt & Peppers, Sugars on each table
	Steve, Sam	Cocktail Party room set up
5:45	Pam & Jane	Coffee cups & Saucers
	Beth, Sue	Bread & Butter Plates
	Tom	Dessert Fork
	Gerri	Dessert Spoon
	Jim & John	Bread & Butter Knives (follow Beth & Sue)
5:30	Steve, Sam	Chafing Dishes set up
	Pam & Jane	Knives
	Beth, Sue	Forks
	Tom, Gerri	Spoons
	Jim, John	Table Numbers & Napkins for center of table
	Jim, John	Table clothes on tables
5:15	All staff	Meeting concerning function
5:00		All staff report

Figure 13–7. A job duty roster for the Lockwood wedding. This form makes it easy for the staff and the banquet manager to have a successful banquet.

attack. If the banquet manager has to leave the room, the staff know exactly what they need to do to set up the room. Notice also that the banquet room is set up on a team system, using an assembly-line method.

The first item on the duty roster is a meeting. Any special instructions about the event can be explained at this time. For instance, Steve and Sam will be told that their primary responsibility before the main meal is to take care of the food at the cocktail party.

By using a duty roster, the banquet manager can easily make changes and correct the situation if there is a problem.

The First Job of the Day

When the banquet manager arrives at the establishment, the banquet room is the first thing checked to see that it has been physically set up. If it has not been, then it must be done. Yes, the banquet manager may have to move tables and chairs into their proper place.

Once it has been determined that the room has been set up properly, the banquet doors that the guests enter through are locked. This prevents guests from entering the room before it is set up.

 # One Great Tip for Wedding Receptions

According to Elsie Panza, whose family has operated banquet establishments on both the East and West Coasts of the United States, there is one piece of equipment a banquet manager should always have at hand to assist in the smooth operation of wedding receptions. It is a roll of scotch tape. She uses it all the time to tape loose envelopes onto gifts, so the bride and groom know who gave them what gift. It is a small detail, but that is the key to the banquet business. No bride or groom ever has to wonder, "Who did this gift come from?"

Planning the Place Setting and Cover

The banquet manager also plans the place setting and cover for the banquet. This information is also obtained from the notes the banquet manager made for the equipment that is needed. Figure 13-8 is the place setting for the Lockwood wedding. One setting is set on one table in the banquet room before the staff arrive. It is called the sample setting.

For the Lockwood wedding, the banquet manager has decided to use a variation of the Russian banquet setting. The dessert spoon and fork are placed above the starter plate. The coffee cup is already in place. All this is done to save time. If this were Russian banquet service, the coffee cup would be brought when the coffee was served. It would not be preset. In American Banquet Service, however, the coffee cup is preset. The napkin will be folded in the shape of a candle and placed in the red wine glass.

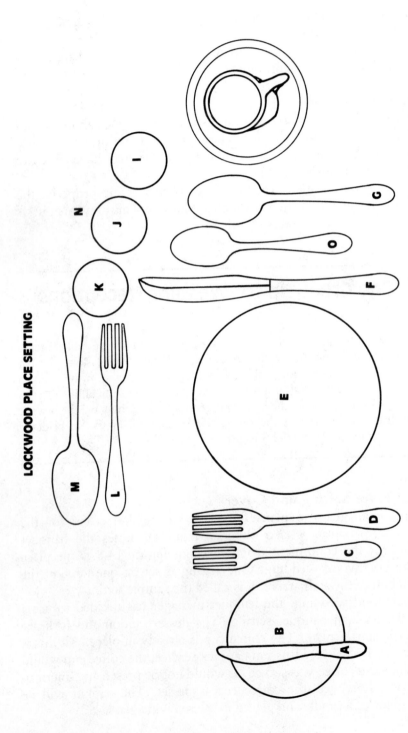

LOCKWOOD PLACE SETTING

Figure 13–8. A diagram of the place setting for the Lockwood wedding. This is a guide that the service staff will use when setting up the dining room. There will also be a sample place setting situated on one table to guide the service staff. This is the key for the Lockwood Cover: A, bread and butter knife; B, bread and butter plate; C, salad fork; D, main course fork; E, 7″ plate that the pineapple will be placed on; F, serrated steak knife; G, fruit spoon; H, saucer & coffee cup with handle at 5 o'clock; I, champagne glass; J, red wine glass; K, water glass; L, dessert fork; M, dessert spoon; N, napkin folded in candle fold, placed in wine glass; O, coffee spoon.

Setting up a sample place setting eliminates any questions the service staff may have.

Direction of Setting Up the Room

The proper way to set up a banquet room is to set the tables farthest from the kitchen first and work back toward the kitchen. If, for some reason, the tables are not completely set up when the guests arrive, the service staff do not have to carry items through the guests to the tables in the farthest part of the room. They can continue to work their way back toward the kitchen.

Serving the Party

Once the banquet manager has the event organized and the service staff are aware of their pre-party assignments, a decision will be made concerning the best method to serve the food to the guests.

There are three styles of service used in American banquet service to serve a party. The first is referred to as the *station method;* the second is the *follow-up method;* and the third is called the *combination method.*

The Station Method

In this method, each service person is assigned two tables of either eight or ten guests, for a total of between sixteen to twenty people. The service person is solely responsible for the service at those two tables. This system is best used when a large staff of temporary workers are hired to serve a large party. The advantage of this system is that the banquet manager knows who is responsible for service at all the tables.

This system has two main disadvantages. It is the slowest type of American banquet service. Also, guest tables usually will not be served in the proper order. For example, if Pam had tables 1 and 2, she would serve the guests at table 1 their food. Then she must return to the kitchen to obtain the food for table 2. It the meantime, the service person who has table 3 has already served that table. Table 3 is served before table 2, which is shown in Figure 13-9.

Another potential problem with using the station method is that service people will only set up their own tables. They will not assist in the setting up of the total banquet room. To avoid this problem, the banquet manager must not give out station assignments until the room is set up. Then the service people should be brought to the tables for which they are responsible, so there will be no mixup concerning which table should be served by whom.

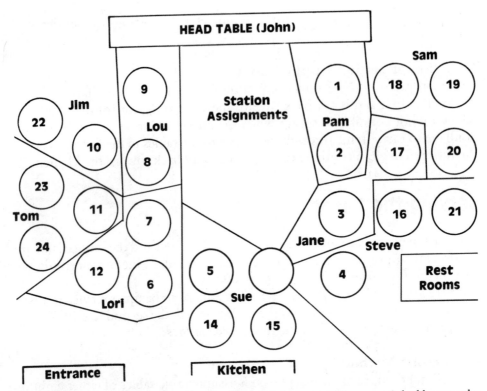

Figure 13–9. Service stations for an American style banquet. This system is bad because the tables are not served in order. Table 18 will be served before Pam can serve table 2.

The Follow-Up Method

This is the most efficient method and quickest service if the staff can master the system. It takes planning, cooperation, and leadership by the banquet manager, the head service people, and the remaining service staff.

For the Lockwood wedding, the staff would be broken up into two teams of five. The responsibility of serving the food and removing the dirty dishes in the banquet room would be divided in half, as shown in Figure 13-10. Each group would have a head service person to supervise its side of the room. Three members of the team would carry the food into the banquet room. The other two (including the head service person) would serve the food to the guests. The head service person would instruct the other service person in the correct order of service. Each team would obtain its food from an assigned plating area in the kitchen.

When it is time to clear the dirty dishes, all five members of the team work together in removing the dishes. They work from the head table backwards

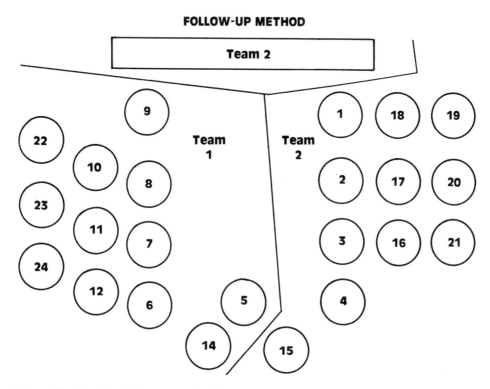

Figure 13–10. The follow-up method for serving a banquet. The most efficient method and quickest service. The tables served first are closest to the head table.

toward the kitchen doors. The banquet manager should be in the banquet room making sure that the all guests get served and that the service is done correctly.

The advantages of this type of service are that it is fast and that all the guests are served in proper order. This is considered the best serving system from the kitchen's point of view, because the food is picked up quickly from the kitchen.

The main disadvantage is that it is difficult to teach temporary workers to use this system. They generally lack the organization and teamwork that is needed.

The Combination Method

This system combines the best features of the follow-up and station methods. Serving the food is done by the team system. However, clearing dirty dishes and serving beverages is the responsibility of a service person who is assigned a station.

The advantage of this system is that it can be used with either permanent or temporary service staff. The only key people that must be employed are head service people. Another advantage is that tables are served in the proper order. Finally, confusion on the part of the service staff (Did we clear the dishes from table 14?) is eliminated.

The only disadvantage is that it is a slower system than the follow-up method.

The banquet manager should decide which of the above systems to use based on the capabilities of the staff and the organizational qualities of the manager. In addition to the above-mentioned styles of services, there are other variations of the three styles that banquet establishments use. For example, a variation of the station method is to have two service staff be responsible for four tables, but have them work as a team. One would carry the food from the kitchen, while the other would serve the food. Regardless of the system the banquet manager decides to use, the main determination in choosing one over the other must be guest satisfaction.

Whichever method is used, the banquet manager must be in the dining room at all times when the food is being served and the dirty dishes are being cleared. It is the manager's job to correct mistakes and oversee service.

Proper Order of Serving the Party

The banquet manager has to know the correct order in which to serve the guests at a banquet. The head table is always the first table served. Next served are the tables in front of the head table. The service of the rest of the dining room would follow in a logical manner, going from the head table to the back of the room.

Figure 13-11 illustrates the floor plan for the Lockwood wedding. This is the way the guests should be served. The head table is served first, then the order is tables 1 and 9, 2 and 8, 3 and 7, 5, 6, 4, 18, 10, 17, 11, 16, 12, 19, 22, 20, 23, 21, 24, 14, and 15.

Often guests farthest from the head table receive their food before the guests nearest the head table at a banquet. This should never happen.

The banquet manager has to inform the service staff of the proper serving order. This information may be put on the duty roster; however, it works better when the banquet manager verbally communicates the correct order to the key staff.

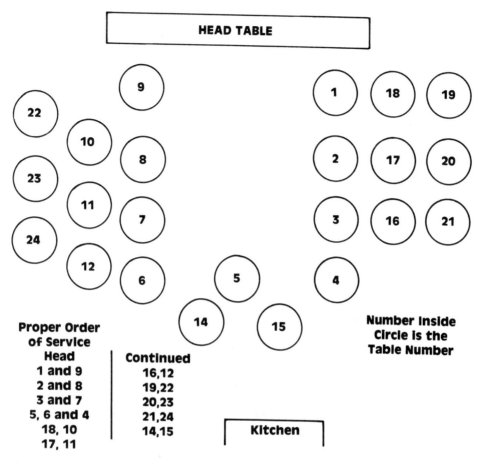

Figure 13–11. The proper sequence to serve the Lockwood wedding. The head table is served first, then the order is tables 1 and 9; 2 and 8; 3 and 7; 5, 6, 4, 18, 10, 17, 11, 16, 12, 19, 22, 20, 23, 21, 24, 14, and 15 last.

Serving Cocktail Parties

Many times the guest obtains the first impression of service at the banquet establishment during the cocktail reception or party. For this reason, both liquor and food service must be accomplished professionally and with dignity.

The bar manager is responsible for the performance of the bartenders, as the chef is for the cooks. A duty roster sheet, which the bar manager completes, should also be provided for the bar staff.

When the host arrives, the banquet manager should introduce the host to the bar manager. It is also an excellent idea to introduce the host to the bartenders. This is done to eliminate potential problems during the reception. For instance, if a guest desires a brand of liquor or drink different from those that have been ordered, the bartenders know who has the authority to approve changes.

The food being served at the cocktail party should be ample to provide the guests with appetizers before the meal, but not so abundant as to spoil their appetite for the main meal. It should be presented attractively.

When the host requests service staff to pass hors d'oeuvres and drinks, it is called *butler style*. The staff passes the food carried on trays. They will have with them cocktail napkins, which are offered to the guests when an hors d'oeuvre is taken. The staff have to be knowledgeable of all items on their trays and be able to explain these items to the guests. Throughout the cocktail party, the staff are circulating throughout the room picking up dirty glasses and plates, changing ashtrays, and replenishing the food.

Tips about Cocktail Parties

Always position bars away from entrances to the room and away from food tables.

Plan on staggering the service of hors d'oeuvres. For example, at a cocktail hour, do not serve them all within the first fifteen minutes of the event. Plan to serve one batch at approximately fifteen minutes after the start of the party; another batch should be held back until there are twenty minutes left in the cocktail hour.

The more food that is put out during the cocktail hour, the more food the guests will eat. Guests very seldom will take the last hors d'oeuvre. Instead they will wait until more food is brought out. Therefore, if you have to make food last, don't be too quick to bring out more food.

Plan on about five pieces of food per person at a cocktail party before a meal. Supplement the food with a bread and cheese table.

Tip Cups

One repeatedly controversial issue is tip cups for bartenders. Tip cups are placed on the bars to allow the guests to give extra money (to insure prompt service) to the bartenders.

Ending the Cocktail Reception

The banquet manager needs to have a method to end the cocktail party. It must be done without offending the guests or the host. This involves tact and diplomacy.

About ten minutes before the cocktail party is scheduled to end, the banquet manager locates the host and informs him or her of the exact time that the cocktail party will end. If a dinner follows the reception, it is critical that the party be ended on time; otherwise the food may be ruined. If no other meal is planned, the host can either end the party or extend it, depending on the policies of the establishment (which were set forth in the policy sheet).

If a meal follows the reception, the banquet manager would then circulate around the room informing the guests that dinner will be served shortly. The guests are asked to proceed to the dining room. Often this information is conveyed by making an announcement via a microphone.

Once the host agrees to end the party, the bars have to be shut down quickly. This is a critical moment in a party. The best way of closing bars is to have a prearranged sign with the bartenders. When the sign is given, the bartenders should finish serving the drink they are serving, inform the guests that the bar is closed, and walk away from the bar.

Running the Banquet Party

When the doors to the banquet room are unlocked, the room has to be completely set to receive guests. All food that is supposed to be preset should be in place, and the service staff should be ready to serve the party.

The main responsibility of the banquet manager now is to get all the guests seated and the meal served. If the host has arranged seating for the guests, everyone will have a seat and the meal can commence. However, if there are no seating arrangements, the banquet manager is responsible to see that every guest has a seat. This may involve breaking up groups of four or six people and having them sit with guests they do not know.

There is a way to avoid having this problem occur again. When the party does not have seating arrangements, select the table that is in the worst location (farthest from the head table, next to the kitchen) and place a reserved sign on it. That way no guests will sit at that table. The establishment should most likely have the extra table because the banquet establishment usually oversets by 10%. Guests coming in early will generally fill up all the other seats. When the latecomers arrive, there is a table left for them. If they don't show up, there is one less table to serve. It works all the time!

Serving and Clearing the Meal

Once all the guests have been seated and the introductions, blessings, or toasts have been given, the service staff can serve the meal.

It becomes the responsibility of the banquet manager to inform the service staff, as well as the kitchen staff, when to serve the meal. No one should serve any food, beverages, or rolls without being told by the banquet manager.

The same is true of clearing the dirty dishes. No service person should clear any dirty dishes without authorization from the banquet manager.

The objective in having the banquet manager tell the service staff when to serve and clear is to ensure that all the guests are served approximately at the same time.

Giving the Number to the Chef

One of the ways the banquet manager ensures a good working relationship with the kitchen is to keep the chef informed about the progress of the party. In order to have a successful banquet, the banquet manager and head service people should count the number of guests that are seated. Once the number of guests has been verified, the banquet manager should give that number to the chef. If there are more or less than the chef planned, adjustments can be made at that time. When late guests arrive, the chef should be informed immediately.

Obtaining Guest Orders for Two Main Course Choices

To facilitate the serving of two main course items to the guests, the banquet manager requests the guests to place their colored tickets at their place setting. The service people collect the tickets and record which and how many guests are having each item.

When the service people go into the kitchen to pick up the meals, they obtain the correct number of each item for each table. When a follow-up system is used, this requires much more organization from the staff. Again a reminder: All guests at the table should be served at approximately the same time. A banquet house should not serve all the chicken meals and then serve all the beef meals; but each table should receive the correct number of beef and chicken meals.

Controlling the Function

Some hosts will only pay their bill based upon the number of meal tickets that are collected. Under these conditions, the banquet manager should have a person in the kitchen collecting tickets from the service people. For example, when the service person picks up ten meals, that person should give ten tickets to the collector. At a buffet, a service person is stationed at the beginning of the buffet line to collect tickets.

The service persons should be taught that if a guest does not have a ticket, the banquet manager is to be summoned immediately. The banquet manager then checks with the host of the party to determine if the person is really a guest or a crasher of the party (which happens often at conventions and weddings).

As soon as the meal has been served, the banquet manager informs the host of the number of guests that the banquet house has served. If there is a discrepancy, the host and the banquet manager can count the number of guests and solve the problem.

Buffets

When the host chooses the option of having a buffet, the banquet manager is responsible for having the buffet set up and ready for the guests at the scheduled time.

All buffets have a few basic principles. It goes without saying that all hot food must be served hot and all cold food must be served cold. Buffet lines are arranged so guests will not have to stand in a long line waiting for food. The buffet has to look neat and the food must be appetizing.

Figure 13–12.   An attractive-looking buffet in the courtyard area at a hotel. (Photo courtesy of The Desmond Americana)

Use of Buffets

As you have read, buffets are great for hosts who want their guests to have a choice of meal items. Buffets are also great for serving a meal in a room that is located a distance from the kitchen. For instance, using a buffet at a pool is an ideal way to increase the use of the area around the pool, and in turn the revenue of an establishment.

Buffets are a lifesaver when the establishment has a limited amount of function rooms. As an example, a group would like to have an all-day meeting with lunch. The banquet house has only one room that will accommodate the guests. The solution is to have the meeting set up using tables. The host and banquet manager schedule a 30- to 45-minute break before lunch is served. By using a buffet, the establishment can serve the guests lunch. The service persons will not have to set up the guests' tables, as they would at a sit-down meal, as the guests pick up all their utensils and food from the buffet. Again, this is another event that takes much organization by the banquet manager to make it a success.

Organization of the Buffet

If at all possible it is best to have separate islands for the different parts of the meal. There can be a separate table for beverages, one for appetizers and salads, one for main courses, and another for dessert.

One buffet line is needed to serve every 100 guests. The establishment can use ice carvings to keep food cold and chafing dishes or heating units to keep food warm. Food can be displayed on mirrors, in ice carvings, or in edible bread items.

All condiments are to be placed in front of or next to the food they accompany. For example, next to the ham would be mustard. It is recommended that the condiments be placed in monkey dishes (small cup-like dishes), which should have underliners beneath them. The proper utensil to obtain the condiments will be available, which should be placed on the underliner.

The Setup of the Buffet

Figures 13-13 and 13-14 illustrate the setup of a buffet. The first item at the beginning of the buffet line should be clean plates. The banquet manager instructs the service people to check not only the top of the plates but the bottoms also for cleanliness.

The buffet is usually arranged in the same manner as a meal would be served. Appetizers are placed first on the buffet line, followed by salads. Then the main course items, along with the starches and vegetables.

BUFFET SETUP

Guests obtain their food   this direction

PLATES	APPETIZERS	SALADS	Main Course Items	STARCHES	VEGETABLES	ROLLS & BUTTER	SILVERWARE	BEVERAGES

Figure 13–13. The buffet is usually arranged in the same manner as a meal would be served. Appetizers are placed first on the buffet line, followed by salads. Then the main course items, along with the starches and vegetables.

The rolls, butter, utensils, and beverages generally are the last items on the buffet line. Ideally, they should be on a separate table. By placing them at the end of the buffet line, it becomes easier for the guests to select the food and carry their plates without having to balance their utensils with their food. Of course, if the banquet establishment wants the guests to take less of the main course items, they will position the rolls and butter, along with the utensils, immediately after the plates.

Service Staff Jobs at a Buffet

The amount of service assistance is limited by the service staff at a buffet. As you have read, the amount of service depends on the style of buffet that is chosen by the host of the party. However, there are some jobs that have to be performed at a buffet that are not performed at a sit-down meal.

Service persons will be positioned behind the buffet line to assist the guests with their food, as they are in Figure 13-15. The service persons will portion out the food for the guests. They will also answer questions about the food, clean up any food spills, and replenish the food. Their job is to keep the buffet line looking neat and clean, and the food appetizing.

One of the problems the banquet manager wants to avoid is having the guests wait for food. Service persons are instructed to replenish food when

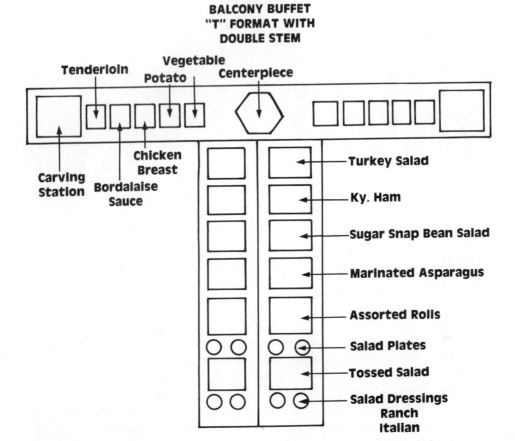

**TURF CLUB
BALCONY BUFFET
"T" FORMAT WITH
DOUBLE STEM**

Figure 13–14. A planned buffet setup using a "T" format with a double stem. The chef has planned where each item on the buffet table will be placed.

there is between one-third and one-fourth remaining on the tray or in the pan. The banquet manager assigns an employee to act as a runner. It is the job of the runner to obtain food from the kitchen and bring it back to the buffet line when told to do so by the service person. More food is obtained from the kitchen in a clean tray or pan called an *insert*. The runner brings the new tray to the buffet line. The old tray is removed and replaced by the fresh tray of food; the food is not transferred from one tray to another. The remaining food is brought back into the kitchen. There the tray is replenished and garnished to be used again.

Figure 13–15.   The service staff behind the buffet line. Their job is to portion out food, answer questions, clean up any spills, and replenish food. (Photo courtesy of The Desmond Americana)

Some establishments place signs near the food, which explain the item. This is recommended; however, it is more effective to have knowledgeable service staff explaining the food items. If the signs have only the name of the item, it may necessitate that the guests ask questions about the food.

Controlling the Traffic Flow

Another problem that has to be avoided is having all the guests rush up to the buffet table at once to obtain their food. The banquet manager has the responsibility of having the guests proceed to the buffet table in an organized fashion. This is how it is done.

When it is time to serve, the banquet manager announces that the guests may proceed to the buffet when their table is called. Informing the guests that they will be called to the buffet alleviates their fears about the establishment running out of food, even if they are the last table to be called. This system allows for a more controlled and civilized manner of serving a buffet.

The first person who has the honor to see and choose the food at the buffet is the host. The banquet manager invites the host's table up to preview the buffet before anyone takes food. After the host's table guests take their food, the banquet manager invites other tables up to obtain their food from the buffet. To keep everyone calm, the banquet manager circulates among the guests telling them when it will be their turn. The next table is invited to proceed to the buffet when there are three or four people waiting in line to obtain their plates. Using this method eliminates many problems that are associated with buffets.

If during the preplanning for the event the host informs you that the buffet must be served quickly, more buffet lines should be set up.

Chafing Dishes

Chafing dishes are used to keep food hot on a buffet. All employees need to know how they work and how to set them up.

The chafing dish consists of a frame, two pans, and a top. The top pan fits into the bottom pan, leaving two to three inches of space between the two pans. The bottom pan should be filled with about an one inch of **hot** water.

Underneath the bottom pan, there are one or two containers that hold a can of jellied liquid that will burn for about an hour. This is referred to as canned heat. Sometimes, through careless handling and misuse, the container that holds the canned heat is lost. To solve the problem, an inverted bread and butter dish can be used as a substitute for the container. One problem to avoid is that of placing the canned heat too close to the bottom of the pan. When that occurs the flame from the canned heat will be smothered and it will go out, resulting in cold food.

Approximately ten minutes before the function starts, the service person should light the canned heat. The flame will heat up the water. When the water is heated, the top pan of food may be put into the chafing dish. Use the top to cover the dish. The chafing dish will act like a steam table. The heated water creates steam; the top pan does not let the steam out of the chafing dish, and the food stays hot. During the buffet, the service staff checks to make sure that the canned heat does not go out. If it does, it is replaced with another can of heat. The service staff have to be careful to avoid being burned when taking off the covers or replacing a pan of food in the chafing dish.

Final Tips on Buffet Setups

The buffet should look as appetizing as possible. Many times even though the food is spectacular, the buffet looks boring. This is because the food is not displayed with any imagination.

Platters of food can be raised by using an inverted bread dish. Additionally, height may be created on the buffet table by using crates or boxes covered with linen. Flowers or food items are placed on these covered crates. Dishes with pedestals also add interest and height to a table.

Finally, stand back and look at the buffet. Then make adjustments to the items on the buffet table. These adjustments should be made based on the texture of the dishes, the color of the food, and the position of the items. The banquet manager may position an item away from its normal place to make the buffet more appealing.

Keeping Food Hot

Besides using chafing dishes to keep food hot on a buffet, the banquet manager must know how to serve food hot at a sit-down meal. When the banquet manager has to serve a banquet in a room that is adjacent to the kitchen, a detailed plan (as you read about earlier in this chapter) has to be set up with the chef. In addition, all plates should be heated before the food is placed on them. Some establishments have special heating cabinets, others put the plates in the oven. If hot food is placed on a cold plate, it will get cold.

When the banquet is served at a room distant from the kitchen, the food is generally transported in hot carts. Some are electrically heated while others use a form of canned heat to keep the food warm. Again, the key to keeping food hot is to preheat the cart. Once the food arrives at the location, a cook assists in taking the food out of the carts. This cook is responsible for the appearance and quality of the plates. Often, if the menu item requires a sauce, the cook puts it on at this area, which is called the staging area.

Timing is critical in making sure the food is available to be served to the guests when it is scheduled. If the party is to be served at noon, the banquet manager has to plan how long it will take to plate the food in the kitchen, transport it, and serve it, so the guests will obtain their meal at noon.

Now that the reader knows about buffets and how to keep food hot, let us get back to serving the Lockwood wedding.

The Sequence of Service for a Sit-Down Meal

Using the Lockwood wedding as a guide, the sequence of service will be explained. The first three steps contain a reminder of proper service using American banquet service.

1. The appetizer course is served (from the guests's left side by the service person using his or her left hand). It may be set as a part of guest's place setting (as was the pineapple).

2. Two roll baskets are served. They are placed in the center of table by the service person (using the left hand). The rolls should be put in a location that is easy for all the guests to reach. (A small tip: rolls and coffee are a lifesaver when the food is not ready to be served on time. Have the service person serve them to the guests and keep replenishing them. It gives the guests something to eat and drink, but more important it appears to them that everything is under control. If the guests were not being served some item, they would be wondering when the food will be arriving.)
3. The plate, spoon, and pineapple are removed by the service person (using the right hand, from the guest's right side).
4. The salad is served. At times, the salad can be preset on the table. It should be placed to the left of the salad fork.
5. The salad plate and fork are removed. The champagne glass should also be removed. If the guests have not finished their champagne or salad, instruct the service person to ask if they may be taken away. If the answer is negative, the service person should move the salad out of the center of the place setting and put it to the left of the guest's setting. The service person should also check to see if water glasses and roll baskets need refilling. If they do, the service person should take the roll baskets back to the kitchen and bring them out with the next course. If he or she has time, the service person can refill the water glasses from water pitchers. Ashtrays should be changed, if needed. (Water pitchers, ashtrays, extra utensils, and napkins should be set up at strategically located service stations in advance of the banquet, so service staff do not have to waste time obtaining these items.)
6. The main course is served. Meat is positioned in front of guests so the first cut made by the guest is into the most tender part of the meal. (Remember: serve all the guests at one table, before serving another table. If the banquet establishment is using a station service setup and the service person cannot carry out ten dinners on the tray, have another service person carry out the remaining dinners so all the guests at the table are served at approximately the same time.)
7. Red wine should be poured by the bartenders. When the service person places a prime rib meal, the bartender should follow by pouring red wine to the guest.
8. The coffee course is served. The service person must use a coffee shield. Tea should be placed in an individual pot above the coffee cup. A wedge of lemon should be served with the tea. At times, the banquet manager can have the service staff put a whole pot of coffee on each table. The guests can pour the beverage themselves. This method is used especially for breakfast meals or when the host is on a limited time schedule.

9. The main course dishes are removed, along with utensils, red wine glasses, bread and butter plates, salt and pepper shakers, and rolls and butter. The only items left on the table are the utensils for dessert, cream, sugar, water glasses, and ashtrays.
10. Dessert is served, along with more coffee.
11. Dessert dishes, water glasses, utensils, and all items with which the guests have finished are removed. The banquet manager should also have an organized system for putting away items when they are returned to the kitchen. For example, the salt and pepper shakers should always be placed in the same location when they are cleared from the tables.

The banquet manager must be flexible when serving a meal. There are many parts to the meal. Some things may happen that the banquet manager has no control over. The ability to be flexible and to think quickly enough to use whatever items are necessary to keep the guests pleased are critical for the banquet manager. The above is simply a suggested serving sequence. There may have to be adjustments made in the sequence to satisfy the needs of the guests.

The Problem with Latecomers and Early-leavers

At many parties, guests will arrive after a few courses have been served. When this occurs, the banquet manager approaches the table and asks the guests if they would like to eat. If the answer is affirmative, the guests are served as quickly as possible whatever courses they desire. It may involve bringing out the pineapple course and salad course together.

You may also experience the guest who must leave in a hurry, before the meal will be served completely. Try to accommodate this type of guest also. This can be done by serving the guest the main course before or while other guests are eating their salad.

Both of these types of guests create a problem for the banquet manager. Using tact and diplomacy, the banquet manager can please the host and the guest by accommodating these individuals.

Banquet Checkbacks

To be a truly effective banquet manager, it is imperative to check the satisfaction of all the guest tables after the main course has been served to see if the meal and service were satisfactory.

An experienced banquet manager will know if the food has been satisfactory by observing the guests' plates. This is the ubiquitous quality needed by the banquet manager. The type of inquiry the banquet manager will make will be determined by the situation that is observed. For instance, if guests have not eaten their meal, inquire if they would like another choice (if it is possible). A fact to remember is the following: influencing one guest at a banquet has the potential to sell an additional banquet for many guests. It is easier to obtain business from people who have experienced your operation rather than trying to create a whole new market.

When the opportunity arises that the banquet manager can be introduced to the guests, take advantage of this situation. It will be beneficial for future business.

Throughout the event, the banquet manager should be constantly communicating with the host. The host has to be informed of what will happen next (such as the cake cutting ceremony). The banquet manager continues inquiring to find out if everything meets the host's satisfaction.

Keep in mind that musicians and photographers love to work at an establishment where the banquet manager informs them of the time and location of events at the function. If the banquet manager makes it easy for these individuals to do their job, it will benefit the establishment, because they will recommend the establishment to potential clients.

Managing the Meeting Room Business

Another type of business that the banquet manager may have concerns meeting rooms. Knowing the correct way to set up the rooms is important, but just as important is knowing how to manage the meeting room business.

Coffee breaks are often scheduled in the meeting rooms that the banquet establishment has to set up. As in other types of banquet management, the key to having repeat conference business is to make sure all items are in place and the room is correctly set up for the guests before they arrive.

Items such as water, glasses, pads, pencils, and ashtrays, if they are desired, should be on the tables. One water pitcher should be available for four guests. When the coffee break is scheduled for a specified time, make certain that the coffee and food arrive on time.

The timing is critical, but just as important is what happens while the guests are having their coffee break. During the break, the banquet manager should have a staff in the meeting room, replenishing the water, cleaning ashtrays, and freshening up the room for the remainder of the meeting.

Again organization is the key to successful meeting room business. All the equipment needed to freshen up the room should be set up outside the room in advance of the coffee break. At break time, the staff simply enter the room and replace, for example, the empty water pitchers with full ones.

Presenting the Bill to the Host and Rebooking the Party

The banquet manager's last job on the day of the function should be to present and explain the bill to the host. Payment should be obtained and the host should be thanked for holding the function at the establishment.

Finally, if the function is an annual event, ask the host if it may be rebooked for the following year. If the function was a wedding reception, ask the host to recommend your establishment to any future bride and groom.

And once again, thank the host for the opportunity of having served him or her! Of course, in a few days, you will send the host a hand-written thank you note.

Breakdown of the Function

When it is time for the party to end, inform the host. As the guests and host are leaving the banquet, assist the host with presents, the top of the wedding cake, or any other items with which he or she needs assistance.

Once the guests have departed, there is still work to be done. The banquet manager should have a system for cleaning up the dining room. The dirty dishes and equipment must be brought into the kitchen in an organized fashion. For instance, the staff should go into the dining room with big pots and glass racks. Glasses on the tables should have their contents dumped into the pots. The glasses can then be put into the racks, ready to be washed. Using a system like this eliminates confusion and breakage in the kitchen.

Finally, when the banquet room and kitchen are cleaned up to your satisfaction, the employees should be thanked and dismissed. And you, the banquet manager, should feel proud that you have just completed another great function!

Chapter Summary

1. Based on information from the function sheet, the banquet manager must determine the amount of service staff, bar staff, and kitchen staff needed.

2. The three styles of service used in American banquet service are: the station method, the follow-up method, and the combination method.
3. Managers must be flexible enough to deal with such unexpected occurrences as equipment shortages, latecomers, and early-leavers.

Review Questions

1. You have a doubleheader booked (two parties, one after another) in the same room. The first one is for 300, followed by a party for 150 guests. You only have an hour between the two parties. At the end of the first wedding reception, the father of the bride sees that everyone is having a good time. He tells the band to play an extra hour. What problems do you anticipate, and how could this situation have been avoided?
2. Using the banquet function sheet, complete the banquet checklist form by filling in how much equipment would be needed to serve the Lockwood wedding.
3. Using the banquet function sheet, state what utensils can be used over again and how you would accomplish it if you were a banquet manager.
4. Do you think that tip cups should be allowed at the Lockwood wedding? Should they be allowed at other events?
5. A group of eight guests were drinking and talking at the cocktail party and have just arrived in the room. All the other guests have been seated. There are enough seats to accommodate the eight guests; however, they must split their group up. Two people have to sit at one table, four at another, and two at a third table. They refuse, and want to sit together. What do you do to solve their problem?
6. The host has a party of four hundred, which must be served within fifteen minutes. Your room can physically hold only enough tables for two buffet lines. How would you solve this problem?
7. What is a chafing dish? How is it set up, and what is its purpose?
8. When should a buffet be used for a party? What are the advantages and disadvantages to a host in using a buffet?
9. What is the first and last thing a banquet manager has to do on the day of a function? Why are both of these jobs important?
10. What is a duty roster? Why is it important, and how does it help the banquet manager?

Appendix A

Eight Easy Napkin Folds

The Tent

1. Lay the napkin out flat in front of you.
2. Fold the napkin in half.
3. Fold the napkin in quarters.
4. Fold the napkin into a triangle.
5. Fold the napkin into a triangle again.
6. Place the open end of the triangle facing the guest's seat.

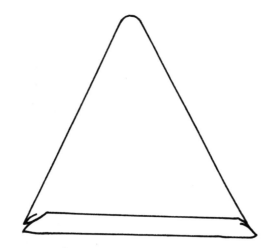

Figure A–1.   The Tent Fan Fold. An easy fold to learn.

The Cuffed Roll
(Great to use on a buffet)

1. Lay the napkin out flat in front of you.
2. Fold the napkin in half.
3. Fold the base of the napkin up about three inches.
4. Turn the napkin over.
5. Going from left to right, make three (3) even folds.
6. Place silverware into the pocket.

The Cuffed Roll

Figure A–2. The Cuffed Roll. An ideal fold for buffet service.

The Candle

1. Place open napkin in a diamond shape.
2. As if napkin were a clock, fold 6 o'clock point up to 12 o'clock to form a triangle.
3. Fold the base of the triangle up two inches so that it looks like a pirate's hat.
4. Turn the napkin over so that the fold is hidden. The shape should still be a triangle.
5. Roll the napkin evenly from right to left, forming a candle.
6. Tuck the tail into the cuff formed by the fold.
7. Stand the candle in a wine glass at a place setting.

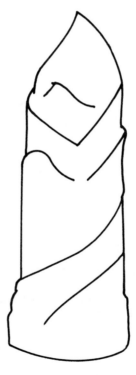

Figure A–3. The Candle. A great fold to give the impression of height.

The Lilly

1. Lay the napkin out flat in front of you.
2. Fold the napkin into quarters.
3. Fold the napkin into a triangle, so that the solid base is in front of you.
4. Make sure there are five ends at the top of the triangle.
5. Starting with the left base, accordion pleat the napkin from left to right.
6. Place in a wine glass.
7. Separate out the five ends.

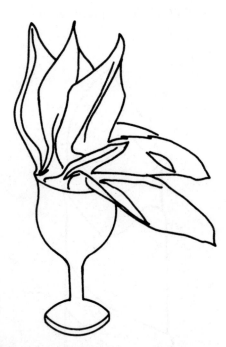

Figure A–4.   The Lilly, which can either be placed at the cover or in a wine glass.

The Crown

1. Lay the napkin out in a diamond shape.
2. Fold the napkin into a triangle, with the point at the top and the base facing you.
3. Take points 3 o'clock and 9 o'clock and fold them up to point 12 o'clock.
4. Take the 6 o'clock point, fold it up three-fourths of the way toward 12 o'clock.
5. Crease the base of the napkin.
6. Still holding onto the point (6 o'clock), fold point down to base.
7. Turn napkin over.
8. Place three fingers at the base of the napkin (or four, if you have a small hand) in the center of the napkin.
9. Wrap the right side around your fingers and tuck it under them.
10. Take the left side and fold it so you can tuck the left side into the pocket made by the first fold.
11. Stand the napkin up and face it toward you.
12. Peel the two outside "wings" of the napkin down.

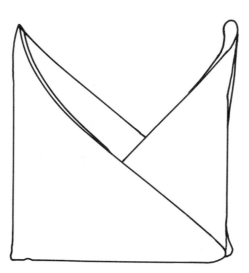

Figure A–5. The Crown. An excellent fold to use either at the cover or on a cover plate.

The Easy Cone

1. Lay the napkin out in a diamond shape.
2. Fold the napkin into a triangle, with the point at the top and the base facing you.
3. Take points 3 o'clock and 9 o'clock and fold them up to point 12 o'clock.
4. Turn the napkin over.
5. Take the 6 o'clock point, fold it up one-fourth way toward 12 o'clock.
6. Turn the napkin over.
7. Place three fingers at the base of the napkin in the center of the napkin.
8. Wrap the right side around your fingers and tuck it under them.
9. Take the left side and fold it so you can tuck the left side into the pocket made by the first fold.
10. Turn the napkin over and place it in the center of the place setting.

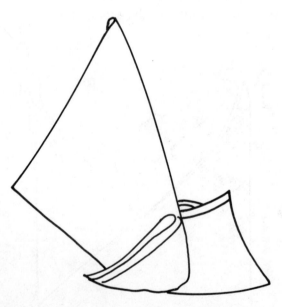

Figure A–6.   The Easy Cone. As its name implies, an easy fold for the service staff to do.

The Cock's Comb

1. Lay the napkin out in front of you.
2. Fold into quarters.
3. Fold into a triangle so that the base is in front of you and that the points of the napkin are at 12 o'clock.
4. Make sure that the five ends are in the 12 o'clock position.
5. Take 3 o'clock and 9 o'clock and fold them so that the sides of the triangle meet in a parallel line (this will leave a cone shaped triangle).
6. Take the bottom of the cone (old points 3 o'clock and 9 o'clock) and fold under the base of the napkin to form a triangle.
7. Crease the napkin with your right hand while holding it in your left hand. This is now lengthwise.
8. Place the napkin lengthwise and separate the top four ends.

Figure A–7. The Cock's Comb. A fold that adds intrigue to the place setting.

The Fan

1. Fold the napkin in half.
2. Arrange the napkin so it is lengthwise in front of you.
3. Working up from the bottom, accordion pleat the napkin three-fourths of the way to the top.
4. Holding the pleated end in your right hand, fold the napkin in half so that the pleats are on the outside of the fold.
5. The pleated part is now at the right-hand side of the napkin.
6. Take the bottom of the unpleated part with your left hand and fold it into a triangle so the triangle forms a base for the fan. Tuck the triangle into the pleats.
7. At this point, a rubber band can be placed on the napkin and the napkins can be used when needed. (This is an optional step.)
8. Stand the napkin up on the triangle base. The napkin will fan out.

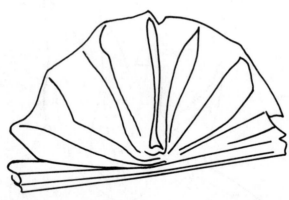

Figure A–8. The Fan. A favorite of many banquet houses, as fan-folded napkins can be done in advance.

Glossary

a la carte restaurant: A business that serves guests individual meals on demand.

American a la carte service: Service in which the food and beverage is served to the guest by either an individual service person or a team method. The food is plated in the kitchen.

American banquet service: Service in which the guest's food is all placed on one plate. Often known as "on the plate, no wait."

back of the house: A term referring to employees who do not come into contact with the guest in their normal line of duty.

banquet: A meal with a menu that was preselected by the host for all of the guests attending the event.

banquet captain: The person responsible for service in a section of the banquet room.

banquet facility: A business that serves groups of guests the same meal, at the same time.

banquet manager: The individual responsible for planning, organizing, and running banquets.

beverage service: The type of alcoholic or non-alcoholic drinks requested by the host at a banquet function.

blocking: A term that means to reserve a certain table at a certain time for a guest.

buffet: A banquet meal at which guests obtain a portion or all of their food by serving themselves from buffet tables.

busperson: A restaurant employee who is responsible for assisting the service person.

captain: Employee who is responsible for an area of the dining room.

cash bar: At a banquet, an arrangement by which guests are required to buy their own drinks, both alcoholic or non-alcoholic.

check-off method: A method of blocking reservations used in a large restaurant.

chef de rang: An individual in French service who finishes off the food tableside.

competency: Serving food and drinks in the correct manner to the guest.

commis de rang: An individual in French service who assists the chef de rang in the service of the meal.

consumer orientation: The act of viewing your business from the perspective of your guests.

cover: The area or space for all utensils (including salt, pepper, and ashtrays) needed for each guest.

dependent needs: A part of *Maslow's Hierarchy*. They are needs that can only be met by someone else, not oneself. The first four needs of the hierarchy are dependent.

deuces: Tables that seat two guests.

diplomacy: The ability to act tactfully with the guest.

dupes: Stands for duplicate guest check. A copy of the original guest check turned into the kitchen or bar to obtain orders.

esteem needs: The fourth in Maslow's Hierarchy of needs. Esteem is the way in which people perceive the individual, which in turn affects the individual's ego.

forecasting: Planning for anticipated business based upon previous history of the restaurant, reservations, and events that are planned for the community which will affect the business.

four-tops: (also *4-tops*) Tables that seat four guests.

French service: A style of service in which final preparation of food is done at the guest's table with flourish and fanfare.

friendliness: A way in which individuals make their guests feel important by talking to them, and by using Maslow's theory to make them feel comfortable in the restaurant.

front of the house: A term referring to employees who work in direct contact with guests.

function: Any use of banquet facilities.

function book: An organized piece of equipment that lists the rooms that the establishment has to rent on a daily basis.

function sheet: A form, prepared by the banquet office, which lists in detail everything that the host desires for the event.

guarantee: The minimum number of guests that the host will have to pay for at a banquet.

gueridon: A cart, used in French service.

head banquet waiter: A person responsible for the success of the party in the room in which he or she is supervising.

Health Department: An agency that issues permits for operation of food service establishments and monitors the cleanliness of the establishment.

host bar: At a banquet, an arrangement by which the host pays for all drinks that the guests consume.

"in the weeds:" A slang term used to describe an employee who has too many people to serve at once.

log book: A document kept at the establishment's host desk. Information included in the book concerns the number of meals served, the weather for the day, any special events, the money generated per hour, and the money per meal period. A section is reserved for messages between the day and night hosts.

love and belonging needs: The third in *Maslow's Hierarchy* of needs. This need deals with the fact that individuals must belong or be accepted by their peers.

Maslow's Hierarchy: A series of five needs that humans must satisfy. Before moving to a higher need, the lower need must be satisfied.

MBWA: An acronym standing for "managing by wandering around."

no-shows: The term applied to guests who do not show up for their reservations.

occupancy rate: A figure used in a lodging establishment to anticipate the number of guests who will be staying in the establishment on a certain night.

open bar: At a banquet, an arrangement by which the host pays for all drinks consumed by the guests. Also called a Host Bar.

open seating: The practice of allowing guests to reserve tables for any time that the restaurant is open.

overbooking: The practice of taking more reservations than the restaurant can accommodate.

place setting: All the utensils, linens, plates, and glasses needed by one guest to consume the meal, arranged in the proper sequence.

physiological need: The first in *Maslow's Hierarchy* of needs. Physiological needs deal with food, water, sex, and sleep.

QSC: An acronym for the standards of business at McDonald's. *Q* stands for quality; *S* for service; and *C* for cleanliness.

rechaud: A small heating utensil used in French service.

reservation: A promise for a table in a restaurant.

reservation manager: A person whose sole job is to plan and organize reservations for the restaurant.

resident time: The time it takes a party of guests to eat their meal and pay their bill.

Russian service: A style of service in which food is placed on silver trays in the kitchen and then transferred from the tray to the guest's plate by the service staff in the dining room.

Russian banquet service: A style of service in which the service staff work as a team. All food is placed on silver trays in the kitchen, and the service staff work in teams of two.

tact: The ability to say or do the correct thing so as not to offend the guest.

safety needs: The second in *Maslow's Hierarchy* of needs. This need deals with how safe the individual feels in his or her surroundings.

sanitation: The process of keeping the restaurant clean of filth- and food-borne diseases.

seating: The tables in a restaurant used for one specific meal period.

self-actualization need: The fifth in Maslow's Hierarchy of needs. Self-actualization comes from the individual, after the dependent needs have been met.

service: Competency and friendliness combined.

service person: The individual who has the responsibility of serving the guests their meals. Often this person is called a waiter or waitress.

shadowing: A method in which a new employee follows a trainer around and observes how to do the job.

station: An area of the dining room, which usually consists of from fourteen to eighteen seats.

sub rosa: A term from Roman times, meaning confidentially.

table d'hôte: A complete meal served to all guests at a fixed price.

turning tables: This means resetting the guest table for another party. The phrase is often used in conjunction with how many times a table is reset during the meal period. For example, the tables were turned over three times means that each table was used for three parties.

turnsheet: A form used to keep track of the number of guests that have been seated at a service person's station for a particular meal period.

ubiquitous: The ability to be everywhere at the same time.

walk-ins: These are guests who patronize the restaurant without making a reservation; in effect, they walk in the door expecting to obtain a table.

waitlist: A form used by hosts that allows walk-ins to be seated in an organized manner.

word of mouth: The most potent form of publicity; this occurs when people tell other people about their experiences (whether good or bad) with the business.

working the floor: A phrase used to mean that the host is circulating around the dining room talking to guests and assisting the service staff.

underliner: A plate that goes beneath another plate to make it easier to serve food. For example, a saucer placed under a soup cup would be an underliner.

utensils: This refers to all forks, knives, and spoons used by the guests to eat their food.

wine steward: The employee of the restaurant responsible for suggesting and selling wines to guests for their meals.

Bibliography

Bartlett, Michael, ed. in chief. "Owners Define Perfect Waiter." *Restaurants & Institutions* (October 28, 1987):26.

BASF Wyandotte Corporation. Food Service Sanitation Manual. Wyandotte, Michigan.

Bernstein, Charles. "Silver and Golden Touches: A Winning Combination." *Nation's Restaurant News* (June 1, 1987):9.

Bernstein, Charles. "Teamwork Service: An Idea Whose Time Has Come." *Nation's Restaurant News* (August 10, 1987):13.

Biehler, Robert F. *Psychology Applied to Teaching.* 2nd ed. Boston: Houghton Mifflin, 1974.

Bruno, Karen. "Marlowe's Bucks Denver's Slump." *Nation's Restaurant News* (March 30, 1987).

Bubonia, Sam. Interview with the author. Albany, New York.

Chaudhry, Rajan. "Banquet Business Forces Monaco's to Close Its Doors." *Nation's Restaurant News* (May 9, 1988):52.

Curran, George. "Bring Waiters into the Fold with Linen Service Training." *Restaurants & Institutions* (October 14, 1987):194.

Curran, George. "Restrooms: Bubble, Bubble, Toilets and Trouble." *Restaurants & Institutions* (September 2, 1987):160.

"Customer Service As Primary Challenge." *Nation's Restaurant News* (May 1987):25.

Dahmer, S., and Kurt Kahl. *The Waiter & Waitress Training Manual.* Boston: CBI Publishing, 1977.

Davis, Caleb. "Peter." Vol. 18, *Collier's Encyclopedia.* Crowell-Collier Educational Corporation, 1969.

Desatnick, Robert L. "Seizing The Competitive Advantage." *Nation's Restaurant News* (September 28, 1987):F68.

Dooley, Susan. "And After All, Isn't That What Eggs Are For?" *Smithsonian* (February 1987):52.

Gerzonich, Barb. Principal Sanitarian, New York State Health Department. Personal interview with the author. Albany, New York. December 1988.

Goodman Jr., Raymond J. *The Management of Service for the Restaurant Manager.* Dubuque, Iowa: WCB, 1983.

Gottlieb, Leon. *The Best of Gottlieb's Bottom Line.* New York: Lebhar-Friedman, 1980.

Graham, Stephen. "Peter I, The Great." Vol. 18, *Collier's Encyclopedia.* Crowell-Collier Educational Corporation, 1969.

Hayes, Jack. "Albrecht Stresses Need to Service America." *Nation's Restaurant News* (March 14, 1988):4.

Herrick, Christine Terhunne, ed. in chief. *Consolidated Library of Modern Cooking and Household Recipes.* New York: Bodmer, 1904.

Hill, Janet McKenzie. The Up-To-Date Waitress. Boston: Little, Brown, and Co., 1906.

Jenkins, Tony. Interview with the author. Clifton Park, New York. 29 September 1987.

Josephson, Matthew. *Union House Union Bar.* New York: Random House, 1956.

Kanner, Robert. *The Art of Waiting Tables.* Videotape, 1986.

Kerner, Robert J. "Catherine De Medicis." Vol. 5, *Collier's Encyclopedia.* Crowell-Collier Educational Corporation, 1969.

King, Carol A. *Professional Dining Room Management.* Rochelle Park, New Jersey: Hayden, 1980.

Koepp, Stephen. "Why is Service So Bad?" *Time* (February 2, 1987):48–52.

Lang, George. "Think Tank: Wonder About Knives and Forks?" *Restaurant Hospitality* (March 1977):36.

Landers, Ann. *Schenectady Gazette.* April 18, 1987.

Lantzeff, George V. "Catherine II." Vol. 5, *Collier's Encyclopedia.* Crowell-Collier Educational Corporation, 1969.

Lebhar-Friedman Books. *Today's Waiter & Waitress.* New York: Chain Store Publishing Corp., 1979.

Lehrman, Lewis. *Dining Room Service.* New York: ITT Educational Services, Inc., 1971.

Liddle, Alan. "Details Make A Difference for Bon Appetit Catering." *Nation's Restaurant News* (October 12, 1987):F3–4.

Love, John. McDonald's Behind the Arches. Toronto: Bantam Books, 1986.

Lundberg, Donald E. *The Hotel and Restaurant Business.* Boston: CBI, 1976.

National Family Opinion Poll. *Restaurants & Institutions* (December 1, 1982).

National Institute for the Foodservice Industry. *Applied Foodservice Sanitation.* 2nd ed. Dubuque, Iowa: WCB, 1978.

Nation's Restaurant News. May 19, 1986. National Opinion Poll.

Peters, T., and Nancy Austin. *A Passion for Excellence, The Leadership Difference.* New York: Warner Books, 1985.

Powers, Thomas F. *Introduction to Management in the Hospitality Industry.* New York: John Wiley, 1979.

"Razzle's Prime Ingredient: Owner Morrone's Personal Touch." *Nation's Restaurant News* (February 16, 1987):62.

Ricupero, Franca. Interview with the author. Schenectady, New York. 3 March 1988.

Romano, Peter J. "Friendliness Works As Well as Discounts." *Nation's Restaurant News* (December 5, 1988):3.

Rose, Frank (Sandy). Interview with the author. Saratoga, New York. 3 October 1987.

Schmidt, Arno B. The Banquet Business. Boston: CBI, 1981.

Sherman, Colleen. Interview with the author. Schenectady, New York. 2 April 1987.

Solomon, Ed. *Service Is an Honorable Profession*. USA: McGarvey's Nautical Restaurant, 1979.

Spiak, Kim. Interview with the author. Albany, New York. 13 June 1988.

Springsfield, Anne Francis. *The Expert Waitress*. New York: Harper, 1894.

Stalica, Michael. Interview with the author. Schenectady, New York. 8 November 1987.

Stein, Jess, ed. in chief. *The Random House Dictionary*. New York: Ballantine Books, 1978.

Tighe, Eileen, ed. "Fork." Vol. 5, *Woman's Day Encyclopedia of Cookery*. New York: Fawcett Publications, Inc., 1966.

Tighe, Eileen, ed. "Knife." Vol. 7, *Woman's Day Encyclopedia of Cookery*. New York: Fawcett Publications, Inc., 1966.

Tighe, Eileen, ed. "Spoon." Vol. 11, *Woman's Day Encyclopedia of Cookery*. New York: Fawcett Publications, Inc., 1966.

"The Best Restaurant in Connecticut." *Connecticut* (February 1979).

The Educational Institute of the American Hotel and Motel Association. *Food and Beverage Management and Service*. East Lansing, Michigan: Educational Institute of the American Hotel and Motel Association, 1969.

The Foodservice Editors of CBI. *The Professional Host*. Boston: CBI, 1981.

Walkup, Carolyn. "Culinary Enterprises Beats Competition With Diversity." *Nation's Restaurant News* (October 12, 1987):F3–4.

Wallace, Jane. "Eating Out: A Pleasure or a Hassle?" *Restaurants & Institutions* (March 4, 1987):16.

Walt Disney Company. *The Disney Look*. Burbank, California, 1987.

Walt Disney Company. *Walt Disney World Show Booklet*. Burbank, California.

Walt Disney Company. *Walt Disney World College Program*. Burbank, California, 1985.

Walt Disney Company. *Walt Disney World & You*. Burbank, California.

Wilkin, Edith A. "Cleanliness Training Important." *Nation's Restaurant News* (October 12, 1987):7.

Williams, Kim. Interview with the author. Schenectady, New York: 25 October 1988.

Index

A

A la carte
  means, 145
A la carte restaurant, 229
A la carte service. *See also*
    American a la carte
    service; American
    service; French service;
    Russian a la carte
    service
  types of, 18, 41
Abbreviations, standard, 137
  using, 139
Accompaniments, 140
Accounting Procedures, 166
Acquired Immunodeficiency
    Syndrome (AIDS), 39
Advertising, 4, 230
Aid, the, 121–2, 154–5
  responsibilities of, 121
  training, 121
Albrecht, Karl. *See* Service
    America
Alcoholic beverages, 141–2.
    See also Beverage
    service; Wine service;
    Wine steward
  a la carte, 285
  drink description (example),
    141
  on guest tables, 284
  mixers, 284
  service, 284
  set-ups, 284
Alcohol laws, 284
Allergies, 138
American a la carte service,
    18, 41–42
  guidelines for, 83–100
American banquet service, 18,
    42, 67–68, 287, 289,
    309, 311–4. *See also*
    Combination method;
    Follow-up method;
    Station method
  guidelines for, 83–100
  menu, typical, 67
  place setting, 45, 47, 59, 67,
    69
    diagram, 68
    space requirements, 60
  sequence of service, 325–7
  styles
    combination method, 311
    follow-up method, 311

station method, 311
American service, 53, 64–66,
    105, 123, 132
Ancient France, 44
Ancient Rome, 43–44, 59, 66
Appearance
  of banquet manager, 233,
    236
  of building, 26
  checklist for, 32
  of employees, 30–31
  first, 26
  importance of, 23–40
  landscaping, 28
  lobby, 26
  parking lot, 26, 28
  policy, enforcing, 32
  of service person, 31–33,
    134
  signage, 26
  standards for employees, 23
  of waiter, 31
Appetizer, 154
Arby's, 10
  Roberts, Leonard, 10
Arrangements, confirming,
    287–9
Ashtrays, 59, 96, 328
  capping, 98
  changing, 96–98, 157, 316
Astrodome Complex, 17, 225,
    286
  Astrohall, 17, 228, 267–8,
    277
  Houston Astrodome, 226,
    268
  Williams, Kim Sibson, 17,
    267–8, 286
Audio-visual equipment, 246,
    254

B

Baked, 141
Banc, 66
Banquet(s). *See also* Function
    sheet; Sample banquet
  assembly line method, 308
  booking of, 232, 262
  checkbacks, 327–8
  definition of, 66
  deluxe buffet, 242
  first, 43
  meals, 276–83
  modified, 242
  origin of word, 66

policies of, 269
purpose of, 226, 277–8
reasons for having, 226–9
running, 317
steward, 306
styles of, 241
successful, 267–8
team system, 308
types of, 227–9
type of service, 241–2
vs. catering, 231–2
waiter, 232–3
what is, 225–6
why, 229–31
Banquet captain(s), 232–3
Banquet checklist, 304
  sample form, 305
Banquet facility
  choosing a, 3
  size of, 245
  staffing, 230, 232–3
  use of. see Function(s)
Banquet management, 229, 232
Banquet manager, 3, 5, 8,
    225, 256, 258, 284, 297,
    327, 329. *See also*
    Ubiquitous
  benefits, 238–9
  disadvantages of becoming,
    239–40
  effective, 327
  is, 233
  job knowledge needed,
    240–1
  job of, 17
  key to, 233
  organizational skills, 238,
    268
  purpose of, 233
  qualifications of, 233–8
  responsible for, 233, 237,
    247, 269, 317, 323
  visibility of, 18
Banquet rooms, 329
  cleanliness of, 38
Banquet service, 66.
  types of, 18, 41
Bar manager, 315–6
Barnsider Restaurant, The,
    110, 132
Bars
  cash, 18
  open, 18
  position of, 316
Bartenders, 75, 284–5, 300,
    302, 315

Bears, The, 219–20
Bechamel, 44
Belmont Hotel, 32
Bench, 66
Bernstein, Benjamin, 31
Best of Gottlieb's Bottom
  Line, The. *See*
  Gottlieb, Leon
Beverage service, 89–93, 154,
  166, 278. *See also*
  Alcoholic Beverages;
  Wine service
  guidelines, 126
  implementing, 18
  merchandising, 143–7
  methods of, 18
  ordering, 214
  organizing, 18
  planning, 18
  pouring, 90–94
  tasting, 142
Blackboard, 148, 175
Blocking, 179–98, 206
Bodmer, R. J., 43
Body odor, 33
Bonus, 113
Booking
  advanced, 262
  firm, 262–3
  person, 246
  rebooking, 329
  tentative, 262–3
Brenensthul, Professor Gary.
  See Schnectady County
  Community College
Bubonia, Sam. *See* DeWitt
  Clinton Hotel, The
Buffet, 138, 241–2, 278, 298,
  318–24
  arrangement of, 320–1
  guidelines, 278
  lines, 319–20, 322
  look of, 324
  organization of, 320
  principles of, 319
  service staff jobs at, 321–3
  set-up, 320, 322
  tips on, 324–5
  traffic flow, 323–4
  types of, 42, 69–70
    deluxe, 42, 70, 241–2, 278
    modified deluxe, 42, 70,
      241–2, 278
    simple, 42, 241, 278
  use of, 320
Buffet service, 69–70
Busperson (dining room
  attendant), 106–9,
  117–9, 121
Business, setting the tone of, 6

Business meetings, 3
Butler
  professional, 43
  service, 298
  style, 316

C

Cafe Provincial, 197
Captain, 106–7, 110, 117,
  132, 160
Carlzon, Jan, 199
Casa Lupita Mexican
  Restaurants, 132
Cash bar, 284–5
Cashier, 176
Caterer, 232, 259, 268
Catering manager, 17
Catering vs. banquets, 231–2
Catherine the Great, 53
Chafing dishes, 320, 324–5
Chairs
  storage of, 38
Chapter Summary, 21, 39, 70,
  102–3, 127, 158, 177,
  197, 220, 242, 264–5,
  294, 329–30
Chart, 189–90
Checklist, 169
Checkoff method, 190
  sheet, 191–4
Checks, 175–6, 209–10
  explaining, 329
  presenting, 329
Chef, 290, 315, 318
  accomplished, 6
  creation, 145, 147, 177, 213
  features, 154
  special, 213
Chef de rang, 51–53, 58
Churchill Downs, 173
Cigars, 95–96
Cigarettes, 95–96
Cleaning procedure, 29
Cleanliness, 170
  acceptable, 23
  of banquet rooms, 38
  during shift, 33
  of eating items, 37–38
  and hospitality industry, 23
  monitoring, 25–26
Coach and Six. *See* Shere,
  Beverlee Soiff
Cobwebs, 38
Cocktail parties, 250–1, 298, 309
  ending, 316–7
  serving, 315–7
  tips about, 316
Code order, 150, 152–3
Coffee breaks, 328

Coffee cup setting, 49–51
Coffee shield, 94, 157
Cologne, 33
Combination method, 311, 313–4
  advantage of, 314
  disadvantage of, 314
Commercial establishments,
  the first, 44
Commis de rang, 52, 58
Common sense, 203
Communicating information,
  213–4
Communication, 290
  oral, 237
  visual, 148
  written, 237–8
Community events, 167
Competency, 74–76
Complaint(s)
  how to handle, 217
  letter, example of handling,
    19–20
Computers, 6, 151, 153, 166,
  170, 184, 188, 193, 197,
  259–60, 268
Condiments, 154, 156, 320
Connecticut Magazine, 75
Consumer orientation, 28, 38
Contracts, 270
Cooking methods, 140–1
  doneness, 141
  preparation time, 141
Copper Beach Inn, 75
  McKenzie, Jo and Bob, 75
Corks, 124
Coryate, Tomas, 69
Cover, 60–61, 309–11
  completing, 62
  definition of, 59
  setting the, 59–60
Credit card charges, 166
Critics, 108
Cross Keys Inn, 59
Cruise ship, 139
Crumbing a table, 101, 157
Crumbing device, 157
Customer service, 6
Customers
  boring the, 8
  disruptive, 13
  former, 4
  displeased, 4
  greeting, 6
  names, tracking of, 7
  unhappy, 4

D

Dais, 66
Daydreamer, 164

Delmonico's, 64
deMedicis, Queen Catherine, 59
Deodorant, 33
Deposits, 262–4, 268, 270
Desatnick, Robert L., 4
    Creative Human Resources
        Consultants, 4
Desmond Americana, 27, 195,
        251, 261–2, 268,
        279–83, 319, 323
    Spiak, Kim, 261–2, 268
Dessert
    merchandising, 145
    tables, 145–7
    tray, 145
Dewey, Thomas, 136
DeWitt Clinton Hotel, The,
        76, 136, 301–2
    Bubonia, Sam, 76
Dining experience
    managing, 189–221
    pleasurable, 199
Dining room. *See also*
        Organization of dining
        room
    manager, 3, 117
    operation of, 199–200
    organizing, 117, 159–78
        team system, 117–8
    physical layout, 188
    service personnel, 106. *see
        also* Busperson;
        Captain;
    service person; Wine
        steward
        qualities of, 106–110
    service styles, 105
    staffing, 117
    visibility of, 18
Diplomacy, 233, 236
Director of beverage, 160
Director of food, 160
Director of service. *See* Host
Disabled guests, 215–6
Discounting, 6
Dishes, dirty. *See also* Plates
    removing, 83–84, 98–100,
        118, 157
    stacking, 85
Dishwashers, 237, 306
Disney, Walt, 28, 30
Disney, Walt Productions, 30
Disney World College
        Progam, Walt, 10–11,
        29
Disney World Company,
        Walt, 9–11, 19, 28–32,
        55, 57, 74–75, 77–78,
        95, 135, 146, 180–2,
        205, 218

College Relations
    Coordinator, 9
    Tony Jenkins, 9
    "The Disney Look", 30–31
    Traditions Orientation
        Session, 135
    Training, 9–10
Disneyland, 30–31
Dress codes, 32
Dress rehearsal, 290
Drink stations, 250
Dust, 38
Duty roster, 307, 314–5
    sample, 308

E

Early-leavers, 327
Ego gratification, 14. *See also*
        Maslow's Hierarchy
    example of, 14
Ego needs. *See* Maslow's
        Hierarchy
Egyptian, 57
86 items, 148–9
    definition of, 148
Employees
    competency of, 113
    evaluation of, 116, 132
    finding, 6
    manual, 110
    morale of, 173–4
    scheduling, 173–7
    selection of, 131
    smell, 33–34
    teaching, 131
    testing, 110, 133
    training, 6, 132
Empress Lilly, 205, 218
Environment. *See* Sanitation
Equipment
    availability, 251–4
    needs, 303–7
    testing of, 255
Escoffier, 58
Esteem needs, 12–14. *See also*
        Maslow's Hierarchy

F

Fern bars, 8, 133
Fink's Mike. *See* Bernstein,
        Benjamin
First-come basis, 179
5 P's, 169–70, 196
Flagler's Restaurant, 180
Floor plan, 136–7
Flowers, 325
Follow-up, the, 121–2
    method, 311–3, 318

Food
    arrival at table, 93–95
    keeping hot, 325
    left over, 230
    merchandising, 143–7
    preparation of, 147, 166
    quality of, 230
    safety of, 24–25
    service of, 166
    stations, 250
    tasting, 142
    transferring of, 102
Food service, philosophy of, 9
Forecasting, 171–3
Forks
    history of, 68–69
    manipulating, 102
Francophile, 53
Franklin, Ben, 14
Freedom of soil, 23
French a la carte service, 102
French revolution, 51
French service, 18, 41–42, 44–53,
        55, 58, 63–66, 117, 132
    guidelines, 101–2
Friendliness, 73
Front of the house, 24
Function(s)
    booking, 247, 258–61, 267
    breakdown of the, 329
    controlling, 318–9
    definition of, 245
    diagraming, 256–8
    examples of, 245
    how to book, 245–66
    managing, 297–330
    obtaining information,
        about, 268–9
    preparing for, 297–8
    purpose of, 274–5
    room availability, 246–7
    room capacity, 246–7
    room setups, 246–51, 256–7
    rooms, use of, 254
    scheduling, 256
    types of, 247
    what is, 245–6
Function book, 259–61
Function sheet, 267–93,
        298–9, 304
    cover letter, 289
    daily, 292–4
    distribution of, 289–90
    example, 271
    other names of, 270
    part one of, 271–3
    part three of, 273
    part two of, 274, 276, 286–7
        example, 288
    purpose, 270

updating, 292
used as, 273
weekly, 292–4
Future business, planning, 212

G

Gallup poll, 5–6
Garnishes, 138–40, 154–5,
    302, 322
German service, 64
Gimmicks, 145–7
Glass tops, 60–61
Glasses, 141–2
    freedom from soil, 37–38
    handling of, 23, 34–36
    storage of, 34–36
Goodman, Raymond J., 65
Gottlieb, Leon, 32
Grand Floridian Beach Resort,
    55, 57, 135, 180–2
Gratuity, 238–9, 273. *See also*
    Tipping
    fixed, 161, 185
Greeting, 204–6
Grooming
    guidelines, 31
    and service person, 31
Guarantee(s), 264, 268, 270,
    273, 285–7, 291, 297
Gueridon, 51, 53–55, 65, 102
Guest(s), 6. *See also* Disabled
        guests
    addressing, 14
    building up trust, 145
    disabled, 215–6
    explaining items to, 147
    explaining restaurant
        policies, 185–6
    greeting, 200
    history, 172
    as a host, 226
    leading, 213
    mood of, 143
    and the order, 143
    problem, 216
    recognition of, 6
    reservations, 182
    seating, 207, 213
    soothing feelings of, 217
    treating of, 14–15
    and waiting, 210–2
Guest Check, 151–5
    placement on table, 157
Guidelines of service, 116–7

H

Hair
    facial, 64

Hall of Springs, 301–2
Hand washing, 36
Health code, 25
Health department, 13, 25, 36
Health hazards, 37
Health laws, 25
Health regulations, 23
Health rules, 25
High chairs, 29
Hill, Janet M., 43
Hixson, Burt, 31
Home base, 149–50
Hospitality industry, 3
    thinks about service, 6
Host, 119, 159–69, 214–6,
    276. *See also* 5 P's
    assigning stations, 171
    definition, 171
    desk (podium), 200, 207
    and eye contact, 201
    final job of, 218–9
    multiple, 204
    obligation of, 200
    perfect, 219–20
    and reservations, 183, 187
    responsible for, 159–61,
        169–70, 199–200, 205
    and scheduling, 173
    should not, 205
    training, 183
Host bar
Host stand, 172, 200, 207
Human interaction, 6

I

Ice bucket, 126, 155
Ice carvings, 320
In Search of Excellence, 9
"In the weeds", 206
Ingredients, 138, 147
Inspection of staff, 176–7

K

King Louis XIV, 44, 46
King Louis XV, 44
Kitchen, 24, 329. *See also*
        Sanitation
    working with, 290
Knives, history of, 46
Kroc, Ray, 28–30. *See also*
        McDonald's

L

La Paloma, 121
Labor cost, 160, 165
Landers, Ann, 145
Latecomers, 327

Lead, the, 121–2, 154–6
Lecturn, 38, 254–5
Lights, 38
    fixtures, 170
Log book, 172, 219
Loud speakers, 212
Love and belonging needs
Love, John, 28

M

Maintenance program, 38
Maître d'Hôtel. *See* Host
Management
    poor, 12
    successful, 18–19
Management of Service, The.
    See Goodman,
        Raymond J.
Managers. *See also* Banquet
        manager; Catering
        manager
    best type of, 7
    and employees, 18
    and grooming, 31–32
    and guests, 18
    and organization, 18
    physical condition of, 18
    qualifications of, 18–19
    and sanitation, 28–29
    setting examples, 29
    style, 12
    successful, 7
    and training, 19
Managing by wandering
        around (MBWA), 7–8
Marlowe's, 12
Maslow's Hierarchy, 3,
        12–16, 146, 285
    knowledge of, 18
    use of, 18
    when to use, 14
McDonald's, 28–29, 32
McDonald's Behind the
        Arches. *See* Love, John
McKenzie, Jo and Bob. *See*
        Copper Beach Inn
Meal
    clearing, 317–8
    getting prepared, 132
    merchandising, 132
    parts of, 132
    sequence of, 154–8
    service of, 132
    taking order, 132
    types of, 276–83
Media, 25
Medieval society, 57
Medieval times, 59, 66
Meeting rooms, renting of, 228

Meeting setups, 248–9
Melba, Dame Nellie, 58
  melba toast, 58
  peach melba, 58
  sauce melba, 58
Menu, 154, 175–6
  a la carte, first, 64
  childrens, 137
  concepts, 12
  imaginative, 6
  ingredients, 132
  innovative, 6
  knowledge of, 138–41
    lack of, 133
  learning, 132–3
  memorizing, 75
  planning, 275–6
  preprinted, 278–83
  preselected, 225
  presenting, 9–10
  prices, 65
  pronunciation, 132
  selection, 276
  set prices, 259
  studying, 75
  testing criteria, 142
Methods of service, 118–23
  individual service person
      method, 118–20, 132,
      174
    disadvantages of, 118
  team system, 118, 120–2,
      132, 154, 174. *See also*
      Aid, the; Follow-up,
      the; Lead, the
Michelin guide, 108
Microphones, 254, 317
Modern Hostess, The, 43
Moment of truth, 199, 210,
  247
  example of, 203
Monaco's Palace, 231
  Monaco, Baldino, 231
Morrone, Nicholas, 6
  Razzle's, 6
Musicians, 328

N

Napkins, 62, 287, 306, 309
  cocktail, 90, 154, 316
  folding, 62–63, 331–8
  history of, 62
  types of, 62
Napolean, 51, 53
National Family Opinion, 5
National Institute for the
      Foodservice Industry,
      The (NIFI), 23

Nation's Restaurant News
      (NRN), 4–6, 35–36,
      59, 120
New York Racing
      Association, 107
New York State Chiefs of
      Policy Organization,
      272
No-shows, 183, 186, 213
  how to alleviate, 196–7
  preventing, 196
  reducing number of, 196

O

Old Journey's End, The. *See*
      Philippi, Carol
Open bar, 284–5
Open seating, 193, 196
Order forms, 150–1
Order taking, 147–55
Organization of dining room,
      159–78
Overbooking, 182–3, 186,
      188–9, 191, 261
  avoiding, 193, 196
  definition of, 260
  problems of, 196

P

Palace Cafe, The, 120
Panza, Elsie, 309
Passion for Excellence, A, 7
Payne, Bob and Pat. *See*
      Bears, The
Perfume, 33
Permit, 25
Perquisites (perks), 238–9
Peter II, 53
Philippi, Carol, 6, 202
  The Old Journey's End,
      6–7, 26, 63, 202
Photographers, 328
Place setting(s), 309–11
  adapting, 49
  styles of, 41–71
Placemats, 60–61
  types of, 62
Planning meeting, 269
Plates. *See also* Dishes
  freedom from soil, 37–38
  handling of, 23, 34–36
  monkey, 155, 320
  placement, 156
  removing, 95, 157
  scraping, 95
  stacking, 95
  starter, 155
  storage of, 34–36

Platter, silver, 54
Podium, 204, 210, 214, 254–5
Policies
  memorizing, 75
  studying, 75
Policy sheet, 269–70, 286
Procrastinators, 167
Professional Host, The, 163
Promotion(s), 4, 177
Public address system, 153
Publick House, The, 84

Q

QSC (Quality, Service, and
      Cleanliness), 29
Qualifying business, 261–2
Quality Control, 55

R

*Random House Dictionary,
      The,*201, 276
Razzle's. *See* Morrone,
      Nicholas
Rebooking, 329
Rechaud, 51, 53
Recommendations, 4
References, 21–22, 40, 71,
      103, 178, 221, 295
Reis, Leslie. *See* Cafe
      Provincial
Reservation(s)
  accepting, 179–86, 193
  advantages of, 182
  benefit of, 182
  book, 184
  creating policy, 181
  definition of, 179, 182
  disadvantages of, 182–3
  factors, 180, 183
  form, 184–5, 188
  information to obtain, 184–5
  list, 194, 207
    example of, 208
  and meal times, 189–90
  multiple, 193
  not honored, 216–7
  not taking, 186–7
  open, 193
  organization of, 196
  pad, 189
  people taking, 193
  planning, 179–98
  policy, 209, 217
  preplanning, 196
  problems with, 183
  system, 165
  taking, 183–4
  training, 183

Reservation manager, 5, 194
 care of the, 6
 concern of the, 6
Resident time, 183, 195–6,
 217
Restaurant. *See also*
 Reservation(s)
 business, 63
 career in, 12
 choosing a, 3, 29, 108
 and etiquette, 145
 experiences at, 3
 failures, 12
 history of, 172
 location of, 179
 and Maslow's Hierarchy, 13
 patronizing a, 5
 physical layout of, 136, 166
 policies, 185
 profitable, 199
 and the service person,
  135–6
 success for, 116–7, 131
Restaurant owners, 73
Restaurant reviewers, 73
Restaurants, American
 types of service, 105
Restaurants & Institutions, 11,
 31
Restroom. *See* Sanitation
Return business, 199
Review questions, 21, 39, 70,
 103, 127–8, 158,
 177–8, 197–8, 220–1,
 242–3, 265–6, 294–5,
 330
Richelieu, Cardinal, 46
Rigi-Kulm, 58
Ritz, Cesar, 58–59
Roberts, Leonard. *See* Arby's
Rockefeller, Governor, 255
Role playing, 143
Room rentals, 264
Rose, Sandy, 46
Royal Caribbean Cruise Lines,
 Inc., 14–15, 139
Rules, bending, 203
Runner, 322
Russian a la carte service, 18
Russian banquet service, 18,
 41–42, 53–56, 58,
 64–66, 69, 132
 guidelines, 101–2
 place settings, 55–56, 59, 69

S

Safety needs, 12–13
Sales goals, 12
Sales manager, 232

Sales tax, 273
Sample banquet, 298–303
 equipment planning, 303–4
 serving, 301, 315
Sanitation, 23–40. *See also*
 Health department;
 Safety needs
 responsibility for, 24
 visual, 23
Sauté, 140–1
Savoy Hotel, 58–59
Scandinavian Air System, 199
Scheduling, 171–3
 employees, 173–7
 parties, 289
 setting up, 287
Schenectady County
 Community College,
 214
Seating, 107
 arrangements, 291–2
 procedure for, 291
Self respect, 13. *See also*
 Maslow's Hierarchy
Selling
 additional items, 145–7
 aggressiveness, 147
 key to, 144
 suggestive, 143–4
 typical, 144
Servants, 43
Service American, 200
Service. *See also* American a la
  carte service; American
  service; French service;
  Methods of service;
  Russian a la carte
  service; Russian
  banquet service; Seven
  deadly sins of service;
  Styles of service
 beginnings of, 43
 best in world, 9–10
 competent, 8
 definition of, 3, 5, 8
 examples of, 3
 excellent, 73
  key to, 9, 75
  what is, 8–9
 facts about, 4
 guests think of, 5–6
 guidelines for, 73–103
  chart, 85
 how accomplished, 75
 impersonal, 6
 importance of, 3–22
 ineffective, 10
 methods of, 117–23
 names of, confusion over,
  41–42

personal, 5
poor, 73
 reason for, 12
 what is, 10–12
for preseent and future, 3
psychology of, 12–16
quality of, 230
reasons to provide, 3–8
responsibility for, 6–8
seven deadly sins of, 200–4
styles of, 41–71, 105–28,
 132
superior, 8
types of, 3, 41–42
Service manual, 75
Service person, 6, 8, 106,
 108–10, 117, 134–42,
 214, 247
 appearance, 31–33, 134
 and grooming, 31
 and guests, 24
 what should know, 134–42
 writing the order, 137
Service staff, 237
 obligation of, 200
 organizing jobs for, 307–11
 training, 131–58
Service stand, 124
Serving, 117, 153–8
 a booth, 91
 as critical part of meal, 153
 direction, 90
 guidelines, 84–100
 helpful hints, 100–1
 hors d'oeuvres, 316
 how to, 9
 a meal, 131–58
 the party, 311–4
 sequence, 86, 105, 117
Serving a meal, 131–58
 proper order, 314
Set, 285–7
Setting up the room, 311, 320
Seven deadly sins of service,
 200–4
SeVille Room, 287
Shadowing, 9–10
Shere, Beverlee Soiff, 6
 Coach and Six, 6–7
Sherman, Colleen, 75, 94
Shoppers, mystery, 10
Sideboard, 79, 81
Sidestand, 78, 157. *See also*
 Traystand
Sidetowel, 76–77, 81–82,
 88–89, 92–94, 101,
 122, 124, 157, 165
Sidework, 114–5, 154, 171,
 175
Silver platter, 54, 102

Silver tray, 54
Sit-down dinner, 250, 321,
    325
  sequence of service, 325–7
Slavery, 43
Spiak, Kim. *See* Desmond
    Americana
Special of the day, 144–5, 175
Sponder, Ross. *See* Palace
    Cafe, The
Spoons
  history of, 57
  manipulating, 102
Staff meeting, 290
Staffing, 172
  forecasting, 173
Station(s), 79, 105, 107,
    110–3, 118, 163
  assigning, 113–4, 171
  definition of, 64, 110
  increasing, 113–4
  scheduling, 174–5
  setting up, 105, 111
  size of, 110, 112, 120
Station method, 311–2
  variation of, 314
Statler, Ellsworth M., 38
Steerman's Quarters, 205
Stevens, Harry M.,
    Corporation, 46
Strauss, Johann, 59
Styles of service, 41–71, 132.
Subrosa, 44
Substitutions, 117
  policy for, 140
Supersititions, 44
Survey, 5
Swamped, 206

T

Table(s), 247. *See also*
    Blocking
  assigning, 206–7
  claiming, 212
  dessert, 145–7
  diagram of, 207
  head, 249, 314
  reserving, 188–97
  shape of, 252
  size of, 251
  space between, 253
  special requests for, 206
  special shaped, 253–4
  storage of, 38
  types of, 247, 251
Table setting, 23
  presetting, 36–37

Tablecloths, 60–61
  drape of, 62
  types of, 62
Tact, 168, 233, 236
  definition of, 168
Telephone courtesy, 183
Tests, 133
  written, 75
TGIFridays, 32
TIME, 5
Tip cups, 316
Tipping, 64, 163
  reporting, 161
Training, 12, 19, 74, 116–7,
    147. *See also* Disney
    World Company, Walt;
    Serving a meal
  booklet, 134
  follow-up, 75, 116
  handling of utensils, glasses,
    and plates, 35–36
  manual, 12, 132–3, 138
  methods, 75
  program, 143
  role playing, 12
  serving a meal, 131, 58
Trays, 76–83, 102, 122, 154,
    156, 316, 322
  dessert, 145–6
  loading, 82–85
Traystand, 77, 79–80, 86
Truman, Harry S., 136
Tschirky, Oscar, 64
Turner, Fred. *See* McDonald's
Turning tables, 217
Turnsheet, 207–8
Typhoid Mary, 36

U

Ubiquitous, 3, 31, 164, 328
  being, 16–17
  manager, 16
  service, example of, 16
Underliner, 155, 320
Uniforms, 33, 162
Unions, 113
Up, 209–10
Up-to-Date Waitress, The.
    See Hill, Janet M.
Utensils. *See also* Cover
  and freedom from soil,
    37–38
  handling of, 23, 34–36
  location of 49–50
  and presetting, 37
  spacing for, 59
  storing, 34–36

V

Valet, 44
Vegetarian, 4
Ventilation, 53
Victoria and Albert's, 55, 57,
    146, 181–2
Videotapes, 12
Visual aid, 25
Voisin, 58
Voltaire, 53

W

Waiting times, 210–2
Waitlist, 211–2
  forms, 218
  information gained from,
    213
Waitresses
  duties of, 43
  textbook for, 42–43
Waldorf Astoria, 43, 64
Walk-ins, 179, 182, 211, 219
Wallace, Jane. *See* Restaurants
    & Institutions
Walls
  moveable, 255
  soundproof, 255
Warehouse Restaurant. *See*
    Hixson, Burt
Water pitcher, 328–9
Williams, Kim Sibson. *See*
    Astrodome Complex
Wine, 145–7, 155
  beaujolais, 127
  breathing, 127
  conditions of purchase, 125
  coolers, 127
  knowledge of, 123
  pouring extra, 156
  presenting, 123–5
  red, 124, 126–7, 155
  rosé, 126–7
  serving, 123, 126
    temperatures, 126–7
  sparkling, 124, 126–7
  sweet dessert, 126–7
  unacceptable, 125–6
  white, 124, 126–7, 155
  why host tastes, 124
Wine service, 18, 105, 123–7
Wine steward, 106–7
Winthrop, Governor John, 69
Word of mouth, 4–5, 165
  campaign, 40
Working the floor, 168,
    214–5, 218